Fight Sports
and the Church

Fight Sports and the Church

Boxing and Martial Arts Ministries in America

RICHARD WOLFF

McFarland & Company, Inc., Publishers
Jefferson, North Carolina

This book has undergone peer review.

ISBN (print) 978-1-4766-7387-5
ISBN (ebook) 978-1-4766-4213-0

Library of Congress and British Library
cataloguing data are available

Library of Congress Control Number 2021000759

© 2021 Richard Wolff. All rights reserved

No part of this book may be reproduced or transmitted in any form or by any means, electronic or mechanical, including photocopying or recording, or by any information storage and retrieval system, without permission in writing from the publisher.

Front cover image: mixed martial artist in boxing ring
(Shutterstock/Andy Gin)

Printed in the United States of America

*McFarland & Company, Inc., Publishers
Box 611, Jefferson, North Carolina 28640
www.mcfarlandpub.com*

For all
faithful fighters

Table of Contents

Acknowledgments	ix
Preface	1
Introduction	7
1. The History of Fight Sports and the Church	27
2. Cultural Reflections on Fight Sports and the Church	47
3. Ethical Issues Regarding Fight Sports and the Church	83
4. Case Studies of Fight Sports Ministries	111
Conclusion	147
Postscript	167
Chapter Notes	171
Bibliography	183
Index	193

Acknowledgments

I wish to express my thanks to those who have contributed in various ways to the completion of this book. Academic research and writing may at first glance seem to have little in common with training in fight sports or engaging in public ministries. Even so, just as fighters and pastors seemingly do much of their work in solitude, like writers, they nonetheless could not accomplish what they do alone. As boxers rely on their trainers and ministers their parish staff, so too writers rely on the support of unseen others who merit recognition for their contributions. And so, here is my own version of a post-fight center-ring address, wherein I publicly express my thanks to those who helped me in completing this project.

First, to those academics at this project's "ringside" I proclaim my gratitude. This begins with members of the faculty and staff at the Lutheran Theological Seminary at Philadelphia (recently merged with the Lutheran Theological Seminary at Gettysburg to form the United Lutheran Seminary), where this project formally began. This includes members of the dedicated library staff who located and sent numerous articles and books to me at my then-residence in New York. It also includes academic-administrative leaders, such as members of the graduate school staff, who supported my work on the project. In particular I wish to thank John Hoffmeyer, Associate Professor of Systematic Theology, for thoughtfully commenting on drafts of the manuscript. His careful reading and critical insights helped immensely. Above all my sincere thanks goes to Jon Pahl, the Peter Paul and Elizabeth Hagan Professor in the History of Christianity, for his unceasing guidance and support. His challenging remarks and substantive ideas for new directions for this research were crucial in its achieving its final form.

Also in my corner have been those more directly involved in fight sports. Foremost among these is my long-standing boxing and martial arts trainer Carmine Caracciola, with whom I have enjoyed many between-the-rounds conversations about fight sports and their relation to broader matters, including those of religion and the church. These conversations were the impetus that helped spur my interest in various scholarly pursuits related to boxing, including this one. Further, his example as one wholeheartedly devoted to achieving goals once set served as an example for me both inside the ring and out, and bolstered my commitment to completing various projects, the present study as a case in point. I also must express thanks to the student members of the Valparaiso University Boxing Club for which I serve as adviser and trainer. Working with these young aspiring boxers has allowed me to put into practice approaches discussed in this book, and their receptiveness and enthusiasm has been inspiring.

This leaves those at this project's ringside who are fully engaged in ministries. Hence, my next note of thanks goes to the martial arts and boxing ministry leaders who spoke with me for this book, completing a series of interviews during which they shared stories of how they and their fight sports ministries developed, and the role that faith has played in both these ministries and their own lives. I truly appreciate their candor and willingness to share reflections and personal insights with me, and hence all who read this book. My deepest appreciation therefore goes to each of these fight sports ministry leaders: Michael Birch, Teejay Britton, the Rev. J. Brown, the Rev. Craig Cerrito, Charles Clark, Paul Doyle, Cristino Felix, Mike Joyce, the Rev. Jarrod Lanning, Pastor Mark Morrow, Mike Mosley, the Rev. Servando Perales, Sonia Ramos, the Rev. Thomas Richards, Ruben Silvas, Andrew Truong, and Steve Wilson. It is they and those like them who inspired my interest in examining the issues explored herein. I admire their work, respect their dedication, and appreciate their faithful service.

On a more personal note, I must thank those who have been in my corner for the longest time. Circumstances of my life made the year I worked most heavily on this book among the most challenging I have ever faced. My family was there to support me throughout this period, including in my undertaking of this research. My next note of thanks therefore goes to them for supporting me in innumerable ways throughout that year and this project. Foremost among these are my parents, Richard and Carol. For all of their support and faith, I am forever grateful.

Finally, to those who provided various other types of support, I am beholden. This includes the late Benilde Montgomery, O.S.F., with whom I spoke regularly and at length about issues regarding boxing, religion and the church; Frank Zagottis, who provided technical support and steady encouragement; the faculty, staff and students of Dowling College, who encouraged my developing academic interest in boxing and the church; and my colleagues at Valparaiso University, who have wholeheartedly supported my research in boxing, religion, and culture. In particular I wish to thank Communication Department chair Lanie Steinwart and the members of my academic department, as well as those in Valpo's academic leadership, who supported my research and helped provide me with the necessary time and resources to complete it. Lastly, I thank the students of my college seminars on boxing, media and culture, who enthusiastically and thoughtfully reflected with me in the classroom on the relationship of fight sports to society, the church, the media, and ministry. To these and others go my heartfelt thanks.

Preface

Ever since I was a kid, I have loved boxing. Not that I practiced the art—at least not then. I simply admired those who did, for many reasons. I admired the dedication it took to be really good at their craft. I admired the courage it took to face an opponent and stand their ground, with nowhere to hide. I admired boxers' various styles and the very form of boxing: swift bobbing and weaving; spry footwork; the defensive postures that instantly transform into explosive counterpunching; the feints, jabs, crosses, and hooks. All of it. Boxing drew me in and, although I did not yet formally train in the sport, it stood its ground over time as a growing fascination for me—like a fighter patiently advancing on an opponent, slowly but surely.

As a youngster, I was somewhat timid. Even so, I knew who I was and in what I believed. At the heart of my belief system, I was a church-going Christian. I believed in turning the other cheek. I believed that the meek were blessed, for they would inherit the earth. I believed in allowing oneself to suffer persecution and even violence for the sake of one's beliefs. Such were among my religious commitments at the time. Because of this, Saint Stephen the martyr had special meaning for me; he was stoned to death for his faith and did not fight back even then. And, of course, there was Christ himself, who would not let his followers take up arms to defend him in the Garden of Gethsemane, and who ultimately was hung on a cross, demonstrating his love for others in an act many would see as a moment of not only sacrifice, but also chosen meekness, submission and surrender.

This all resonated with my experience. Small for my age and armed only with a philosophy of gentleness and commitment to Christian ideals as I then saw them, I was bullied and would not fight back. I submitted when faced with aggression or any expression of animosity. My response, as might be expected, made the bullying worse. Not being willing to fight made me all the more of a target. I had the courage of my convictions and a well-integrated sense that what I was suffering was born out of my deeply held religious convictions. I came to believe that there was a kind of courage in being willing to suffer for one's religious beliefs. And I had Christ, as

I then saw him, as a role model. I was content to be treated as I was because my response to mistreatment held a place in my firmly established religious beliefs.

Still, I admired those who took another stance: the fighters—those who stood up for themselves and others. I respected those who showed courage and strength in a different way than I did. Even the bullies, I somehow admired—especially those that knew how to handle themselves in an altercation. I particularly admired those who used their strength and courage to stand up to wrong. I recall one occasion when a much bigger youngster whom I did not even know stood up for me against a bully who was taunting me in the gym locker room. As I was being tormented, he saw an injustice and decided to step in. With strength and self-assurance and doing nothing more violent than holding the aggressor to the wall, he intervened for me and warned my bully not to bother me again. In a way, as I saw it, he had expressed a kind of love—one that would use strength and skill virtuously, to protect another.

Therein lies a paradox, and one that to this day underlies my thinking about the relationship of fight sports to Christianity. It involves differing attitudes toward confrontation, aggression, justice and love. I recall being regularly preoccupied by this contradiction in my own thinking, so much so that even as a youngster I sought out and read material about Christianity and nonviolence. At the library, I picked up a book written by philosopher Jacques Ellul—*Violence: Reflections from a Christian Perspective* (1969). Ellul wrote of the incompatibility of Christianity with violence. I was particularly impressed with a section in which he dismissed as unrealistic the placement of limitations on the use of violence, even if one intended to do good; that if one plans only to use enough defensive force to dissuade an opponent from further attacks, this will result in an escalation on the opponent's part, and necessitate an escalation of one's own commitment to violence. Hence, any act of violence, he argues, is an implicit commitment to use as much force of which one is capable, and to do as much damage to an opponent as one can, given the recognized likelihood of escalation.[1] To a youngster with both a problem being bullied and a Christian commitment, this further solidified my commitment to faithful meekness, in the name of peace.

Even so, I was drawn to fight sports, and particularly boxing. Increasingly, I admired the skill, confidence, and styles of boxers. I respected their spirit and their courage to stand and fight an opponent. How was I to reconcile this admiration with my philosophical inclinations? At the time, the nuances of Ellul and those similar to him may have been lost on my young mind. He and others (Thomas Aquinas, Thomas Merton) write mostly of systemic violence, and the role of violence and nonviolence in struggles of the state. Still, while the context may differ between governmental and individual uses of violence (or nonviolence), there is some crossover applicability in the underlying principles. While I self-consciously accepted the passive role of one who expressed love by turning the other cheek in my childhood experiences, I must also admit to having had a repressed awareness that some of this was practical, given my size and lack of training in self-defense techniques and fight sports. Notably, I did not condemn others who were bullied and fought back. In fact, I accepted theirs as another reasonable response to violent confrontations—just not one for me, given my physical and practical realities, and theological proclivities.

Meanwhile, boxing's slow advance in my life continued. As a boy, I loved to play with a toy boxing bag my father had given me, and already felt a determination to hit it as accurately as I could. When I grew older, I bought a rather odd contraption—a doorway-mounted heavy bag—in order to practice striking. Eventually, I shared my interest with others, one of whom surprised me one birthday with a gift certificate for private boxing lessons at a Manhattan gym. I was finally pursuing a long-held dream to learn the "sweet science." It is noteworthy that this occurred at a time when I was older and no longer subject to bullying. I was now able to pursue the art of boxing for its own sake, more as a sport than as a form of self-defense. Over time, I not only had a chance to grow as a fighter, but also to think about boxing from the perspective of an adult, in a more mature and objective fashion. On another trip to the library, I discovered Joyce Carol Oates' classic collection of essays *On Boxing*. Reading this book helped increase my intellectual and enthusiast's appreciation of boxing, including its history and cultural impact, and encouraged me to pursue more conceptual reflections on fight sports.

Years later as a seminary student and young college professor, my commitment to boxing progressed as I turned extra space in my house into a "boxing room." Over time, I filled it with whatever equipment I could afford and fit in it. What started as a space with a speed bag and some gloves evolved into a small home boxing gym—one complete with a heavy bag, round timer, jump ropes and other tools of the trade. In short, I was finally "all in." More importantly, I started working with a trainer. This took my commitment to a whole new level. I practiced every day. I was focused on perfecting each punch, movement and combination. Over time, I joined nearby boxing gyms to learn different styles from various coaches, and for the chance to train with others. My interest exceeded the purely physical, as boxing became part of my academic work. I researched and wrote about boxing films. I developed and taught an interdisciplinary seminar on boxing, one that looked at it historically, culturally, sociologically, medically and, alas, ethically. Slowly, my earlier theological ruminations on fighting and its related religious issues came full circle, as I once again took up an interest in the relationship of boxing with Christianity.

By now a graduate of one seminary degree program and a student in another, my interest in the paradoxes of fight sports and Christianity reignited. I read articles and books on various related subjects: ethical reflections on violence and non-violence from a Christian perspective; historical discussions of boxing's relationship to the church; critical considerations of the relationship of fight sports and violence to culture and Western masculinity. While many of the arguments were internally consistent and raised fertile ground for thought, not all of what I read rang true to my own experience and theological perspective. A growing interest and beginning study in Brazilian jiu-jitsu (BJJ) added broader context to my experience with fight sports. Reading books and articles about boxing and martial arts that articulated fight sports' appeal from a practitioner's perspective, sometimes from outside of an explicitly Christian perspective, impressed upon me a growing appreciation for fight sports and those who devotedly studied them. I sensed that, while abuses of fight sports were a reality (such as for intimidation, or dominating others for self-aggrandizement) and that not all ways of practicing fight sports would resonate with Christian values, there nonetheless were philosophical and theological matters needing further consideration, and that appropriate Christian engagements with fight sports were indeed possible. In short, I learned there were more nuances to the practice and appreciation of fight sports from a Christian perspective than I had previously considered.

Discovering others who likewise thought about the relationship of fight sports and the church, and even practiced boxing and martial arts as committed Christians and church leaders, piqued my interest. Upon learning of the existence of boxing and martial arts ministries which not only purported to do good but also to teach fight sports as a means of Christian discipleship, I was all the more committed to pursuing a comprehensive, scholarly exploration of this phenomenon. Some of the fighters and ministry leaders I encountered differed from me in terms of how their theology related to their practice—but this in itself was another reason to pursue these differences as part of a serious reflection on boxing and martial arts ministries. I committed to uncover the range of thinking about Christianity and its relationship to fight sports attested to in history, culture and practice, particularly as a form of church-based ministry, and reflect upon the various approaches and issues involved, including the theological. I myself do not find every approach to Christian uses of fight sports to be sound, but I also do not think, as some critics do (as we will see), that dismissing at the outset all such Christian engagements of boxing and martial arts, in ministries or otherwise, is justified. To do so does not fully consider the substantial range of practices, experiences and faithful reflection I have discovered in various fight sports ministries and practitioners, which is pertinent to a fair, comprehensive consideration of the matter. In fact, I find many ministries and their practices to be not only sound, but also admirable, theologically and otherwise.

I still believe in nonviolent means of conflict resolution. Even now, I am personally willing to walk away from confrontation under the right circumstances, to avoid violence. If in doing so the only blow is to my ego, that is a blow I am secure enough to take. Part of the reason for this (as is emphasized by some of the fight sports program leaders we will consider) comes from knowing I am *choosing* that path, rather than having it forced upon me as my only option, as was the case when I was younger. Knowing I *could* fight back in self-defense makes walking away somehow more honestly principled, even perhaps honorable. Even so, I no longer uncritically accept Ellul's proposition that any act of violence is an implicit commitment to the use of full force, and have learned that others agree with me. I know that I would stand up for others or myself under the right circumstances. Many trainers teach that choosing not to fight is both respectable and preferable—but that knowing how to handle a violent confrontation, should one arise, is certainly defensible, although given to a set of ethical considerations. Some well-known trainers even suggest that retreating is an honorable, preferred option to take, once a situation involving violence has been adequately controlled and choosing to stay might only lead to more violence. This means teaching students to have the discipline and confidence it takes to withdraw or diffuse a situation by use of the minimally necessary force, should the need to protect oneself or others arise. That those others might be too frail, untrained or timid to stand up for themselves makes this approach to training, for me and many others, all the more laudable. There is an expression of love in that, I believe: to be willing to risk one's own well-being in order to protect another. It may even mean loving the attacker, or at least showing mercy enough to end a conflict quickly and with as minimal a use of force as possible.

In short, I now believe it is indeed possible to train in fight sports and in fact use them—in real life situations, at a training gym, in the ring or octagon, and even as part of a church ministry—and remain true to Christian principles and values. However, I also believe there are limits to and abuses of such training and fighting. Clearly there are those who simply enjoy dominating others or take advantage of their strength and skill to commit immoral acts. Based upon experience and study, I have come to believe that some people justify the use of violence in fight sports on the basis of what I and others consider a flawed theology, just as I am convinced that theologically acceptable approaches to fight sports and fight sports ministries exist. There are genuinely sound uses of boxing and martial arts programs in the church, for evangelism, pastoral care, formation, fellowship—and, indeed, fun. Some see more limits to acceptable parameters for boxing and martial arts ministries than I do, while others outright oppose any such programs. My cognizance of this range of positions, my own experiential and critical journeys, and my interest in lending a voice of reform, perhaps, to discussions of best practices and informed theologies grounding boxing and martial arts ministries leads to the present study. To quote Saint Paul as he writes in 1 Corinthians 9:26, I do not box "as though beating the air," but as one with purpose and a genuine interest in thoroughly and honestly grappling with the issues involved. My aim is to examine the relationship of fight sports and the church from historical, cultural, practical and theological perspectives, and ultimately to articulate parameters to help determine what form an authentic, well-grounded practice of boxing and martial arts ministries might take in both the life of the church and that of the faithful, one that remains true to religious ideals and ideas about discipleship.

Introduction

Boxing and the church—to some these may seem an odd combination, even incompatible. Boxing in most people's minds is about violence, while the church advocates turning the other cheek and making peace. In boxing, one seeks to dominate an opponent and impose one's will, whereas the church promotes love and concern for others' needs. Boxing rewards victories achieved by trying to harm an adversary; the church advocates praying for one's enemies. It is a compliment in professional boxing to say one has a "killer instinct," and boxers are told to punch "with bad intentions"; the church, in contrast, recognizes as blessed those who are meek and merciful. Even the settings where one finds each practiced are in contrast: boxing's raucous stadiums where aggressive outbursts and primal behaviors are the norm, versus the church's cultured, decorous sanctuaries that traditionally welcome contemplation and reflection.

Then again, St. Paul uses boxing metaphors to inspire Christians to endure hardships and achieve great things. Plenty of famous boxers are renowned for their devotion to the Christian faith. Undefeated heavyweight champion Rocky Marciano attended Mass amidst his training schedule, and once read St. Augustine before an important fight.[1] Boxer-turned-ordained-minister George Foreman wrote an autobiography titled *God in My Corner: A Spiritual Memoir* (2007). Eight-division world champion Manny Pacquiao, the Catholic boxer turned Born-Again Christian, prays for his opponents' safety before fights.[2] Many qualities boxing teaches are recognized virtues in Christianity, from discipline to camaraderie and strength of character. In part for these very reasons, mainstream Christian organizations, from the Young Men's Christian Association (YMCA) to the Catholic Youth Organization (CYO), have incorporated boxing into their programs. Popular culture, particularly that of movies, has regularly depicted an association between boxing and the church. This is perhaps most famously so in the opening scene of the archetypal boxing film *Rocky* (1976), wherein the aforementioned contrast between the serene setting of the church and that of the boxing gym is captured in the very opening shot, one which

8   Introduction

Rocky Balboa, played by Sylvester Stallone (right), takes on a journeyman, slugging it out with Spider Rico (Pedro Lovell) in the ring of Resurrection Gym, while a mural of Christ looks on. From the opening scene of *Rocky* (1976).

further suggests themes of sacrifice and redemption. Inside a church converted to a sports hall, the camera tilts down from a giant mural of a white robed Christ holding the communion bread and cup, to two men boxing in the dimly lit ring of Resurrection Gym, where posters promoting professional boxing matches hang beneath Jesus—who is the only onlooker not shouting.

The affirmative association of boxing and the church, however surprising it may seem to some, has enjoyed a significant history, and includes church organizations such as the YMCA and CYO, theological treatises of those representing the so-called "muscular Christianity" movement, and cultural depictions not only in boxing films like *Rocky*, but also in church-set films such as *Boys Town* (1938), *The Bells of St. Mary's* (1945), and others. Equally noteworthy are the voices of those critical of this association, particularly coming from church leaders and theologians who question the ethics underlying boxing.

The increasing popularity in recent decades of professional mixed martial arts (MMA) has only raised the stakes of this argument for advocates and critics of the church's relationship with fight sports. In many ways more extreme than boxing, its more restrictive forebear, MMA nonetheless enters the same historical, theological and cultural arena in which boxing has stood, and its relationship with the church demands similar reflection. This includes the practice of individual martial arts forms on which *mixed* martial arts are based. Raising the stakes even higher is the growing practice of boxing and martial arts ministry programs, offered nowadays by churches as part of the larger phenomenon of sports ministries, or sometimes offered as separate programs related to the church. This makes an investigation of the association of fight sports with the church all the more timely and pertinent.

The purpose of this study is to undertake a comprehensive, scholarly examination of fight sports in relation to the church, focusing attention on both boxing and martial arts. The analysis will consider a range of perspectives, from the historical, to the cultural, ethical and theological. The historical will trace these sports from the muscular Christianity movement of the 1800s to the present and include a look at both proponents and opponents of the church's relationship with boxing and martial arts. The cultural reflection will examine depictions of the relationship of the church and fight sports in popular culture, from books of the early muscular Christianity era through later depictions in film, television and on the Internet. It will also examine what the relationship of fight sports with the church suggests about American culture and gendered experiences of the church, and how this relates to the church's mission. Among the theological issues to be considered are what Christian ethics suggests about fight sports, as well as how boxing and martial arts ministry programs relate to matters of ecclesiology (the study of the nature of the church), Christology (the study of the person, nature and example of Christ), and evangelism.

Throughout, one overarching theological consideration will be on the types of discipleship suggested by differing approaches to fight sports and the church, particularly as this relates to actual boxing and martial arts ministries, the subject of interview-based case studies included ahead, but also in the broader discussions of fight sports' relation to church history and programs, Christian ethics, and American culture. Differing emphases and approaches of fight sports ministries, I will argue, reflect differing understandings of what it means to be faithful, and careful reflection on the relationship of these approaches to one's understanding and practice of discipleship is essential. Ultimately, the study will critically examine which ministries receive more national media attention than others, and how this selective national attention distorts the more prevalent form of discipleship reflected in many other boxing and martial arts ministries. This will lead to the conclusion of the study—an explicit reflection on theologies underlying the practice of fight sports ministries, and a critical discussion of how they relate to models of Christ's example. Ultimately, while acknowledging a range of theologies and models, I make an argument as to which of these expressions of discipleship is most in keeping with ideals of historic Christian theology.

Popularity of Boxing and Martial Arts Ministries

One reason that study of boxing and martial arts ministries is timely is that these programs are becoming more prominent, especially in the public eye. Part of a broader increase in sports ministries, appealing particularly to millennials,[3] these programs provide opportunities for churches to reach out to both their own members and those in their communities who have an interest in sports. Sometimes developed to provide fellowship for congregants, and sometimes as stand-alone programs developed for community outreach, boxing and martial arts ministries are of practical interest to many, and a curiosity to others. That these programs sometimes, though not always, include religious activities, such as prayers, Bible readings and religious reflection, make them all the more interesting for how fight sports programs relate to understandings of the church.

These growing forms of sports ministry are found in a range of congregational contexts in the United States. They are practiced in mainline Protestant, Catholic and evangelical congregations; they exist in rural, suburban and urban settings; and they are found in all regions of the country. Even the titles of these programs range from the simple to the colorful. Some such programs, many of which are included in forthcoming case studies, are: Battlefield Boxing Ministry (in Anderson, South Carolina); Calvary Chapel of Kensington's Rock Ministries' boxing program for boys and girls (Philadelphia, Pennsylvania); Boxing for Christ (San Jacinto, California); Trinity Lutheran Church's Martial Arts Ministry (Landis, North Carolina); the boxing program of Catholic Charities Teen Center at St. Peter's Church, and later the Boys' and Girls' Club (Dorchester, Massachusetts); the Christian Karate Association's schools (in various locations, including Post Falls, Coeur d' Alene; Moscow, Idaho; and Byram, Mississippi); St. Paul's Lutheran Church's Pocono Tang Soo Do Karate Club (Tannersville, Pennsylvania); the Rock Church's kickboxing, karate, and mixed martial arts ministries (San Diego, California); a "Fight Church" ministry, once in development at Canyon Creek Church (Lynwood, Washington); "Victory Mixed Martial Arts Ministry" at Victory Church (Rochester, New York); the Concord Karate Club, at the Concordia Lutheran Church and School (Fort Wayne, Indiana); Church Street Boxing, part of the SonRise Church ministry (Salem, Oregon); Escape Ministries' West Side Boxing and Fitness program (Holland, Michigan); the Christian Boxing Academy (Jersey City, New Jersey); Victory Boxing Club (Omaha, Nebraska);

a boxing and MMA program at the Victory Ministry and Sports Complex (Joplin, Missouri); Fight 4 Life's "Fitness and Boxing Ministry" (Birmingham, Alabama); Cross for Christ Boxing, a boxing ministry at True Foundation Outreach Center in Columbus, Mississippi; and the Fist of God boxing ministry in Baltimore (formerly the Cross for Christ Boxing Gym). One estimate places the number of mixed martial arts ministries in U.S. evangelical churches alone at more than 700.[4] Without a doubt, these ministries are a considerable part of contemporary American church life.

Attesting to the curiosity these ministries generate is their media attention. Movies, as well as print and broadcast news stories about boxing and martial arts ministries demonstrate public interest in these programs. To wit, the documentary film *Fight Church* (2014), directed by Daniel Junge and Bryan Storkel, features pastors who lead mixed martial arts ministries in their congregations and who fight competitively. The film also includes professional MMA fighters who publicly proclaim their faith and its relation to their vocation, alongside ministers who question the ethics of the sport and its appropriateness for a Christian's life. A news feature originally produced for the Public Broadcasting System (PBS) television program *Religion and Ethics Weekly*, and later revised for presentation on PBS's *Newshour*, spotlights an inner-city boxing ministry in Baltimore, the Cross for Christ Boxing Gym (since renamed Fist of God). The Bishop of the worship center with which the ministry is affiliated explains its significance as "a part of our ministry to help children, young men and women, to be able to reach their own potential through an activity that creates discipline."[5] Print media have likewise featured stories about fight sports ministries, including *The New York Times* ("Flock Is Now a Fight Team in Some Ministries" and "Pastor with a Punch"), *USA Today* ("Churchgoers Turn the Other Cheek in the Boxing Ring" and "High School Coach Dies in Church Boxing Match"), *The Los Angeles Times* ("This Minister Can Preach Virtues of Boxing—and Practice Them"), *Christianity Today* ("Pastor's 'Fight Ministry' Incorporates Mixed Martial Arts; Sees it as Counter to 'Feminised' Church"). Online news sites, such as *The Conversation* ("Mixed Martial Arts and Christianity; 'Where Feet, Fist and Faith Collide'"), have also reported on the phenomenon.[6] Clearly, between the ministries themselves and the media attention they generate, we find both a significant trend and growing public interest in fight sports ministries. Both the programs and their depictions are worth exploration.

Defining Fight Sports Ministries

What, then, exactly are these programs teaching, and what range of activities is signified under the auspices of the terms "boxing," "martial arts," "mixed martial arts," "fight sports," and each of these in ministry? Beginning with the last term, "fight sports" encompasses a range of activities where the objective is to engage in physical combat with another person, the objective being to outscore, submit or disable them. Wins in fight sports are thus awarded by scoring points (such as for getting past an opponent's defenses with a strike), achieving a submission (when an opponent is forced to concede to another) or, in harsher forms, incapacitating an opponent. Many of these are "ritualized" forms of fighting or combat; while dominance over another is the objective, rules are present to limit injury and create a setting for "fair play." Even in professional mixed martial arts (perhaps the most extreme of popular fight sports), certain activities, such as eye gouging, are not permitted, while a host of rules in boxing are designed to protect fighters, such as in the prohibition of hitting an opponent when at least one of their knees is on the ground (thus permitting a downed fighter time to recover), or hitting an opponent behind the head. The very presence of a referee—a judge, a representative of "the law"—is a civilizing force in what might otherwise become a free-for-all brawl. Thus, fight sports include: boxing, kickboxing, and the martial arts of karate, muay thai and taekwondo—all of these considered "striking" sports because they emphasize thrusts with fists, feet and legs; wrestling and the martial arts of judo and jiu-jitsu—referred to as "grappling" sports, because one manipulates or entangles an opponent's body to achieve a "pin" or "submission"; fencing and stick fighting, which use weapons; and, finally, combinations of these forms, called "mixed martial arts."[7]

Beginning with this last category, "mixed martial arts" combine various techniques culled from individual martial arts, each chosen for a particular offensive or defensive situation, to respond to the strengths of one's opponent or capitalize on the strengths of the individual fighter. Some fighters will be more expert in striking sports, others at grappling; and many will have a primary "stand up game"—that is, a form that emphasizes striking—and a primary "ground game"—some form of grappling, be that wrestling, Brazilian jiu-jitsu (BJJ) or another. Thus, mixed martial arts, as one expert defines them, are "any competitive contest whereby participants can punch with a closed or open hand, kick, wrestle, and perform submission techniques under strict guidelines in a professionally supervised setting."[8] Although practiced under other names in particular regions (such as vale judo, Portuguese for "anything goes," in Brazil), the mass popularization and commercialization in the United States of the term mixed martial arts, and the sport itself, emerged largely in 1993, with the debut of the Ultimate Fighting Championship (UFC).[9] This is a contest where combatants fight in an octagonal cage, which is why it is sometimes called "cage fighting." Having a reputation for brutality, these competitions differ somewhat from those involving the individual martial arts on which they are based, to say nothing of the practice of training in these forms, apart from formal competitions, as is the practice of some fight sports ministries.

There are many individual martials arts, each emerging from a particular geographic area or "tradition," and each taking a different approach to combat and how best to engage in it, leading to a martial art form's "philosophy" and "strategy." While there are scores of martial arts forms, several stand out for their prominence in schools and training centers in the United States. These include Brazilian jiu-jitsu, karate, taekwondo, judo, and muay thai. Brazilian jiu-jitsu is among the most popular forms of martial art taught in the Americas. Based on an earlier Japanese form, BJJ is a grappling system that uses chokes and pressure applied to joints, using various "holds" to achieve submissions. Based upon adaptations to the Japanese system made in Brazil by the Gracie family (still among the leading proponents and teachers of the art in the United States), a basic concept in BJJ is that a smaller opponent may submit a larger one, using its techniques.[10] Karate, another martial art, is mainly a striking form, using knees and elbows, kicks and punches, including "open hand" techniques. It originated in Japan's Okinowan islands as a hybrid form, with aspects borrowed from Chinese martial arts, and it spread from there to mainline Japan and the world. This form may be the most prominent martial art depicted in American popular culture, promoted by stars like Chuck Norris and in movies like *The Karate Kid* (1984).[11]

Another striking form is muay thai, the "art of the eight limbs," which originated in Thailand and uses hands, elbows, feet and knees to hit or take down an opponent, with its signature move being the powerful, low roundhouse kick.[12] Taekwondo, from Korea, features kicks—high ones, aimed at the head—thrown from spins and leaps, while also incorporating punches, throws and blocks.[13] Very popular worldwide, taekwondo is an Olympic sport, as is judo. Based on the idea that a fighter (particularly a smaller one) may use the force of an opponent against him or her, judo emphasizes throws and the redirection of force (applying the proverb "when pulled, push; when pushed, pull"), while also using other martial arts techniques.[14]

"Boxing" in the United States is best known in its Western form. Written of in classic works such as *The Iliad* and *The Odyssey*, both of which directly compare it to war, boxing was introduced as an Olympic event in Greece in 688 BC.[15] Practiced in a manner that was more barbaric than the modern version, the ancients recognized "no rounds, rest periods, weight classes or points systems," nor the prohibition of hitting a downed opponent; a fighter won when his opponent could no longer continue.[16] Boxing's next major iteration was in the form of the bare-knuckles fights of London, championed by the pugilist and self-promoting businessman James Figg

(1695–1734), who made of prizefighting a successful "commercial amusement."[17] Famously, Jack Broughton created a set of rules that barred hitting a downed fighter, who was given 30 seconds to rise and fight or be considered "knocked out of time"—that is, "knocked out."[18] Further refinements in the rules emerged with the London Prize Ring Rules of the mid-1800s, until the well-known Queensberry Rules were finally established in 1867; these form the basis of modern boxing, and include many now-standard stipulations: that rounds, previously of indeterminate length, last three minutes; that the interval between rounds is 60 seconds; that wrestling is barred; that a fighter has to beat a ten count to continue if knocked down, or else forfeit the fight; and, most importantly, that padded gloves must be worn.[19] While the Queensberry Rules were an attempt to make the game more civilized, and hence more appealing to upper classes as spectacle, they also, according to some, helped emasculate the sport.

Nowadays, boxing is practiced in a range of contexts, involving both men and women. It is taught locally at commercial clubs and gyms, although typically (unlike many other popular sports) not in public schools.[20] Many gyms offer non-contact fitness boxing, where participants train using bags and perform exercises. Many colleges have boxing programs, which range from fitness-oriented clubs to intramural and inter-collegiate competitive teams.[21] Amateur boxing, including that of the Olympics, typically involves more safety-focused rules. Participants are required to wear protective headgear, matched with others of their experience level, overseen by more hawkish referees, and scored mainly for winning points (that is, hits), making knockouts and impact injuries less common. It is in professional boxing, where fighters use lighter gloves (with less padding), do not use headgear, and where many spectators take singular pleasure in knockouts, that more risk and injury are involved. Even so, boxing is heavily regulated by state commissions and, while there have been high profile "death bouts," studies have shown that other sports (such as swimming, equestrian and motor sports, and even fishing) are actually more likely to result in death, or lead to serious head injuries (these include cycling, skiing, football, baseball, and equestrian sports) than boxing.[22] Then again, recent findings have also shown that chronic brain damage is fairly common among professional boxers.[23]

Other individual fight sports adapted from their Western forms, which also contribute to the "mix" in mixed martial arts, are kickboxing and wrestling. Although many Asian-derived styles incorporate or even emphasize kicks among their techniques, the particular form most associated with the term "kickboxing" in the United States developed in the 1970s as a mixture of Western and Eastern influences. Based upon American boxing style and requiring the use of regulation gloves, American kickboxing also permits the use of kicks and karate chops.[24] The resulting form is now taught at many local venues and has inspired a range of practices, from that solely for cardiovascular fitness to competitive kickboxing training programs and tournaments. Finally, wrestling plays a role in mixed martial arts. As a basic fight sport, various styles of wrestling have developed around the world, including Asia and Africa.[25] Even so, its Western practice, developed from the ancient Greco-Roman form and now taught, trained for, and used in scholastic, collegiate and Olympic competitions, often finds expression in the collection of styles used by MMA athletes.

While an overview of these "fight sports" most prominently practiced in the United States nowadays, alone or as part of MMA, helps set the background for a consideration of how these relate to sports ministry programs, this is only part of the picture. One must also consider the range of contexts within which these sports are engaged. Hence, an athletic ministry program might take an approach to practicing fight sports that emphasizes (1) conditioning or physical fitness, (2) self-defense, (3) recreation, or (4) competition.[26] In fact, an individual ministry may incorporate one, several, or all of these objectives into its program. This choice will result in a different range of activities, possibilities, appeals and concerns, and this will be a particular concern in the forthcoming discussion of the ethics of fight sports ministries. It is nonetheless noteworthy that if an objection or concern should arise regarding programs that take a particular approach, this does not necessarily mean that this objection would apply to others.

A sports ministry may, for example, use boxing or kickboxing for conditioning purposes, as a form of physical exercise for fitness. Many gyms offer classes in "cardio kickboxing" or "boxing boot camp," where participants use the moves and equipment of those fight sports for health benefits, but do not spar or prepare to compete. This practice would be least controversial, and yet still use the forms and techniques of a fight sport for physical and social benefits. Alternately, some ministries might emphasize the teaching of a fight sport's techniques for the purpose of self-defense. Participants would learn various philosophies, strategies and techniques of the form being studied (boxing, karate, BJJ, or whatever) in order to protect themselves and others. In this context, some programs might take a more aggressive approach to teaching self-defense than others, even bordering on competitive-style sparring. Others might be less competitive. To square off with others while emphasizing the fun, playful aspects of a sport or form would involve the above identified recreational use. The creation of an environment that emphasizes growth, mutuality and play is essential here; providing this is achieved, the resulting atmosphere may foster learning, exercise, and mutual support. Finally, a formally competitive approach would likely incorporate all of the above approaches and add to them in various degrees, with the goal of applying the skills and strategies learned and practiced to dominate an opponent and win a fight. The openness to escalation, and the degree to which that potential intensification is tolerated or even encouraged, is an essential ethical consideration, which we will address in a forthcoming chapter.

Those designing or reflecting upon the approach of fight sports ministries should consider the context, audience and mission of a given program, as well as how it relates to church values and the model of discipleship it presents. The resulting choices may be influenced, for example, by whether one is designing an outreach ministry aimed at involving "at-risk" urban youth, or a program made to appeal to a broad range of congregational participants, including adults, with an emphasis on fun. Theoretical and practical reflections on these matters will be the central focus of chapters ahead, including in upcoming case studies of various such fight sports ministries around the United States, based upon interviews with their program leaders. For now, it is significant to recognize the range of approaches from which programs may choose in developing fight sports ministries, and that each may be appropriate for different circumstances, and present different challenges and appeals.

As to the benefits of fight sports ministry programs, many of these are shared with the benefits of sports ministry programs in general. For the individuals involved, these include not only increased physical fitness—that is, a stronger body—but also making participants stronger in mind, community-engagement and spirit—emphases, as we will see, that are explicit goals of many fight sports ministries. Hence, the communal aspect of training promotes fellowship and social involvement. Leaders also tout the potential of such programs to develop character, spiritual "formation," and leadership skills, particularly as participants contemplate matters such as fair play, how to work well with others, and their own dedication to self-improvement and excellence. All of these are matters which will be central discussions in the forthcoming chapters on ethics and case studies. Regarding boxing's benefits to society in particular, even church-affiliated boxing programs have held a historically important place in readying citizens for successful military service, as we will see in the chapter on the history of fight sports and the church. These are some of the benefits of past and present fight sports ministry programs for both individuals and society.

Fight Sports Ministries and the Church

As for how fight sports ministries relate to wider concerns of the church, aspects of several theological disciplines naturally arise in a comprehensive reflection on boxing and martial arts ministries. Church history will help to understand how such programs developed vis-à-vis broader trends and concerns in the church, and how contemporary fight sports ministries relate to their antecedents. Christian ethics, including reflections from biblical perspectives, will help in reflecting upon the benefits and ethical boundaries of boxing and martial arts programs, and the principles that should guide consideration of what is and is not acceptable in the practice of such ministry programs. As these programs often are seen as part of a church's mission to reach various groups, matters of evangelism arise, as do reflections on church and society, in considering how the interaction of church and fight sports is reflected in broader culture. Inasmuch as the sports under consideration are often considered "masculine" and their use historically has been employed in efforts to "re-masculinize" what some see as a "feminized" church, issues of gendered ecclesiology (the expression of gender traits in the overall character of the church) arise, and likewise do so in relation to reflections on history, ethics and evangelism. Finally, Christology is involved in the form of the conception of Christ that derives from or influences leaders' approach to their sports ministries, and how this advocates particular types of Christian discipleship. As we will see, there are those who literally depict Christ as a pugilistic fighter, just as there are those who envision Christ in other ways, such as a shepherd, and use these models to guide what is considered appropriate for training programs and Christian behavior.

As mentioned, an ongoing, particular focus of this study will be on the kind of discipleship suggested by the specific practices of various fight sports ministry programs. This involves how leaders approach a fight sports ministry and its participants; what goals leaders set for participants; what sort of relationships with others leaders encourage; and what values leaders model. All of these considerations bear witness to broader matters of discipleship, which are on display in everything believers do—including in church sports ministry programs. Clearly, discipleship involves more than just sports ministry; however, inasmuch as discipleship is reflected throughout a Christian's life, it is also inclusive of this, and so how discipleship relates to the specifics of sports ministry programs merits attention. Does one value victory over another more than helping others to thrive and achieve? What attitude does one's approach reflect about violence and mercy, vengeance and sacrifice, glory and grace? Indeed, while some practitioners say they fight to evince God's glory, others emphasize a mindfulness of how their training relates to God's love—a love that appreciates the gift of play and fellowship with others, honors the body, helps others achieve and advance—sometimes even at the expense of one's own glory; and, should one be forced to engage in self-defense, a love that may show mercy even to an assailant. How these issues are raised, considered and practiced also depends upon the particular goals of a boxing or martial arts ministry, be those for fitness, self-defense, recreation or competition, as each objective raises different possibilities and concerns. In sum, those behaviors, attitudes and values leaders model for participants and put into practice say something about their understanding of faithful discipleship. These are therefore important matters to consider in reflecting upon fight sports ministry programs, all of which we will consider ahead.

Scholarship on Fight Sports and the Church

Scholars and church leaders alike voice an awareness of the need for more reflection on newly raised issues arising from culture's and the church's increasing engagement with sport, including in the context of sports ministry programs. This is increasingly important for boxing and martial arts ministries, given their growing prominence. Reflecting upon the need for more scholarship on the intersections of sports and the church, one theologian, recalling remarks by theologian Dietrich Bonhoeffer, observes the need for the church to contribute more to our understanding of play and game, asserting that "for far too long the church (and specifically its scholars) have passed on such an endeavor"; he calls on theologians "to think deeply and critically about God's intention for sports and their current role in society today."[27] Author and pastor Michael Shafer, who has written on the theology and ethics of sports from the Christian perspective, laments the dearth of Christian theologians' reflection on these subjects, and calls for "a richer understanding of how [...] faith offers formative principles to guide" that reflection, and to "provide spiritually meaningful reasons for participating in sport."[28] Nick J. Watson and Brian Brock, two professors studying sports, culture and religion, note the limited literature regarding the church's reflection on boxing and mixed martial arts, particularly among ethicists, and issue a call for more.[29] Hence, while growing numbers of newspaper and magazine articles, television segments and documentary films evince a burgeoning popular interest in reflections on the church's engagement with boxing and martial arts, and while ministries involving these sports are of considerable numbers and on the rise in American congregations, thorough theological reflection on the phenomenon is wanting.

Observing that "Christians tend [to] see sports as something altogether separate from the serious matters of life," another critic calls for greater development of a "theology of sport," so as to provide "a fuller, more biblical view of sports," concluding with the observation that "we need to see sports not as something without purpose and meaning, something secular, but instead as something with purpose and meaning, something sacred."[30] Indeed, conceptualizing a comprehensive understanding of the relationship of sports in general with religion in all its iterations is important, particularly for how we might adapt such schemas to the context of fight sports. One such systematic approach that provides a useful framework within which to consider the relation of sports to religion is that of Joseph L. Price, who has developed a five category taxonomy for this task.[31] Thus, Price suggests, the relationship of sports to religion may manifest as (1) in conflict, (2) commingling, (3) conscripting, (4) co-opting, or (5) supplementing the latter. Engaged in the context of fight sports, Price's categories provide a helpful framework within which to consider the range of engagements of fight sports by the church.

Hence, in discussing sports conflicting with religion, Price notes the history of churches' and religious figures' objections to sport for enticing believers to celebrate the profane, or engage in "ungodly" behavior (such as drunkenness, gambling, or rough play, especially on the Sabbath), or in various ways compete with the "rightful" central place religion should hold in the lives of the faithful. Price, in fact, specifically notes that prizefighting's brutality made it subject to criticism by church leaders, who would encourage their followers to reject such spectacular vices as this in deference to one's faith. As we will see in examining the history of the church's engagement with fight sports, there is a well-established history of church leaders using religion to denounce fight sports, just as there is with Price's next two categories: of sports commingling with religion, and religion conscripting sports. As to the first, that of commingling, this category includes uses of sport for missionary work and evangelical outreach, in public expressions of the values and faith of athletes, and in "fusing faith and athletics" in religious institutions.[32] As noted earlier, renowned fighters, such as Rocky Marciano, George Foreman and Manny Pacquiao, among others, have used their status as stars of the ring or octagon to express how their vocation in fight sports reflects their faith. This is a matter to which we will return, when later we consider potential theological misuses of such expressions. More immediately in Chapter 1, this commingling will relate to the history of church organizations' engagement of fight sports to express a particular vision of Christian life, such as in the muscular Christianity movement, as Price himself observes. Indeed, this category of commingling also aptly describes the relationship of sports to religion underlying most fight sports ministry programs we will consider in the forthcoming case studies chapter.

The "conscripted" use of sports by religion applies to efforts to, often in a heavy-handed fashion, capitalize on the values associated with sports for religious purposes. Rather than uses of religion and sports that serve their mutual interests, as in the categories above, this grouping (to adapt an image from Shakespeare's *Macbeth*) might best be thought of as religion dressing itself in the "borrowed robes" of sports, in order to be seen more in the latter's light. Price offers the examples of holding religious events (such as revivals, religious concerts, or appearances by religious leaders) in sports arenas, to capitalize on the associated excitement of the venue. Price also includes herein St. Paul's uses of athletic metaphors to inspire his followers. As I will argue when discussing Christian ethics in relation to fight sports, this inclusion may not fully consider Paul's subversive use of athletic references and pugilistic imagery for his purposes, as he may actually use sports metaphors (boxing or otherwise) to challenge their customary sensibility. Price also explicitly mentions the stained-glass window "sports bay" at St. John the Divine Cathedral in New York, which we will likewise consider ahead, as the images appearing on it include biblical allusions to modern fight sports. Indeed, inasmuch as some "fight pastors" and professional fighters use religious terminology in their ring or cage names (including, for example, "The Pastor of Disaster," "The Punching Pastor," and "The Soldier of God"), use their presence in the octagon or ring to advocate for their faith, or alternately use the pulpit to discuss their engagement in fight sports, these examples befit Price's discussion of religion conscripting sports.

Price's final two categories involve sports "co-opting" or "supplanting" religion. The first involves claims that God intervenes in sporting events, suggesting that God cares about who wins a contest, and that winning reflects God's favor—that God is on the winner's "side." This may well apply to some of those fighters who claim that their victories reflect God's glory, an assertion I will interrogate later when considering theological reflections on fight sports and issues of discipleship. Price also mentions the co-opting of religious language in the context of sports, as in using the sporting terminology of a "sacrifice" (in baseball), an "immaculate reception" or "Hail Mary" pass (in football), or, similarly, a "Hail Mary" punch in fight sports— that is, one thrown in desperation, with wild abandon, in hopes that it will "land" and disable an opponent. The "supplanting" of religion by sports, Price's final category, concerns how some fans treat sport itself as a religion, showing a devotion usually reserved for more traditional religious subjects, but here afford such devotion to a sport, team, player, or (in the present context) fighter. By approaching sports with such devoutness, and finding a "religious significance in the ritual dimensions of sports activities," some enthusiasts may thereby raise the "profane" world of sports to the status of the "sacred," not only in their treating sport with such devotion, but also by ritualistically engaging in the sporting activities in a manner that replaces the functions of "traditional" religion.³³ This, then, is how Price's taxonomy may be useful for considering not only the relation of religion to sports in general, but also, for our purposes, to fight sports, and fight sports ministries in particular.

As to full length works considering sports and the church, several excellent historical books look broadly at Christianity and sports, tracing the development of the muscular Christianity movement in America, beginning with its British roots. Foremost among these are Tony Ladd and James A. Mathisen's *Muscular Christianity: Evangelical Protestants and the Development of American Sport* (1999), Clifford Putney's *Muscular Christianity: Manhood and Sports in Protestant America, 1880–1920* (2001), and William J. Baker's *Playing with God: Religion and Modern Sport* (2007). While these books are pertinent to the study of fight sports and the church, boxing itself is but one of the many sports considered in these works (two of which make only a handful of references to boxing), and martial arts as such are not a significant focus of these works at all. Hence, while these volumes are helpful resources for examining the historical development of the muscular Christianity movement and its relation to fight sports, their focus is much broader than that of the present study, which aims to look more particularly at the relationship of fight sports and the church.

On the other side of the equation are works that cover the history of boxing or martial arts generally, and which may occasionally address matters of fight sports and religion, but which do not themselves focus principally on boxing and martial arts in relation to the Christianity and the church. These works include Jeffrey T. Sammons' *Beyond the Ring: The Role of Boxing in American Society* (1990), Arne K. Lang's *Prize-Fighting: An American History* (2008), Clyde Gentry III's *No Holds Barred: The Complete History of Mixed Martial Arts in America* (2011), and Christopher David Thrasher's *Fight Sports and American Masculinity: Salvation in Violence from 1607 to the Present* (2015). Valuable resources for the historical and cultural chapters of this book, their wider focus is not identical to the more specific aims of the work in hand.

Likewise, ethical and cultural treatments of Christian engagement with sports in general are valuable resources for this study, even though the focus herein is more particularly on how these relate to fight sports. As such, Shirl James Hoffman's *Christianity and the Culture of Sports* (2010) and Michael Shafer's *Well Played: A Christian Theology of Sport and the Ethics of Doping* (2015) are crucial resources for this book. Each expertly offers critical perspectives on the relationship of sports to Christian values and ethics. Nonetheless, although each occasionally discusses fight sports outright, their arguments are more broadly drawn than to look specifically at boxing and martial arts, as is the focus of the present study. Other works similarly look at a broad range of sports in relation to the church, and yet are (at least in part) more practically focused, offering guidance for the Christian practice and appreciation of sports. These include Bryan Mason's *Beyond the Gold: What Every Church Needs to Know about Sports Ministry* (2011) and David E. Prince's *In the Arena: The Promise of Sports for Christian Discipleship* (2016). Notably, Prince's work complements its "practical instruction," including that offered for parents of young athletes, with a discussion of discipleship in sports, albeit one whose strength lies in its emphasis on practical advice, whereas the goal of a similar discussion in the current text is to more fully develop it in a broader theological reflection. Beyond this, some books offer advice specifically on how to start or organize fight sports ministries, or how to undertake instruction in fight sports in the context of Christian ministry, and may include devotionals, marketing tips, advice on developing lesson plans and budgets, and other practical matters. These include works such as John Terry's *Christian Martial Arts: The Passion, the Calling, the Journey* (2009), Wendy Williamson's *Christian Martial Arts 101* (2004), and John Blackman's *Martial Arts Ministry: How to Start a Martial Arts Ministry* (2016).

The unique contribution of *Fight Sports and the Church: Boxing and Martial Arts Ministries in America* is in its focus, scope and approach. Vis-à-vis broader examinations of sports and Christianity, the focus herein is specifically on boxing and martial arts and their associated ministries. The aim is to consider fight sports in relation to the church from a comprehensive range of scholarly perspectives, including the historical, cultural and theological. In contrast to more practically focused books on the subject— which give advice on how to begin, manage and offer instruction in fight sports ministries; how to oversee a child's success in such programs; and how to instill biblical principles in participants via sports—the approach of the present study is more critical and reflective. It draws upon a range of academic disciplines and approaches to examine the relation of fight sports and the church. To balance this, the book also surveys the practice of actual fight sports ministries, employing interviews with ministry leaders to consider how their programs relate to the more scholarly discussions. The resulting work will appeal to various constituencies, including those interested or involved in fight sports ministries, those interested or involved in fight sports training on their own and interested in how this relates to matters of faith, and those with interests in history, cultural studies, media studies, gender studies, ethics, sports and society, the American church, and theology.

To examine current boxing and martial arts ministries, an understanding of how the church's past relation with such programs informs its present is fundamental. Therefore, we begin in Chapter 1 by historically tracing the development of such programs, including considerations of their practices, motivations and approaches. This includes discussion of the muscular Christianity movement as it arose in England and then was transported to the United States. Among the relevant considerations here are the movement's principal proponents and how their advocacy conceptualized of the relationship of the church with fight sports, boxing in particular. Those Christian organizations that offered boxing programs, such as the Young Men's Christian Organization and the Catholic Youth Organization, will receive significant attention, as will later organizations that focused on other fight sports. Also considered will be the voices of historic church leaders who raised moral objections to boxing and fight sports, and what form their opposing arguments took. The overall aim of the chapter is to historically examine the church's relationship with boxing and martial arts by chronicling the development of church-affiliated programs incorporating fight sports, examining the perspectives of those who rose to defend or oppose such sports in general, and to consider what church leaders' advocacy, one way or another, suggests about the perceived relationship of fight sports and the church.

Inasmuch as some of the major, historic boxing and martial arts ministries were developed as a way to combat what some perceived as a feminization of the church, Chapter 2 considers fight sports and the church from the broader perspective of how these relate to larger aspects of culture. Just as some have argued that American culture has become feminized, so too many in the church debate matters of gendered ecclesiology—whether and how the church reflects particular gender traits, and whether and how it thereby appeals more to men or women. In this context, boxing and fight sports ministries are occasionally offered as part of a larger effort by some to "re-masculinize" the church. Likewise, popular books about "men's ministries" figure in this discussion, particularly as they consider how to appeal to and evangelize "traditional" men by promoting masculine activities and models of discipleship. This, as we will see, includes promotion of a "warrior" archetype as a model for male Christian disciples, one with clear ties to fight sports. Many of these works aim to ensure that male church members are able to maintain a strong, rugged, individualist self-image in an organization often associated with refinement, docility and service toward others.

Popular culture, from the muscular Christian age on through today, has reflected these tensions in books, films, television programs and internet imagery. Sometimes it brazenly takes one side, wholeheartedly depicting a strong Christian fighter, as in the main character of Thomas Hughes' novel *Tom Brown's School Days*, or in internet memes that depict Christ himself as a boxer, wearing gloves standing in a boxing ring, as we will discuss. At other times, popular culture attempts to resolve these contrasts by depicting fight sports ministry leaders as quiet, peace loving, and disinclined from using force, but who will use it when necessary. Literary characters from novels of authors ranging from Charles Dickens to Jack Butler depict Christian boxers and martial artists in this way, as do films such as *The Boxer* (1997), which focuses on the leader of a boxing ministry in Northern Ireland who values nonviolence and seeks reconciliation among members of various Christian groups, and TV shows such as *M*A*S*H* (1972–83), with its featured anti-war priest and former CYO coach Father John Mulcahy. Similarly, a martial arts school instructor guided by the Bible and opposed to the use of guns uses his training to help fight crime in the TV series *Sons of Thunder* (1999). Thus, the depiction in popular media of church leaders skilled in fight sports has sensational appeal, while also serving to portray church leaders as both peace loving and strong fighters for the faith. Chapter 2 examines all of this, ending with a consideration of how ritualized violence, such as that in the ring or cage, relates to modern cultural anxieties about masculinity and violence, in the church and elsewhere.

Chapter 3, on fight sports and Christian ethics, reflects upon arguments for and against fight sports, highlighting their use in church-related programs. This discussion begins with reflections on biblical rhetoric (such as that of St. Paul), iconography and themes, particularly about violence and nonviolence, and how these pertain to fight sports ministries. Next, the chapter considers the conception of the body as God's gift and how human being's creation in the likeness of God (that is, imago dei) provides motivations for and against fight sports and their related ministries. Given that supporters of Christian athletics programs often emphasize their positive effects on participants' character and the social benefits of such programs (to say nothing of the physical), Chapter 3 also looks at the stated outcomes of these programs, as well as how ethicists respond. The chapter then looks at ethical issues related to competition, particularly for Christian sports participants, as well as ethical issues related to training for self-defense. Given the central role philosophies of play hold for Christian ethicists considering the ultimate purpose of sport, the chapter also reflects upon this body of thought and its relation to fight sports ministries. Finally, the chapter considers how each of the four goals of fight sports ministries previously identified (for fitness, self-defense, recreation, and competition) relates to the matters discussed, and anticipates the coming discussion of differing models of discipleship.

After these various scholarly reflections on boxing and martial arts ministries, Chapter 4 takes up a consideration of actual fight sports ministries from the perspectives of those involved in such programs. To accomplish this, the chapter incorporates interviews conducted by the author with leaders of fight sports ministries around the United States, representing various religious affiliations, fight sports, and program types. The discussion includes a history of each of these programs, the goals of the programs, what the programs involve, who participates, the types and extent of religious activity involved, and how these ministries understand their relationship to Christianity and the mission of the church. The discussion also applies the matters considered in previous chapters to the practical issues raised by these ministries' leaders. The chapter ends by comparing these programs with those receiving more high-profile media attention, finding that the national media's focus on more sensational fight sports ministries obscures the more measured approach of a vast many others.

Finally, the conclusion brings together the various strands of the preceding discussions and reflects upon the theological presuppositions underlying the various approaches to fight sports ministries. It considers what differing types of practice in fight sports ministry says about their understandings of discipleship. This includes discussions of fight sports ministries as adiaphora (the "indifferent things," which are neither commanded nor condemned), how the approaches of these programs relate to theology (here, contrasting those invoking a theology of glory with that of the cross), and how divergent understandings of discipleship lead participants to different ways of practicing their faith. This last discussion highlights contrasting models of how to understand Christ as an exemplar for Christian behavior—specifically between the models of the warrior or knight, and that of the shepherd. Lastly, the postscript harkens back to the personal reflections of the prologue and considers how the book may be used by various readers, including Christian practitioners of fight sports and those who lead fight sports ministries.

As stated at the outset, fight sports and the church might at first glance seem like an odd combination; however, their combination shares a significant history, reveals provocative issues in American culture, enjoys significant practice, and invokes interesting discussions of ethics and theology. Their intersections concern matters of American history, popular culture, sports and society, gender, the media, and faith. If, as writer and essayist James Ellroy writes, "the Fight World is the Outside World condensed and refracted,"[34] then a study of the junctures of the church with the world of fight sports promises to reveal fascinating issues beyond boxing and martial arts ministries themselves, and reflect broader concerns of society, religion and culture.

1

The History of Fight Sports and the Church

In her classic essay "On Boxing," writer Joyce Carol Oates proclaims that boxing is "a purely masculine activity and it inhabits a purely masculine world."[1] For those looking to establish a "masculine" stronghold in the church, the integration of boxing into church institutions and rhetoric is one way to accomplish that goal. Based on the more brutal sport of bare-knuckles prizefighting, itself created for the ethically suspect purpose of gambling, boxing was at first seen by some as an emasculated form of its more savage forebear.[2] Even so, it was a manly enough fight sport to appeal to those looking to infuse the church with masculine character and appeal, and make it more palatable for male membership. To this end, the professionalization of boxing, together with the outlawing of bare-knuckles prizefighting, helped redeem fisted fighting from its seedy image as a sport that appealed to the more crude tastes of the underclass[3]; this made it all the more suitable for use in a broad range of church contexts. Thus, those looking to define discipleship in a manner inclusive of, and indeed emphasizing masculine character and a "warrior" or fighter's spirit, could use a now more "civilized" fight sport to meet this goal. Even so, others objected to boxing and other fight sports on theological and ethical grounds and used their rather vocal opposition to define their own discipleship as one of safeguarding believers and society from perceived ills, including fight sports.

Historical Support by the Church for Fight Sports

It was at about the time that boxing was becoming professionalized that a concurrent movement was afoot in Christianity. Emphasizing a connection between "manliness and Christian character," the movement was known as that of "muscular Christianity." It first arose in Victorian England in response to a perceived "effeminacy" reportedly brought to the church by seminary graduates and an urbanized society, the latter of which led to poor health and a de-emphasis on physical rigor.[4] First coined in 1857 in a review of a novel by Charles Kingsley, the term "muscular Christianity" came to represent a movement among Christian socialists whose work emphasized in equal parts "athleticism, patriotism and religion."[5] Kingsley himself was a clergyman, and his novels, including the influential *Westward Ho!* (1855), included narrative portraits of what would become recognized as the embodiment of the muscular Christian philosophy; in fact, this novel ushered in an era in which "literature became flooded with pious athletes who knocked their enemies down with texts from the Scriptures and left-handers from the shoulder."[6] It was, however, Thomas Hughes' novel *Tom Brown's Schooldays* (1857), together with others of his writings (including 1887's *The Manliness of Christ*, a treatise about Jesus' masculinity), that became most associated with the movement. Focusing on boys who had hardy appetites for sports, learning, and godliness, the mythic world created in popular culture by the writings of Hughes gained ground for the crusade. Although his writings mostly heralded the virtues of team sports, Hughes did include reference to schoolboys who "enjoyed the pleasures of [...] occasional fistfights at Rugby School"; indeed, he wrote that, while such should be avoided if possible, boxing was one way "for English boys to settle their problems," and that if one was faced with a fistfight, one should not "say 'No' because you fear a licking, and say or think it's because you fear God, for that's neither Christian nor honest."[7]

A similar sentiment is documented by British novelist and historian Walter Besant, who penned a number of works of both fiction and non-fiction examining life in London's less affluent districts in the nineteenth century. In his documentary work *East London* (1901), Besant writes sympathetically of the working-class people and culture he encountered and documented. Noteworthy in particular here are his notes on the efforts of one local vicar to establish a well-functioning church in the area, a church that catered to all of the needs of those living around the parish. While not strictly or self-consciously an advocate for the muscular Christian movement, Besant nonetheless extolls similar virtues as he describes this church's use of boxing to develop strong character traits in young men. Thus, in writing about the efforts of this vicar to help adolescent men rise above temptations of "slum" life, Besant records that the vicar:

> opened a club for lads and the younger men; he provided his club with things that attracted them—rough games and gymnastics; more than this, he gave them boxing-gloves and taught them how to fight according to the strict rules of the prize-ring. You think that this is not the ideal amusement for the clergyman—wait a bit. The rules of the prize-ring are rigid rules; they demand a good deal of study; they make boxing

a duello conducted according to rules of honor and courtesy. Now, when a lad has learned to handle the gloves according to the rules he becomes a stickler for them.[8]

Indeed, in a manner that aptly summarizes the objectives of even modern-day urban boxing ministries targeted at "at-risk" youth (which we will discuss, ahead), Besant goes on to describe the effects of the East London vicar's boxing ministry, writing with a literary flourish that the end result of a young man being given

> fifteen minutes with a stout adversary, two or three returns to earth, and a shake-hand at the end, [is to] knock the devil out of a lad—the devil of restlessness and of pugnacity—give him a standard of honor, and make the rough-and-tumble in the street no longer worthy of consideration.[9]

Thus, through this early urban church boxing program, young men would "contract habits of order and discipline," become "infected" with "honor and honesty, purity and temperance," "lead steady lives and become supporters of order and authority"[10]—and, as Hughes writes, learn not to fear an adversary, or fear a fight.

The embodiment of the muscular Christianity movement's values was not only established in fictional writing and documented in historical accounts of actual parish programs; it also found incarnation in Christian fighters themselves. Hence, anticipating later celebrity-boxers-turned-evangelists in the United States was one such English prizefighter: William Thompson of Nottingham, known in the ring as Bendigo. Bendigo's fighting career lasted from 1834 to 1850, during which time he became a popular champion.[11] He held his title from 1839 to 1850, defending it against a series of rivals, until the "Nottingham Jester," as he was also known, retired.[12] Regularly imprisoned during his prizefighting years, it was after his final incarceration that he quit prizefighting and turned to a career in evangelism. He was so successful at drawing crowds that attendance at his revivals reportedly surpassed that of most of his fights.[13] Bendigo openly used his celebrity status to help draw audiences. Once during a sermon he gestured to his trophies while taking a boxer's stance and announced to the crowd, in a manner linking his past career to his current discipleship, "See them belts? See them cups? I used to fight for those, but now I fight for Christ." Bendigo toured England, using his fame as a fighter to spread the gospel. Though it was said that he could not read the Bible, his "straightforward manly speech" was effective at reaching followers. He was better off fighting the Devil, his followers said, because "he had no man left to fight."[14] Clearly one who embodied the spirit of muscular Christianity in England, Bendigo was an early pugilist to use his fame as a fighter for evangelism.

Eventually, the muscular Christianity movement spread to the United

States, where the term was first used in a denominational journal in 1867. The journal noted that the name met with its approval because "[it] is suggestive of force and that high-strung, nervous energy which by constant exercise has developed its possessor into the stature of a perfect man in Christ Jesus. We need such a Christianity now."[15] In America, the movement became associated with revivals.[16] Indeed, one of the first celebrity muscular Christian figures in the United States was Hezekiah Orville Gardner, or Orville "the Awful," as he was known in the ring—a bare-knuckles era fighter with a penchant for out-of-the-ring brawls. During one such fight in New York City in 1855, Gardner broke a man's jaw and was imprisoned for six months. This experience led to his conversion to Christianity. After this, Gardner traveled, spoke at revival meetings and churches, and "used his celebrity status as a sports hero to [...] convert others to Christianity," particularly those in prisons. This prizefighter's muscular Christian persona and the story of his conversion appealed to listeners, "in part because of his twin connection to sport and revivalist religion."[17]

Evangelical revivalism not only used sports celebrities to draw people to the gospel, it also responded institutionally to draw people to the Christian faith, with the establishment of organizations such as the Young Men's Christian Association, the YMCA. What started in England as a response to problems of urbanization and a muscular Christian effort to attract a different constituency than "only women and effeminate men" would cross the pond when the first YMCA in the United States opened in Boston in 1851.[18] Thereafter, YMCAs quickly spread. The high-profile branch in New York City stated that its mission was "the improvement of the spiritual, mental and social condition of young men," and "to promote evangelical religion among young men of this city and its vicinity."[19] As the institution grew, it moved from church basements, where most had been established, to stand-alone facilities, hundreds of which included gymnasiums. Although other branches indeed included gyms, the New York YMCA, opened in 1869, was the first planned primarily for physical activity. Notably, its features included boxing equipment.[20]

Although their theological moorings may have differed, the evangelical YMCA program, for all its initial emphasis on personal salvation, resonated with some proponents of the liberal social gospel movement, who were "committed to ministering to the needs of the whole person, material as well as spiritual"; as people's need for play was considered essential for their well-being, social gospel advocates supported sport in general, and the muscular Christian philosophy in particular—although their embrace of fight sports was more problematic, given the propensity of such sports to cause harm.[21] Nonetheless, the effort in this era to integrate physical exercise with the church's mission and outreach had broad appeal. This move was made all the more visible by leadership at the Y coming from some of the top evangelical figures of the age. Dwight Moody, the renowned evangelist, led the Chicago Y from 1858 to 1873. At first more interested in using the YMCA as a place for "Bible classes, sermons and edifying lectures," over time Moody came to recommend the establishment of a gym in order to attract young men. The outcome was lackluster. As one attendee recalled of the Chicago gym, there was little more than "a large, dirty, smoky walled room with a few parallel bars, rings attached to ropes fastened to the ceiling, and a few pairs of dirty boxing gloves."[22] Even so, the programs did include pugilism. Other Ys were not as modest, as professional boxers reportedly trained at YMCAs here and there because the facilities were often better equipped and cheaper than that of other athletic clubs.[23]

The move to include physical fitness as an official part of the YMCA's mission was introduced in 1891, when the institution began to develop what became known as its "four-fold program."[24] This introduced a commitment to provide programs that would help develop its participants spiritually, mentally, socially and physically. It was this last area, already present to a degree in the YMCA's offerings, which now not only became formally acknowledged, but also became the Y's primary attraction for membership.[25] Some local YMCAs were already ahead of the curve. The New York YMCA at 23rd Street, for example, had a daily regimen in physical education that included programs to attract men and develop "true Christian manhood," and featured programs in gymnastics and boxing.[26] The success of such programs ultimately helped doubters, such as Moody, to endorse the four-fold program, leading to an institutional commitment to include fitness and sporting programs in the Y's offerings, which, depending upon the location, might include boxing and, eventually, martial arts.

Thus, over time, the YMCA's emphasis on saving souls transformed into a more general emphasis on character development through physical activity. No longer requiring members to pledge to uphold the tenets of evangelical theology, as they once had, the YMCA "virtually separated itself from its initial evangelical moorings."[27] It was enough now to instill a kind of general discipleship defined by hard work, physical strength and fortitude, rather than a strict adherence to a set of spiritual beliefs. This shift in emphasis, although ensuring the continued success of the Y, did not always sit well with those involved, even with some of its previous proponents. One of the leading figures during this transformation was baseball player turned evangelist Billy Sunday. Although he worked with the YMCA in the early 1890s, Sunday eventually came to see sport as a distraction from what he thought should be the proper focus of Christian life and the business of bringing souls to Christ. "The road into the Kingdom of God," Sunday complained about the established church and its institutions, "is not by the bathtub, *nor the gymnasium*, nor the university, but the blood red hand of the cross of Christ."[28] Notably, whereas his predecessors had espoused a postmillennial theology, which seeks to transform society in order to pave the way for Christ's return, including through institutions such as the Y, Sunday's pre-millennialism caused him to disengage with society. After he left the YMCA to become a traveling evangelist, his exploitation of athletics was restricted to using his celebrity to attract audiences, or the use of stirring sports references in his preaching.[29]

It is in this last way, by use of rhetoric, that Sunday nonetheless continued to make a connection between muscular Christianity and boxing. "Jesus was the greatest scrapper that ever lived," Sunday once proclaimed, creating an image of an hard-hitting, pugilistic Savior; broadening his language to include the aggressive bravery of Christ's followers, Sunday added that "the manliest man is the man who will acknowledge Jesus Christ." In fact, he encouraged his audiences to "fight" along with Jesus.[30] With this image of Jesus as a rugged fighter, and His true disciples as tough combatants, Sunday sought to distance himself from what he called "brittle-boned, weak-kneed, thin-skinned, pliable, plastic, spineless, effeminate, sissified, three-carat Christianity."[31] Indeed, not restricting the use of boxing imagery to Christ, Sunday, referring to himself, once declared, "I'd like to put my fist on the nose of the man who hasn't got grit enough to be a Christian."[32] To be good with one's fists would seem to be not only Christian, but also Christlike, in Sunday's view.

Sunday's rhetoric of Christian fisticuffs aside, the YMCA stepped up its own commitment to teach fight sports during the First World War. This venture came after president Woodrow Wilson issued an executive order that the YMCA should help ready the American Expeditionary Forces (AEF) headed to Europe, to ensure that they were well trained before deployment. The training took the form of hand-to-hand combat, including wrestling techniques and boxing.[33] Among the instructors in this effort was former-professional-heavyweight-boxer-turned-ordained-Presbyterian-minister the Rev. Frederick "The Fighting Parson" Wedge. A Christian true to Sunday's vision, Wedge was a rough-and-tumble church leader, a Harvard educated pastor whose aggressive conduct led him as often into trouble as it did to his eventual success. Working with the YMCA, the Reverend Wedge served as a volunteer boxing instructor for the troops stationed at Camp Grant in Rockford, Illinois, saying he did so because he believed that training in boxing could help the soldiers in combat.[34] Demonstrating his commitment to his two vocations, one with the church and the other in the ring, the Reverend Wedge boxed daily, always right before teaching Bible class, which he did still wearing his sweaty attire.[35] Billy Sunday would be most pleased with the Reverend Wedge's example.

The army's promotion of boxing in conjunction with the YMCA helped not only to increase Americans' appetite for boxing, as both participants and spectators, but also to emphasize the perceived relationship between Christian character and fight sports. Hence, in keeping with the tenets of muscular Christianity, a 1918 YMCA document cited the virtue of boxing as "the development of those physical and spiritual qualities that are characteristic of the aggressive fighting man"; indeed, a 1922 YMCA document on the same topic pronounced that "boxing lives because it appeals to the most fundamental instincts in man," which is noteworthy for the implicit endorsement of a fighting spirit as something righteous.[36] After the war, bevies of veterans who had learned to box and come to appreciate the sport in the army meant there was no shortage of amateur boxers ready to fight in America, nor a shortage of spectators to fill the seats at boxing events. Veterans' acceptance of boxing, in fact, helped legalize the sport.[37] As to any anxiety between boxing and a Christian lifestyle, the remark of one 1919 Inter-Allied Games middleweight and YMCA trainee shows the extent to which boxing had become warmly accepted into the muscular Christian way of life, as he declared that, "if Jesus Christ were living today, I believe he would take up boxing."[38]

Even so, as the Y slackened the original full-fledged focus on its religious identity, another organization emerged that would not only herald its church identification and support, but also highlight a boxing program in its effort to raise strong, fighting churchmen—that is the Catholic Youth Organization (CYO). Started in Chicago in 1930, the CYO became an important presence in American urban life from the Depression through the post–World War II era. Shepherding the organization into its early success was Bishop Bernard J. Sheil, a man who was not only courted by major league baseball clubs in his youth, but also "dabbled in boxing."[39] In fact, biographers and historians examining Sheil and his success suggest that his charm stemmed in part from his "vigorous athleticism."[40] For example, one vivid portrait of Sheil describes him as "no sissy priest but a rough-and-tumble scrapper [who could say] a solemn Mass at a certain moment and two hours later [be] prancing around a boxing ring—still in cassock, with boxing gloves added, slapping the ears of a fresh young punk."[41] Having grown up in the era of muscular Christianity's prominence, that Protestant movement not only influenced Sheil himself, but also his approach to the youth organization he would found, as its philosophy and the institutions founded on its principles—most prominently, the YMCA—"became the model for the CYO."[42]

Hoping that the Catholic Youth Organization would provide an alternative to seedier influences of Chicago's inner city neighborhoods, Sheil's vision for the organization was as a place for Catholic youth to find "the first moorings of religion upon which they could restore their faith, recreation through which they could develop their bodies, and education in which they could expand their knowledge and understanding of life."[43] By far, the most successful venture undertaken to raise the visibility of the CYO was its boxing tournaments. Sheil's plan was to displace local gangsters with more wholesome role models; "We'll knock the hoodlum off his pedestal," Sheil declared, "and we'll put another neighborhood boy in his place. He'll be dressed in CYO boxing shorts and a pair of leather mitts, and he'll make a new hero."[44] In fact, true to the mission of even many current-day fight sports ministries, Sheil saw his program, in part, as a way to keep young men in tough neighborhoods from succumbing to crime, gang violence and juvenile delinquency. Having served as a prison chaplain in Chicago's Cook County Jail, Sheil had seen firsthand what became of young men led astray by crime, some of their lives even ending in capital punishment; ultimately holding society itself responsible for not having provided for the "social, moral, and spiritual well-being" of such young men, Sheil set about doing all he could to provide institutional support to keep such adolescents on the right path.[45] Seeing boxing as the most likely means of reaching the very boys who most needed help, Sheil pursued the CYO boxing program with zeal, saying, "If a boy can come to know about God through a pair of boxing gloves—swell!"[46]

The popularity of the program led to the establishment of CYO chapters in other cities; still, the base and model for the program remained in Chicago.[47] That the venture would emphasize character was embodied in the very rules for the CYO boxing program. In addition to being a "duly baptized" Catholic, a would-be CYO pugilist had to receive passing grades in school, avoid vulgar language, and "publicly pledge himself to good sportsmanship, devotion to God and Church, and love of country"; "I bind myself," each boy would promise, "to promote, by word and example, clean, wholesome, and manly sport; I will strive to be a man of whom my Church and my Country may be justly proud."[48] Thus, the CYO helped to define an athletic, populist discipleship, in keeping with muscular Christianity's ideals. Helping, in part, to Americanize immigrants and lead social reform by means of clerical leadership, Sheil's "merger of sport, religion and social activism" not only helped transform the lives of program participants and the conditions of the inner city, but also Americans' isolationist perceptions of the Catholic church itself, giving it increased visibility as a significant participant in American society.[49]

What is more, Sheil used the CYO and its boxing program in particular to promote interracial contact in a pre-civil rights era, at a time when segregation in the city and church might otherwise have kept white and black Americans from regularly encountering each other. Thus, between the Great Depression and World War II, as one historian notes, the Catholic church's "institutional networks that promoted interracial exchange and cooperation, most notably the CYO, [...] created opportunities for tens of thousands of everyday Chicagoans, black and white, to cross geographic and social boundaries in a city deeply divided by racial segregation."[50] Hence, in both the boxing program itself and in its promotional material, Bishop Sheil endorsed ethnic pluralism. To wit, a 1935 photo promoting the program finds nine boxers of various ethnicities smiling at each other, standing in the corner of a boxing ring, holding their fists towards its center; the headline accompanying article reads, "All Races and Nations Participate in the CYO Program." Indeed, this archetypal image of the program had staying power, as a 1950 promotional photo finds four boys of various ethnicities gathered around a ring, each wearing boxing gloves and trunks, holding a sign announcing details regarding the "20th Boxing Classic," with Bishop Sheil himself approvingly looking on, holding one end of the sign.[51] Lest these promotional efforts falsely present too rosy a picture of a city that at times might have seen real interracial tension arise among Chicago neighborhoods, worth noting is a CYO motto directed at black and white youths living in bordering communities, where interethnic street fighting might occur; that knowing motto was "It's more fun to fight with boxing gloves."[52]

Still, by their very design, the CYO and its boxing program promoted interracialism, doing so at a time when other, similar organizations were still segregated. For example, prior to World War II the YMCA provided separate services for African Americans, as many cities had long since established YMCAs devoted solely to black communities and members.[53] Even so, as waves of migration resulted in increases in ethnic minority populations in American cities (Chicago certainly included), so too did the percentage of non-white ethnics participating in the CYO increase, including in its boxing tournaments, such that the organization at one point derogatorily became known among some white congregants as the "Colored Youth Organization."[54] Ironically, a year after the final CYO boxing tournament was held in 1953, the Supreme Court made its ruling in the *Brown versus the Board of Education of Topeka* that led to mandatory desegregation of public schools and other institutions, making Bishop Sheil's interracial policies enacted in the CYO since 1930 ahead of their time by a quarter of a century.[55]

Notably, the CYO did not encourage its young boxers to turn professional. As one historian notes, "boxing glory itself was not Sheil's ultimate goal."[56] While the bishop wanted to provide a safe, wholesome environment within which his fighters could test themselves and each other, ultimately his goals were loftier than that. To draw people, particularly the young, to the Catholic faith; to increase Catholic presence on the national stage; to establish Catholicism as whole-heartedly American; to Americanize its own immigrant members; to make men of character of out of boys, and at the same time keep those youngsters from felonious influences—indeed, to encourage youngsters to fight against those sordid influences; and to promote interracial relationships at a time when this was not yet the norm, and in so doing advance the causes of pluralism and diversity well ahead of their day; these were Sheil's aims for the CYO and its programs, and for the broader American Catholic church itself. In their heyday, thousands of young boxers and spectators took part in the annual CYO boxing tournaments, and its champions travelled far and wide to compete against fighters of other teams from around the country and the world. Ultimately, the boxing program was not only successful in raising visibility for the CYO but also achieving the organization's and Sheil's broader social mission.

His accomplishments were well-recognized then, as now. In 1954, on the occasion of Sheil's resignation as leader of the CYO, the *Chicago Daily Tribune* reflected on his remarkable success with that organization, harkening back to his earlier days as a jail chaplain, as it wrote of him:

> Wise in the ways of the slums, Bishop Sheil appealed to the so-called "tough" instincts of the slum youngsters. The appeal was successful beyond expectation and has endured for nearly a quarter of a century, with the annual CYO boxing tournament bigger than ever. Thousands of young Chicagoans of all races and religions have been influenced by Bishop Sheil's efforts in behalf of the spiritual and physical development of the city's youth.

The article ends by noting how outspoken the bishop had been in his "condemnation of racial and religious bigotry."[57] Alas, with Sheil's resignation, the boxing tournaments ended, the flagship Chicago chapter of the CYO fell into a period of decline, and a remarkable era for boxing and the church drew to a close.[58]

This ended the period of large scale, organized church programs focused on boxing. While other sports-evangelism programs arose, their emphasis was on presenting athletic speakers who modeled a Christian life, or on providing fellowship for young Christian athletes. Hence, organizations like Campus Crusade for Christ (founded in 1951, and now known as "Cru") and its "Athletes in Action" ministry, the Sports Ambassadors (founded in 1952), Venture for Victory (1952), and the Fellowship of Christian Athletes (1954) all provided new outlets for the muscular Christian ideology.[59] Although each a success in its own right, none focused particularly on boxing or martial arts, in favor of other, largely team sports. This is not to say that fight sports did not flourish in American society after the heyday of the YMCA and CYO boxing era. They did, as their presence as commercial ventures and in the church moved more to the local level. Further, various circumstances at the time led to increased interest and growth in marital arts, although not without challenges. Thus, following a pattern whereby the advancement of martial arts would wax and wane given economic, social and religious factors that hindered or promoted interaction between races, thereby facilitating one group teaching its techniques to new audiences, the expansion of martial arts was hurt by unfavorable conditions between the World Wars, such as by legislation that made Japanese immigration and naturalization more difficult. The resulting limitations on Japanese population growth in America, and a social distrust that arose from such conditions, resulted in many Japanese and others "[retreating] into their own community, [and] cutting off contact with European Americans," restricting cultural interaction, and hence restricting the full sharing of Asian fighting styles.[60] The internment of Japanese people in World War II certainly further hindered such interaction.

Even so, there was some progress between the wars. Interest in judo was aided by a popular touring team of Japanese practitioners in the 1930s, and interest in the potential contributions of jiu-jitsu to police work for both training in unarmed combat and outreach to troubled youth helped keep the expansion of martial arts training alive. This period even saw the first acceptance of white members into an American karate club, notably one housed in the basement of a Christian church—the First Methodist Church of Honolulu.[61] While the Second World War was an impediment to the interactions between races that might otherwise have fostered the spread of martial arts on American soil, servicemen stationed overseas nonetheless learned Asian martial arts and brought interest in these techniques back home with them. Particularly noteworthy was interest in Asian striking arts, such as karate and taekwondo.[62] Thus, in a fashion similar to the process by which boxing flourished due to troops training during World War I (including at YMCAs), a growth in the practice of Asian martial arts resulted from Americans' experiences during World War II. Eventually, this would result in the growth of training in martial arts across the nation, both as business ventures and in church sports ministries.

Thus, the growth of local academies and chains that taught various styles, such as those of Gracie Jiu-Jitsu, and Tiger Schulmann's Karate and Martial Arts, increased the commercialization and visibility of martial arts in the United States, as did increasing attention paid in popular culture. This included movies ranging from *Way of the Dragon* (1972) and *Kickboxer* (1989) to *Warrior* (2011), and television shows from *The Green Hornet* (1966–67) to *The Ultimate Fighter* reality TV series (2005–present), alongside the rise of popular Hollywood action stars from Bruce Lee and Jean-Claude Van Damme, to Chuck Norris, Jackie Chan, Jason Statham and

Scott Adkins. These academies, films, TV shows, and artists helped American interest in martial arts thrive. While no grand, widespread church-based programs on the order of that of the earlier CYO boxing program manifested in the form of church organizations wholly devoted to martial arts,[63] these techniques have nonetheless been practiced over the years in Christian organizations, albeit, again, at the local level. Hence, for example, the YMCA's Sports Camps, introduced in the 1960s and 1970s, have offered specialized programs for various sports, including camps devoted to judo.[64] Nowadays, as a search of program offerings by the group's neighborhood sites reveals, local YMCA programs in martial arts are common. Some church associations have arisen that specialize in teaching martial arts, such as the multi-site Christian Karate Association, founded in 1994 (discussion of which is forthcoming). Further, as will be discussed in the upcoming case studies chapter, a sizeable number of local congregations offer martial arts programs. The same is true for boxing.

As we will see, fight sports ministries of today proffer particular understandings of discipleship, much as the muscular Christian movement of the past presented its own distinctive program emphases. The various modern emphases range from a focus on character development to fitness and fellowship or embody an outreach ministry to at-risk youth. They are led by devoted believers, eager to provide programs for the benefit of congregants, neighbors, and those in need. Even so, those church members who enthusiastically support fight sports programs for what they may offer participants (befitting Price's aforementioned category of the "comingling" of sports and religion), or who find no objection to the public staging of secular boxing matches and other fight sports, find their counterpart in those who see such activities as outside acceptable bounds for Christians (a manifestation of Price's category of religion and sports "conflicting"), many of whom have outright opposed fight sports. It is to these church leaders and their efforts that we now turn.

Historical Opposition by the Church to Fight Sports

While some churches have used boxing and martial arts to evangelize, establish "masculine" appeals for the church, or illustrate their openness to popular, secular pursuits, others have used ethical opposition to boxing to establish moral authority over aspects of modern secular life. Thus, alternately used to entice followers or assert ethical standards and leadership, fight sports' role in the public life of the church has been multi-faceted; depending on a church's or church leader's goals, such sports may be either promoted or prohibited. As we will see, those taking a moralist's position

1. The History of Fight Sports and the Church 39

have an equally long history as those supporting or practicing fight sports, and their opposition to fight sports has taken various forms.

Opposition to boxing from clergy goes back to the beginnings of the muscular Christianity movement. In 1860, for example, English clergy took to the pulpits to condemn the Sayers-Heenan fight, a bout that lasted more than two hours and resulted in a draw, but not before the brawl left both pugilists significantly battered. In response, the clergy sought increased legal measures taken against prizefights, resulting in a somewhat tepid ordinance that denied railway companies (who transported spectators to remote locations where bouts were staged, away from law enforcement) from profiting from promoters.[65] Similarly, a Methodist periodical criticized a "mob" for its behavior as it gathered on the streets after the 1840 Tom Hyers–James Sullivan fight in New York. The writer contrasted the crowd's unruliness with the more refined behavior of a children's choir singing in a nearby church, in a manner later critics considered an example of an "uptown" pundit demonstrating "class prejudice" in a denunciation of downtown degeneracy.[66] Not all who acknowledged potential problems with fight sports from a Christian perspective were completely against them. Congregationalist preacher Henry Ward Beecher, for example, once confessed to his congregation his "naughty" indulgence in following prizefights, only later to promote "muscular games" for the sake of fitness, making him an early accommodationist in regard to the relation of sports to religion.[67]

As time went on, more opposition arose from religious leaders, who used various avenues to raise their concerns, from sermons to publications and other forms of organized resistance. Hence, a Congregational preacher and social gospel proponent, Washington Gladden, sermonized in 1866 about the proper relationship between sport and Christianity, finding that most sports were perfectly acceptable for Christian lifestyles and ethics; Gladden did, however, condemn some sports—namely those which might prove harmful or even fatal to the athletes involved, surely to include boxing. Not wanting his remarks to be misconstrued, Gladden later published his ideas in a short volume, entitled *Amusements: Their Uses and Abuses*.[68] In fact, therein he singles out fictitious muscular Christian acolyte Tom Brown (the literary creation of Thomas Hughes, previously discussed) for his enthusiasm for "brutal," "sinful" amusements, and for advocating on their behalf with such "gusto."[69] Also reaching publication were reflections in the Methodist *Christian Advocate*, which criticized boxing as "public exhibitions of unspeakable brutality," and an article in Nashville's *Baptist and Reflector*, which called boxing "a brutal and degrading spectacle."[70] Notably, these oppositional voices are similar to those raising concerns in the modern period, which denounce sports such as boxing because they often involve "gambling or physical harmfulness."[71]

Sometimes opposition arose not to boxing in general but to a particular fight. For instance, as preparations were underway to stage a bout between Australian boxer Jim Hall and American champ Bob Fitzsimmons in St. Paul, Minnesota, on July 22, 1891, a protest by clergy and their followers helped derail the event. To publicize their moral opposition to the fight, a bout which had been in the works since May, St. Paul clergy, including Archbishop John Ireland, gathered about 5,000 concerned citizens, "whose deep earnestness and great indignation," wrote one newspaper reporter, "found a vent in applauding the strongest kind of denunciatory speeches"; these speeches included that of Ireland, who assailed boxing for its "lawlessness and vulgar animalism." This protest happened on July 20, even as trains were bringing in fans eager to watch the fight.[72] The outraged clergy demanded that the governor, mayor, and sheriff take action to halt the match. On the day of the fight, Governor William Merriam did just that by bringing troops to surround the exhibition hall and cut off access, refusing everyone entry. The bout's organizers had hoped that the fight, illegal and punishable as a misdemeanor, would be allowed to come off anyway, and that any penalties would be applied afterwards; however, given the cleric-led opposition and the resulting use of armed troops by the governor two days later, the fight was called off, "to remove all possibility of disorder and bloodshed."[73]

For yet another Fitzsimmons fight, religious leaders also staged a protest against boxing—this time in response to his 1895 bout just outside of Dallas, Texas, against "Gentleman" Jim Corbett. Even as the stadium was being erected, the governor, Charles Culberson, sought passage of anti-prizefighting legislation in response to a plea from the Dallas Pastors' Association which, according to one boxing historian, lobbied the governor and "condemned prizefighting as inherently brutal and characterized prizefighting patrons as the sorts of people that triggered epidemics of crime and debauchery."[74] Using his attorney general to clarify uncertainties about conflicting laws governing prizefighting, Culberson eventually prohibited the fight, leading its organizers to seek an alternate locale.[75] With Corbett no longer willing to fight under the circumstances, the organizers tried to pit Fitzsimmons against another pugilist, this time in El Paso, just along the Mexican border; the clergy of this town, however, proved no less formidable than those of Dallas in their public denunciation of boxing. They created the El Paso Ministerial Alliance to publicly oppose staging a fight in their city.[76]

Seeking finally to bring together reigning champ "Gentleman Jim" with challenger Fitzsimmons, the organizers looked to Nevada, where a makeshift arena was built to accommodate the fight. Famously, the filming of the bout led to the first feature-length movie ever produced, as the match was shot in its entirety and distributed to audiences unable to watch the fight in person.[77] This also gave religious leaders anywhere the film might be screened reason to raise moral objection—as indeed they did. Positioning this opposition as part of a larger Purity Crusade, religious groups and leaders, led by the Women's Christian Temperance Union, supported legislation to censor such fight films, saying that doing so would "protect our boys from brutality."[78] Meanwhile, even in Nevada, public opposition by religious leaders arose. A Methodist minister in Cleveland sermonized on the fight, excerpts of which were published in the New Haven Register under the title "Nevada's Shame and Disgrace"; it complained, in part, that

> this state, this deserted mining camp, revives brutality by an exhibit that must make its Indians and Chinamen wonder at Christianity.... Such exhibitions promote criminality by feeding the bestial in men. They debauch the public ideal. Such men sell their bodies for merchandise as surely as the harlots in the street.[79]

Other members of the clergy, decrying distribution of the filmed fight, denounced boxing as "not the manly art, but the art of the devil," and interpreted public interest in pugilism as a reflection of the nation's "moral degeneracy."[80]

Later fights met with similar religious criticism. The sensationally hyped interracial fight in 1910 between Jack Johnson and James Jeffries, for example, resulted in an organized national effort by business and church leaders to halt the match. When this effort failed, the focus shifted to stopping distribution of the fight film, warning that "decent" youth who might see the movie needed protection from "the agents of the pugilistic world."[81] Similarly, the upcoming Independence Day 1919 fight between Jess Willard and Jack Dempsey brought forth a coalition of clergy to oppose it, in the form of the Federated Churches of Ohio. Notably, their opposition was scorned by the Army, Navy, and Civilian Board of Boxing Control, who suggested the moralizing clergy were behind the times—that boxing had become a "wholesome pastime," and that church organizations like theirs that raised opposition to boxing "served only to discredit religion."[82] Not long thereafter, both the Presbyterian Church and the Methodist Episcopal Church condemned the much-anticipated 1921 fight between Jack Dempsey and George Carpentier.[83] One Baptist preacher characterized the staging of this fight as "a relapse into paganism which glorified brute power," and a "moral carbuncle."[84] Both Presbyterians and Methodists also objected to the 1927 Jack Dempsey versus Gene Tunney fight (famed for the controversial "long count," when Dempsey delayed retreating to a neutral corner after downing Tunney, possibly affecting the fight's outcome), the Methodist Church calling the bout "unrepresentative of American life and a disgrace to the city of Philadelphia." The state's governor, however, defended boxing, observing that teaching men to fight could be helpful in wartime, and that prizefighting events were much better controlled than in the past.[85] The fight went on.

Religious arguments likewise arose in relation to efforts to legalize boxing and were not unlike later arguments against the legalization of mixed martial arts (a discussion of which is forthcoming). For example, New York's 1900 Lewis Law, which permitted boxing in private clubs between members, led to such opposition. (As a workaround, professional boxers were granted the requisite club membership so they could legally fight in the venues.[86]) In response, a "highly organized campaign" by Brooklyn clergy led to the requirement that private clubs not be permitted to charge admission fees for such events, thus posing a challenge to unchecked profitability of the exhibitions.[87] When boxing was fully legalized in New York by the Walker Law in 1920—a measure still in force in New York, with amendments, and which became the template for the legalization of boxing throughout the United States[88]—religious leaders were once again there to argue their points. From the Episcopal Church rose two voices, one on each side of the matter. The Rev. William Chase spoke against the bill, with support from organizations such as the Women's Temperance Union, warning that the legislation would lead to "brutalized ring exhibitions" and promote gambling.

On the other side was rector Dr. B.W.R. Taylor, who was supported by veterans and sports enthusiasts, and who opined, "For the men who oppose boxing.... I say they are lacking in sporting blood and true manly spirit." He was not alone. At the law's hearing, the legislature was presented with a list of nine hundred clergy favoring the bill.[89] Army chaplains also voiced their support for the bill.[90] Another proponent was Anthony J. Drexel Biddle, a millionaire and former Marine born to a Quaker family, who founded an international Bible society. A boxer and boxing fan, he contacted the membership of his society, asking that they each send a telegram to the New York governor declaring their support for the bill. Partly because of the bill's particulars (which included provisions for licensing, to hold organizers accountable for the responsible staging of events, and to establish a commission to oversee pugilistic activities), the Bible society's membership was satisfied that legalization would keep boxing from succumbing to the dangers of underground recreation.[91] Thus, despite others who opposed it, the support of these religious figures helped the Walker Law pass.

In a move that might have reflected an awareness of the need to appease those opposed to the law in religious communities, the governor appointed as first head of the New York State Athletic Commission an "iconic leader" of the muscular Christianity movement, William Muldoon. A former fighter, respected as much for his victories as his morals and healthy lifestyle, Muldoon did everything possible to allay the fears of those who were concerned with unethical practices in boxing, such as by withdrawing credentials for judges and referees having ties to gamblers, opposing over-commercialization of the sport (which might lead to corruption), and using his influence to persuade boxers to fight in charity fund raisers, a move which "helped win over boxing critics."[92]

As boxing grew in social acceptance and legality over the years, opposition from church leaders and others became increasingly futile. This did not, however, stop other types of ethical criticism of fight sports from arising in religious circles. When the famous "sports bay" stained glass panel was being proposed for the Episcopalian Saint John the Divine Cathedral in New York, some church people raised concerns as to whether it was appropriate to depict sports and religion as compatible. On the other hand, there was much enthusiasm for the project, which gained support from high profile athletes and benefited from fundraisers, including boxing matches staged at the "Mecca of Boxing," Madison Square Garden.[93] Ultimately, in response to criticism, boxing was not included among the modern day sports represented in the colorful panels. It and other more ethically questionable sports (notably, other fight sports, such as wrestling) were only hinted at by the inclusion of carefully selected biblical episodes, such as Jacob wrestling the angel, and David fighting Goliath.[94] The project, begun in the 1920s, was finally completed just after World War II.[95] Other ethical concerns with boxing arose not long thereafter, when New York State boxing commissioner Robert K. Christenberry published a "scathing expose of boxing" in an issue of the highly popular *Life* magazine. Touted in his introduction to the article as "a Presbyterian Sunday School teacher," Christenberry called for the need to free boxing from mob influences, and to protect the health of young boxers.[96]

A decade after that, the exact same set of concerns led *Sports Illustrated* magazine to invite Catholic priest and professor Father Richard A. McCormick, whom the *New York Times* later called "the dominant voice in Roman Catholic moral theology" in his day,[97] to assess the ethics of boxing. Introducing the article by noting that boxing was at the time "under fire" from various sources, including clergy and religious publications like the Vatican newspaper, because of serious injuries or deaths in the ring and "alleged" criminal influences in the sport, the magazine then published the Reverend McCormick's ethical reflections on professional boxing. After acknowledging the reasons why many defend the sport, including that boxing provides "splendid opportunity for physical development, alertness, poise, confidence, sportsmanship, initiative and character-building," the Reverend McCormick then contrasts this with those who find it morally wanting. He includes in this discussion the observation that boxing is the only sport wherein the "immediate objective is to damage the opponent," and that, for those who watch such fights, it encourages "brutish instincts." After reflecting on the Catholic church's official silence on the matter of condemning professional boxing, which, in addition to other practical reasons, he attributes to a lack of clarity of the issues involved and the acknowledgment that many voices raise reasonable arguments, Father McCormick himself ultimately opines that in its then-current practice, professional boxing "would have to be labelled immoral." Notably he also encourages further debate instead of a conclusory blanket denunciation, observing that "premature conviction slams the door to enlightenment as effectively as refusal to face the moral issue." Thus, although offering his own opinion, this Catholic moral theologian is careful to recognize the church's official silence on the matter, and that others do raise reasonable defenses for the sport.[98]

Indeed, as Father McCormick recognized, a range of voices in the church endures to this day and, although religious opposition to the sport of boxing has waned over the years, it still exists, notably alongside supportive voices. Hence, despite the fact that charity fights were staged for Catholic Big Sisters as far back as the 1920s, and the CYO embraced boxing to achieve its mission, the Catholic journal *Civilta Cattolica*, which is "vetted and approved by the Vatican," editorialized in 2005 that boxing is "contrary to Christian morality and gravely damaging to man, his life and dignity," as the journal's argument was characterized in a National Public Radio report; the news source quoted the journal directly, as it called boxing an "immoral enterprise," "merciless and inhuman," and "a form of legalized murder."[99] Even so, Pope Francis recently accepted a commemorative championship belt from the president of the World Boxing Council (WBC), one of the major international fight sanctioning organizations. Saying it was awarding the pontiff the honor in recognition of his "kindness, virtue and hope," the WBC press release, accompanied by photos of the pontiff accepting the belt, dubbed Pope Francis a "Champion of Faith."[100] Although not necessarily denoting his sanctioning of the sport, the meeting nonetheless indicates an openness to dialogue by the pontiff, who is quoted in the WBC's Twitter coverage of the event as charging the official sanctioning body with the duty to "build bridges." Nonetheless, Pope Francis' photographed acceptance of the belt from an organization so central to the sport of boxing is one example of how images in popular culture balance competing ethical challenges to fight sports raised by religious figures.

As for objections raised to the relatively more recent phenomenon of mixed martial arts, the sport has not received as much official, well-publicized reaction from churches and church leaders. Perhaps because of its newcomer status (the first Ultimate Fighting Championship took place in 1993, with the popularity of MMA swelling after the debut of *The Ultimate*

Fighter reality TV series in 2005), and perhaps because it attained greater legitimacy after 2001, when the New Jersey State Athletic Commission first codified a now-standard set of "unified rules" for MMA fights and thus sanctioned the sport,[101] churches and their leaders have not weighed in to the extent they did for boxing in an earlier age. It may also be that since many of the concerns with boxing raised by those opposed to it also apply to professional mixed martial arts, there has been no pressing need to reiterate those concerns specifically for MMA. To be sure, there are individual clergy who have voiced concerns, such as Catholic parish priest Father John Duffell, a leader in the movement staged to keep professional mixed martial arts fights from becoming legal in New York (as they now are), and whose efforts are recounted in the documentary film *Fight Church* (explored more fully in a later chapter). In his efforts to oppose legalizing professional mixed martial arts fights, Father Duffell appeared multiple times before the New York legislature to oppose the bill, which ultimately passed it in 2016. His condemnation is summarized by his assertion that "nothing about the gospel is revealed in cage fighting," as he told the press in 2014, concluding that "cage fighting is about hating one another."[102]

Notably, other clergy (also featured in the documentary *Fight Church*, alongside Duffell) also went on the record, albeit supporting church-based MMA programs, as well as defending their own participation in cage fighting. Pastor Preston Hocker of Freedom Fellowship church in Virginia Beach, Virginia, for example, shared that he values his church's MMA program for its contributions to evangelism, emphasis on character and community building, and teaching of self-defense and discipline. He notes that his church does not allow younger members to cage fight—only to train in the techniques of mixed martial arts, as part of the church's MMA club. "I think most people that criticize me or criticize Christian fighters in general either don't understand the sport or don't understand Jesus," Hocker told the press. Indeed, this pastor's remarks, as do those of Father Duffell, reference differing notions of Christian discipleship—what it means to be a follower of Christ. Hocker says his fight club has taught him to forgive others, just as one young club member says it has taught him that he need not fight when bullied, because with training he now has more self-control. Meanwhile, Father Duffell, referring to training in fighting techniques as part of a church program, counters, saying, "You can't use non-gospel values to reveal gospel values, it just doesn't go."[103] And so, the ongoing historical account of fight sports' place in relation to the church, argued by those on both sides, continues.

A consideration of the moral issues involved with fight sports and the church is the subject of a later chapter, which systematically considers various matters of Christian ethics in relation to fight sports in general, and boxing and martial art ministries in particular. Notably, as we have seen, those who historically opposed fight sports from a Christian perspective did so with a particular understanding of Christian discipleship—one that treated opposition to fight sports as a means to preach reform to those in society whom they believed were pursuing wayward morals. Meanwhile, others advocated for the place of fight sports ministries in the church, doing so with another vision of Christian discipleship in mind—one concerned with strengthening a believer physically, as much as spiritually and morally. The focus of muscular Christianity on character development grew alongside its concern with providing an image of masculine discipleship, at times explicitly related to "manly," even pugilistic depictions of Christ. Indeed, these matters are themselves related to broader issues regarding gender, the church's mission and character, and how fight sports and their association with masculinity relate to the intersections of the church and culture. This, then, is the subject of the coming chapter.

2

Cultural Reflections on Fight Sports and the Church

The history of fight sports and the church is bound up with issues of gender, ecclesiology and evangelism. The effort to "re-masculinize" a church perceived as too feminine, passive, and refined was a basic appeal, for many, of the muscular Christianity movement. The church thus used boxing and other athletic ministries both to reshape the gendered image of the church, and reach out to "masculine" men, as traditionally defined. This chapter will begin with a reflection on arguments about the feminization of culture and how it relates to matters of the church, including issues of ecclesiology and evangelism, and how these matters are engaged in popular books geared towards men's ministries programs. It will next pursue a related matter: examining depictions of fight sports and the church in popular culture, more broadly. Here we will see that church leaders have been depicted as "fighters," as has Christ himself, so as to allay any fears that their religiosity makes them less strong, particularly as regards those whose focus is on the pursuit of peace. Finally, we will look at modern America's cultural view of ritualized combat, from the perspectives of both spectators and participants, as a means of partaking in activities that serve to prove one's strength, heroism, and masculine grit. In many ways, all of these elements trace what some see as an enduring "crisis of masculinity," and how it plays out both in church history itself and popular culture's depictions thereof.

On Gendered Ecclesiology, Evangelism and Culture

Joyce Carol Oates' assessment that boxing is *the* masculine experience par excellence is surely applicable to a review of the historical development of muscular Christianity and its philosophy. Her essay "On Boxing" offers further insights about boxing's place in contemporary reflections on masculinity-as-a-religion, and debates about the gendered church. Oates writes, "Boxing is a celebration of the lost religion of masculinity all the more trenchant for its being lost."[1] The "lost" place of masculinity, in the church as in society, and the resultant loss of male church membership, is a discussion that has deep roots in scholarly reflection, and continues to this day in both academic and popular literature.

The origin of the modern discussion of this issue arises, in part, from Ann Douglas' classic treatise *The Feminization of America Culture* (1977). Herein, Douglas argues that with a shift from rural, agricultural to urban, industrialized society, women's influence over culture diminished, as did that of the clergy. This resulted in a symbiotic relationship between these two factions, whereby educated, domestic women, who had limited influence outside of the local church, championed the very "virtues" that their exclusion from more powerful roles in society imposed on them; meanwhile, the clergy adapted and catered to these values, since the primary audience judging their work was women. Hence, "both liberal ministers and literary women had lost practical function within American society and were anxious to replace it with emotional indispensability; they turned of necessity from the exercise of power to the exertion of 'influence.'"[2] This led, among other things, to a valuing of the sentimental, nostalgic and "softer emotions," and a de-emphasis on "physical vitality."[3] In contrast with Christologies of the muscular Christian past—such as Billy Sunday's "scrapper" Christ and Thomas Hughes' "manliness of Christ"—the emphasis of feminized religion focused on atonement, and in particular a version of it that extolled the qualities of meekness, suffering and submissiveness.[4]

While Douglas' analysis is of Victorian era culture and how it affects modern mass culture, the general subject of her work set off debates about contemporary manifestations of feminization, including in analyses of the contemporary church. Hence, college professor and Dominican nun Kaye Ashe reflects on such matters in *The Feminization of the Church?* (1997), as does scholar Leon J. Podles in *The Church Impotent: The Feminization of Christianity* (1999), doing so from opposite perspectives. Ashe begins with Douglas' analysis and concludes that feminism is a positive, corrective influence on a church with patriarchal history and emphases; it extols gifts women and women's perspective bring to the church, notably including a different ("feminine") perspective on matters such as "body, power [...] and violence."[5] Thus, religious cosmologies that construct a "hierarchic, authoritarian and violent" worldview—the "dominator" model—support the common understanding of "real men" as strong, in a manner that justifies (as she sees it) their use of violence against women, other men, and even nations and the world; to correct this, she proposes a theology and ecclesiology that equates power with "responsibility, love and nurturance."[6]

Ashe sees feminized religion and its critique of dominance as a necessary contribution to the church and its theology and ecclesiology.

In contrast, Podles' concern is for how a church with an overemphasis on feminine imagery and character (as he sees it) is causing men to leave the church—men, that is, of "pronounced or even normal masculinity," and in particular, therefore, "young men, athletic men, and uneducated men."[7] Men, Podles argues in neo-muscular Christian fashion, need competition, a struggle, and even an opponent to fight, together with camaraderie and rituals of initiation into manhood—and a church that can supply this, ideally in both imagery and practice, will attract men. Noting men's appetite for athletics, Podles observes that sports supply these elements and, while he does not necessarily advocate the use of athletics in evangelism (although he acknowledges some churches use them for this purpose), Podles yearns for a church that in whatever fashion possible appeals to men by providing the "masculine" experiences he says men crave.

His concerns echo those of Patrick M. Arnold in his book *Wildmen, Warriors, and Kings: Masculine Spirituality and the Bible* (1991). Arnold posits that a feminized "soul-life" in the modern church has led to a "wounded masculinity," and a crisis for "masculine spirituality."[8] He maintains that men thrive on competition and are naturally drawn to combat, aggression and violence, including "ritualized" fighting.[9] Finding supportive source material in the ancient world and Bible, Arnold looks to archetypes, including that of the warrior, to help men find models with which to understand their role in spiritual life and the church. His prescription includes programs to entice men to return to church, including initiation rites, and prayer or support groups. While not calling for martial arts or boxing ministries specifically, Arnold's thought and emphasis of the warrior archetype resonates with many seeking to establish such a "masculine" presence in the church. Indeed, his observation that conservative and evangelical Protestant churches do a better job than others at attracting men today may help account for the aforementioned noteworthy success of martial arts ministries in these churches.[10]

Similar to Podles and Arnold, author Joseph Gelfer reflects on gender and the church in his book *Numen, Old Men: Contemporary Masculine Spiritualities and the Problem of Patriarchy* (2009). One point of commonality among his and their analysis is that of the warrior archetype—a model evoking the fighter. Hence, in its most positive manifestation, as yet another book about archetypes records, the warrior model (expressed ecclesiastically by hymnody such as "Onward Christian Soldiers," and biblical figures such as King David) inspires this model's adherents to be "energetic, decisive, courageous, enduring, persevering, and loyal to some greater good."[11] Whereas writers like Podles and Arnold are appreciative of this and other archetypes, Gelfer is concerned that they fixate on a single dimension of "masculinity," failing to appreciate a diversity of ways in which one may be masculine; further, he is concerned that archetypes uncritically accept essentialist understandings of what it means to be male/female, and that the warrior's association with sports imagery and violence may "go a long way to promoting an unsavoury [sic] model of masculinity."[12] Although his conclusions may take time to influence more popular writings about masculinity and the church, Gelfer (self-identified in his book's preface as a straight man) finds a solution to the extremes of gendered ecclesiology in the form of non-binary queer theology and "gay spirituality," which, he writes, challenge the essentialist, dualist understandings of gender in the church and allow for a more nuanced, balanced approach—one that does not uncritically accept concepts associated with "masculinity" (such as those tied to competitiveness and violence) that he says, for the most part, support patriarchy.[13]

Anticipating the focus of more popular books about matters of gender and Christianity is a volume that has much in common with the above academics' concerns; this is Nate Pyle's *Man Enough: How Jesus Redefines Manhood* (2015). Herein, Pyle advocates for an expansive definition of masculinity, to include various masculinities, in the plural.[14] He questions the prominence of the warrior model in a discussion of the "manly" hunter Esau and his quieter, more domestic brother Jacob, noting that it was the latter's descendants that God honors by calling His people.[15] Pyle makes the case that we should value men who are willing to be vulnerable and servile, and who find strength in weakness. Noting that Christ's coming was a knowing acceptance of such a vulnerable, weakened condition, Pyle finds in Christ's earthly life examples of taking on such humbled states. In Christ's washing of his disciples' feet; in his acceptance of being the one who bleeds, rather than the one who makes others bleed; and in Christ's very crucifixion, Pyle finds exemplars for men to embrace vulnerability and submission.[16] "The Bible," Pyle writes, "inverts the cultural mandate placed on men."[17] His hope is that men may learn to abandon their own strength to accept their weakness in order to learn to depend on Christ and his strength, and realize that the Gospel frees men from the need to "prove" themselves.[18] Pyle advocates for a model of discipleship that is less focused on machismo and more on vulnerability. The suggestion is that by trying to dichotomize gender traits in overly simplistic and binary ways, we exclude our ability to embrace not only various legitimate ways of being men, but also the call in the Garden of Eden for men and women to work together, without divided spheres of gendered agency, in order to be good stewards of God's creation. Rather creatively, Pyle ends by suggesting that God's call in Genesis is for men (and women) to be gardeners—caretakers of the earth

2. Cultural Reflections on Fight Sports and the Church

and God's creation—and that, perhaps, we would only need warriors if creation, in practice or perception, had "lost its integrity."[19]

While the above academic writings openly grapple with intricate issues of gender, ecclesiology and evangelism, popular books on similar subjects are, unsurprisingly, much less nuanced, if nonetheless impassioned. Here we find the argument that the warrior or fighter mentality is not only appropriate, but also necessary for men to feel accepted in the church. David Murrow's popular *Why Men Hate Going to Church* (2005), for example, identifies men with the warrior model, saying "battles speak to men's hearts"; and while not specifically arguing for fight sports ministries in the church, he does suggest churches need to provide men with opportunities for "risk" and "adventure."[20] Explicitly using fighter imagery, Craig Groeshel's *Fight: Winning the Battles That Matter Most* (2013) consistently takes up the warrior archetype as one to which modern Christian men should aspire. With an image on its cover of a boxer with his knuckles wrapped, Groeshel's book encourages men to "fight like a man," because God wants men to fight for something greater than themselves, and to be "not just a warrior but God's warrior"—the warrior, he writes, God made each man to be.[21]

Books attesting to the power of the warrior model and which explicitly encourage martial arts or boxing training as a means to spiritual empowerment demonstrate the strength of interest in fight sports for some Christians, be that of a more mystical or physical nature. Notably, published works that take their point of entry as fight sports themselves, and not the church's more figurative use of archetypes, are often more inclusive, as some of these books are openly targeted at both men and women, perhaps to increase their potential market. Hence, popular books titles include *The Way of the Christian Samurai: Reflections for Servant-Warriors of Christ*, by Paul Novak (2007); *Warrior Code: Applying the Tenets of Bushido to the Service of the Master*, by Luis Alberto Martinez (2006); *Spirit Warriors: Strategies for the Battles Christian Men and Women Face Every Day*, by Stu Weber (2003); *Shadow Boxing: The Dynamic 2-5-14 Strategy to Defeat the Darkness Within*, by Henry Malone (1999); *Martial Arts: The Christian Way*, by Wendy Williamson (2002); *Christian Martial Arts 101*, by Wendy Williamson (2004); *Christian Martial Arts: The Passion, the Calling, the Journey*, by John Terry (2009); and finally *Tapped Out by Jesus: From the Cage to the Cross* (2011), an autobiography by Ultimate Fighting Championship (UFC) heavyweight Ron Waterman, who would (like earlier fighters of the muscular Christianity era) go on to become an evangelist.

At least from the perspective of popular interest, it seems there are many who see little conflict between Christianity and fight sports. Just as importantly, the focus on the Christian warrior or fighter, be that actual or metaphorical, throughout these popular works traces discussions of gendered ecclesiology, providing a culturally "masculine" image-option for Christian followers, which might help make church membership more appealing to those men concerned with a feminized image of Christianity and the church. Of course, as the above discussion of more academically based reflections on gendered ecclesiology suggests, the assumptions underlying these concerns may (for some) need interrogation and reconsideration. Nonetheless, in terms of the announced historical effort to re-masculinize the church via muscular Christian means; the intervening academic reflection on gender and ecclesiology; the more modern-day focus on the warrior archetype in men's ministries literature, together with efforts to evangelize men; and the growing literature on the Christian fighter, we find throughout culture, high and low, a conscious consideration of the relationship of fight sports and the church. So, too, do we find the use of fight sports employed in fictional popular culture, including novels and movies, invoked to present a carefully balanced image of the church and its leaders. Therefore, we turn now to a critical examination of such fictional church leaders who engage in fight sports, the reasons why popular culture presents such images, and what tensions these depictions attempt to resolve.

Pop Cultural Images of Fight Sports, Ministry and the Church

Popular depictions of boxing and the church capitalize on an apparent contradiction—that culturally we often expect representatives of the church to be docile and peace loving, but also admire leaders who are strong, tough and stand their ground. While Oates describes boxing with adjectives like "brute," "primitive" and "inarticulate,"[22] the church may be described in contrasting terms: "refined," "enlightened," and "expressive." Further, while Oates writes that boxing is "totally identified with the body,"[23] the church is often identified with the spirit. The exploration of surprising character contradictions when church leaders are depicted as boxers makes for dramatic interest, if not also clichés.

Before looking at contemporary examples of popular culture's depiction of boxing, ministry and the church, we will first look at several of the foundational, once-popular works in the muscular Christianity movement, since we will return to the philosophies therein when considering the role of ritualized violence in relation to modern experiences of "masculinity" (at this chapter's end), in addition to observing how these writers'

2. Cultural Reflections on Fight Sports and the Church 53

philosophical works find expression in fictional books. For this task, we will look in particular at the writings of one of muscular Christianity's leading figures, Thomas Hughes. We will begin with an examination of books wherein he expresses his philosophy, and then look at his best-known work of fiction to see how his ideology finds expression in popular, narrative form. To accomplish the former, we will look at two of Hughes' works—*The Manliness of Christ* (1880) and the anthology *True Manliness* (1880)—before considering how the philosophy therein is expressed in his popular novel *Tom Brown's School Days*. Hughes' purpose in the first two works is to define masculinity and show how it is best exemplified in the person of Jesus Christ. The first of these books (*The Manliness of Christ*) takes up this charge with greater focus, while the second offers a series of meditations, many of which focus on Jesus' "manliness."

Much of Hughes' writing on manliness focuses on courage. While not being synonymous with manliness, he opines, it is nonetheless one of its core components. In fact, Hughes explicitly discusses boxing and wrestling to explain that courage can be tested and honed in athletic activities, while also noting that it nonetheless cannot be equated with success in such sports. Counting persistence and the endurance of pain and danger as among the constitutive qualities of courage, he observes that a courageous fighter facing a better trained or bigger opponent may show remarkable courage, but is unlikely to achieve victory.[24] He continues, noting that courage and manliness may be as much a quality found in a weaker man as in a strong one—that mere strength or athleticism does not define manliness, since a strong athlete may also be cowardly.[25] Hughes says courage is most fully and profoundly displayed in the pursuit of truth, which, he observes, is best demonstrated in the figure of Christ, whose life he characterizes (not far afield from Billy Sunday's characterizations of Jesus) as a constant fight. The period of Jesus' ministry, he says, exemplifies a man facing daily challenges and opponents, and rising to each occasion by courageously standing for truth to the point of heroism. He writes that daily life "teems with occasions which will try the temper of our courage," though admittedly on a lesser scale for average men than that facing Christ, or even the dangers faced by other men, offering the examples of soldiers in battle, firefighters, or others engaged in high profile acts of heroism:

> And in this life-long fight, to be waged by every one of us single-handed against a host of foes, the last requisite for a good fight, the last proof and test of our courage and manfulness, must be loyalty to truth—the most rare and difficult of all human qualities.[26]

Already, it is not difficult to see why the institutionalization of the muscular Christian philosophy in the form of YMCA, CYO and other programs would include "character building" sports, intended to both strengthen both one's body and hone one's courage.

It is also apparent how the need to successfully respond to tests of one's manliness in daily life *requires* daily scuffles, which are necessary to prove one's "manly" credentials. These challenges might be physical (as in Hughes' examples of men facing heroic acts) or more socio-political (as that faced by Christ). A lack of sufficient challenges might, in fact, set-up a crisis for those wanting or "needing" to prove their manliness, as we will later discuss in considering the role of "ritualized combat" to establish "manliness" in modern culture. One needs opponents to fight (as Christ fought Satan, the priests, and the Romans) in order to prove one's manhood. Thus, in the strife of daily life,

> the first requisite is courage and manfulness, gained through conflict with evil—for without such conflict there can be no perfection of character, the end for which Christ says we were sent into this world.[27]

Hughes observes that Christians (explicitly, Christian men) are to be perfect (that is, in his worldview, "manly") just as Christ, who was the purest example of such perfection, that is, "manliness." Indeed, here we may also see the seeds (for some) of the developing concern with the "feminization" of the church, and theological and institutional efforts to "re-masculinize" it, to keep it worthy of being "Christ's" (that is, a "manly") church. Hughes writes:

> The conscience of every man recognizes courage as the foundation of true manliness, and manliness as the perfection of human characters, and if Christianity runs counter to conscience in this matter, or indeed in any other, Christianity will go to the wall.[28]

As that courage requires opponents, conflict and daily fighting to assert itself, the experience of "true manliness" requires regular opportunities to establish one's "manhood." Though not reducible to strength or athleticism, mastery of the body does find a place in Hughes' worldview, as "the least of the muscular Christians has hold of the old chivalrous and Christian belief, that a man's body is given him to be trained and brought into subjection, and then used for the protection of the weak, the advancement of all righteous causes, and the subduing of the earth which God has given to the children of men"; and this is the purpose of "wrestling" and other such sports, he writes: for men to learn to "use their strength readily" and "endure fatigue and pain," to protect others, themselves, "and country if necessary."[29] Indeed, directly contesting those who suggest otherwise, Hughes calls Christianity the home to the greatest fighters in history, and says that Christianity is not, as some suggest, a home for the demure, so much as the fighter.[30]

Hughes' popular writings (not a far cry from the warrior archetype and what we find in popular "men's ministries" books of today) were not confined to the philosophical; his ideas also found expression in fictional writing. In this capacity, none of his work is more expressive of his thinking, or more popular, than *Tom Brown's School Days*. The juvenile novel tells the story of a boy who goes off to school and matures from being mischievous to manly. Tom and his friends are adventurous, leading them to test the patience and expectations of some in the adult world; but Tom also shows courage by standing up to a bully who is much bigger than he, as well as compassion, by taking a new student who is weak and lonely under his wing and protecting this boy when necessary. All the opportunities to learn and grow occur amidst vignettes depicting a life lived with the trappings of faith: prayer, chapel, sermons by "the Doctor" (the school's much respected headmaster), Bible readings and discussions, confirmation, and communion. These are important and natural to Tom, as is his ability to meet everyday challenges and tests of character while growing into manhood. Not one of unusual strength or athleticism, Tom is nonetheless brave and spirited.

Most relevant to a consideration of fight sports and Christianity is a chapter in the novel titled "The Fight." It recounts a fistfight using boxing rules (apparently well known to all the boys) between Tom and a boy from another dormitory, named Williams. Showing a willingness to defend the weak, the fight is over Williams' mistreatment of Tom's frail and lonely friend, Arthur. Defending Arthur against Williams' bullying, Tom agrees to fight, showing his courage. Hughes describes Williams as a big boy, "the cock of the shell" (that is, the dominant one of his dorm), and a boy possessing "great strength" and skill in fighting, which earned him the nickname "Slogger Williams."[31] Indeed, Hughes begins the chapter by addressing the audience, as if to belittle any who might find unbecoming the forthcoming details of pugilistic activity; he warns:

> let those young persons whose stomachs are not strong, or who think a good set-to with the weapons God has given us all, an uncivilized, unchristian, or ungentlemanly affair, just skip this chapter at once, for it won't be to their taste.[32]

Thus, Hughes challenges the reader to rise to the occasion and consider that the forthcoming fight, and fighting in similar circumstances, is best considered a supremely civilized, Christian and gentlemanly pursuit.

Yet before recounting the actual fight, Hughes continues his aside to the reader, providing even more of a defense of fighting. He offers a peek into the nightly ritual of Tom and his fellow dormers, whereby boxing gloves, "those surest keepers of the peace,"[33] were brought out, and the boys had the opportunity to test their skill, learning to size up their chances in a real fight against potential opponents, were they ever required to consider facing one. Hughes shares his notions about the rightful place of fighting in life, which, as important as this is, therefore merits quotation at length:

> After all, what would life be without fighting, I should like to know? From the cradle to the grave, fighting, rightly understood, is the business, the real, highest, honest business of every son of man. Everyone who is worth his salt has enemies, who must be beaten, be they evil thoughts and habits in himself, or spiritual wickedness in high places, or Russians, or Border-ruffians, or Bill, Tom, or Harry, who will not let him live his life in quiet till he has thrashed them.
>
> It is no good for Quakers, or any other body of men, to uplift their voices against fighting. Human nature is too strong for them, and they don't follow their own precepts. Every soul of them is doing his own piece of fighting, somehow and somewhere. The world might be a better world without fighting for anything I know, but it wouldn't be our world; therefore I am dead against crying peace when there is no peace, and isn't meant to be. I am sorry as any man to see folk fighting the wrong people and the wrong things, but I'd a deal sooner see them doing that, than that they should have no fight in them.[34]

Thus writes a founder of the muscular Christianity movement in defense of fighting.

With Hughes' vindication of fighting established, Tom and Slogger Williams' bout resumes. Older and taller than his opponent, Williams is the odds-on favorite; but Tom is more spry than his opponent, and both get in good shots, Williams dominating in earlier rounds, Tom more so in the latter. To be sure, the boy spectators form a human ring and choose official timekeepers, such is their familiarity with the rules of boxing. Further, Hughes depicts the boys as fairly skilled pugilists, who feint and parry, and vary their punches, delivering blows high and low. In the end, the fight is stopped when the Doctor passes by, leaving no clear victor. Tom prefers this (even though at the time he was winning) because it allows Williams and him to become good friends. In the end, Hughes once again addresses the reader, saying that he thought it important to include the episode both to be honest about school life and "because of the cant and twaddle that's talked of boxing and fighting with fists nowadays." He encourages the reader to take up boxing, with words that might well anticipate the ethical discussions and case studies ahead, offering his own perspective:

> Learn to box then, as you learn to play cricket and football. Not one of you will be the worse, but very much the better for learning to box well. Should you never have to use it in earnest, there's no exercise in the world so good for the temper, and for the muscles of the back and legs.
>
> As to fighting, keep out of it if you can, by all means. When the time comes, if it ever should, that you have to say "Yes" or "No" to a challenge to fight, say "No" if you can—only take care you make it clear to yourself why you say "No." It's proof of the highest courage, if done from true Christian motives. It's quite right and justifiable, if done from a simple aversion to physical pain and danger. But don't say "No" because you

fear a licking, and say or think it's because you fear God, for that's neither Christian nor honest. And if you do fight, fight it out; and don't give in while you can stand and see.³⁵

Occasionally conflating spiritual and international fighting with its fistic counterpart, Hughes' apologetics on behalf of the reasons to learn to box are presently of interest for their inclusion of its benefits for fitness, discipline and preparedness for self-defense. As to his admonition to avoid conflict if one can but not to shrink from it simply because of fear, this is but one perspective; and, given the muscular Christian concern for the relationship of boxing to character building, befits the viewpoint one would expect in a fictional work by one of the muscular Christianity's chief proponents. Such is Hughes' perspective on the relationship of boxing, manliness and Christianity.

Hughes was not the only well-known writer of his era to wax fictional on the virtues of fighting for Christians. Charles Dickens himself incorporated muscular Christian themes in his creation of the character the Rev. Septimus Crisparkle in his unfinished final novel, *The Mystery of Edwin Drood* (1870). Described as being a fitness buff bearing a youthful appearance, the Reverend Crisparkle embodies the renowned muscular Christianity proponent Charles Kingsley's philosophy that a manly Christian's athleticism and physical strength are a reflection of his spiritual strength and moral conviction; in fact, Dicken's ties Crisparkle's "mania for exercise" with his "soundness of soul" in passages that additionally incorporate his skill as a boxer, as in the following:

> A fresh and healthy portrait the looking-glass presented of the Reverend Septimus, feinting and dodging with utmost artfulness, and hitting out from the shoulders with the utmost straightness, while his radiant features teemed with innocence, and softhearted benevolence beamed from his boxing gloves.³⁶

In fact, in a manner that anticipates film and television's not infrequent use of pugilism to portray a sensitive or peace-loving religious man as being simultaneously virile, Dickens recounts the Rev. Septimus Chrisparkle's reaction to the arrival of his mother while he is engaged in practicing "the noble art," saying that upon seeing her, he "left off at this very moment to take the pretty old lady's entering face between his boxing-gloves and kiss it. Having done so with tenderness, the Reverend Septimus turned to again [sic], countering with his left, and putting in his right in the most tremendous manner."³⁷ In fact, one modern scholar explicitly relates this fictional portrait with Kingsley's philosophical writings, in which Kingsley argues that through sport one cultivates virtues from bravery to temperance, qualities which are attainable through no other activity.³⁸

Popular writings expressing muscular Christianity's philosophy are not limited to those arising from that movement's nation of origin. One work published in the United States, for example, came from a figure that not only wrote about that movement's ideals, but also lived them. Thus, Harvard educated American boxer-turned-minister the Rev. Frederick Wedge, also known as "Kid Wedge" and "The Fighting Parson," penned a partly fictionalized view of his life story in the semi-autobiographical novel *The Fighting Parson of Barbary Coast* (1912). The book is based upon his service as a street preacher and heavy-handed social reformer. After years of working as a professional boxer, Wedge was converted at a revival meeting in Missouri,[39] and then rather publicly refused to fight just before his next scheduled bout, saying he now believed that fighting was wrong, save for self-defense. He made his newfound objection known in a most unusual way, when

> in the presence of 2000 people, [Wedge] astonished everybody by handing his opponent a tract with the wish that he would read it carefully. The amazed boxer seemed to regard this as a public insult, and he promptly smote the "Kid" on the nose. Wedge then said, "We are told to turn the other cheek." He did so, and was rewarded with a terrible blow which sent him against the ropes. "I have not been told what to do next," said Wedge, "but I guess I can pound you to pulp without interfering with my conscience."[40]

Reports of the ensuing fight document a disfiguring brawl, one Wedge won—whereupon he promised to pray for his opponent, and promptly retired from the ring. Even so, after years of pastoral service in several U.S. states, Wedge started a boxing ministry while serving as pastor of a Baptist church in Wisconsin. Saying the sport could teach character and health benefits to his Sunday School boys, he applied for and was awarded a license for an athletic association, permitting him to teach his young congregants to fight and to stage matches between them.[41] As noted earlier, Wedge later worked with the YMCA to teach boxing to servicemen, sparring with them before teaching Bible classes. Nonetheless, Wedge was a rather colorful figure; during his several pastoral calls in various states and denominational settings, he managed to run afoul of the law for various reasons, including fighting, unruly conduct, and drinking.

Wedge's rough-and-tumble personality is captured in his book. *The Fighting Parson of Barbary Coast* reviews vignettes from Wedge's life: being raised in poverty in California; learning to fight to defend his newsboy's corner from rival "newsies"; raising money for the benefit of his widowed mother and younger sister; becoming a boxer; meeting his wife, "Margaret" (Prudence, in real life); and ultimately graduating college and becoming a pastor. The antagonists of the novel include both a well-to-do, corrupt pastor who is in the pocket of the big businessmen in his congregation, and those business owners themselves, who run factories with appalling working conditions, run illicit businesses such as gambling establishments, "dance" halls, bars, and own the police on the seedy side of town—the Barbary Coast. "Gordon" (Wedge's fictional pseudonym) faces a life-changing experience when he accidentally kills a man in the boxing ring. A benevolent pastor who offers encouragement to Gordon while he is incarcerated champions his legal case. (The earlier mentioned corrupt pastor refuses to extend his help, as he is a rival for Margaret's affections.) The story is shot through with the lingo of fighting and battles, actual and metaphorical. Hence, when counseling the imprisoned Gordon about his interest in pastoral ministry, the kindly minister prays for him, saying, "If it be Thy will to lead him into the ministry, may the same determination that has marked all his battles be with him in his struggles to obtain an education."[42] And later, to offer encouragement, the same minister advises, "I knew that your work in the ring would help you see many things in the right way. Life is a battle. Even the struggle for culture and religion is a warfare."[43] Hence, in true muscular Christian fashion, Gordon's character, forged as a boxer, is deemed an asset to his pursuit of ministry.

And what a ministry it is! Faced with so much "drunkenness and debauchery," Gordon, "this sturdy athletic pugilistic evangel," "thrust himself into the mad sea of iniquity on Barbary Coast"; the parson would go "up and down the brilliant Coast at night, taking his station before one resort and then another," preaching God's love, ministering to those in trouble and tending to their needs at a local mission, where he insisted (against custom) that residents work for their room and board.[44] Soon realizing that he has to focus on prevention rather than rescue, the Reverend Wedge confronts the source of the slum's problems, standing up to corrupt business owners, police, and politicians who prey upon the vulnerable.[45] Thus, "hundreds stopped to hear the fearless preacher, who at great risk of his own life, stood exposing the ways of the dives."[46] Eventually, due to his effort to expose the selfish business owners, the Reverend Wedge is "set up" and almost killed in an alley, willing to sacrifice himself for his cause. When it is exposed that the self-same exploitative factory owner (who was a leading congregant at the aforementioned well-to-do church) owns the illicit businesses, and himself orchestrated the attack on the Fighting Parson, "society and the church were shocked."[47] Having successfully fought the tyrant, Gordon recovers and marries Margaret.

The tale is a product of its era, as it is laden with the message of the social gospel movement, prevalent at the time. Wedge's tale's focus on economic justice and righting conditions that lead to slums, poverty, unfair labor conditions and debauchery reflect the social gospel movement's goals. His wife, "Margaret," is introduced trying to fight for the improvement of working conditions for female factory workers and helping them to unionize—much to the chagrin of both the local minister, who is in the pocket of the factory's owner, and the owner himself. Gordon's whole life story is filled with opponents and obstacles he must overcome to serve the Lord here on earth, as befits the muscular Christian need for opponents to fight, to forge one's courage. He does so to help the exploited and confront injustice found in the socio-economic conditions of the city, which made life miserable for its less-fortunate inhabitants. That he is a boxer establishes Wedge as a formidable force, a strong fighter who uses his might to confront evil and establish God's will on earth by working to change exploitative social conditions. In order to balance any concerns with his combatant nature and approach, Gordon's benevolent minister friend defends his fighting, in both the pugilistic and socio-political forms. Notably, the novel also depicts Wedge as wanting to avoid violence when necessary; though he is able to knock out opponents at will, he prefers to win fights by points, and not injure others. Thus portrayed as as-peaceful-as-possible and a fighter when necessary, Wedge's character here establishes what will become the typical portrayal of clergy boxers in popular culture for decades to come.

One final book to note in the lineage of fight sports ministries fictions is a work of Southern literature, a novel set in civil rights era Mississippi amidst the increasing racial tension of desegregationist activism: Jack Butler's *Jujitsu for Christ* (1986). Balancing biting humor and tender-but-truthful character sketches with serious subject matter and knowing references to historical events, the work is experimental, at times written as stream of consciousness or in the style of casual Southern syntax. Butler crafts a racially tense world populated with black and white characters of varying degrees of self-awareness, social consciousness and virtue. This includes: a frustrated but upright African-American couple trying to raise their family in difficult times; a half-cocked young black man, the friend of one of the couple's sons, whose anger exceeds his understanding; black intellectuals and activists; racist police; and white churchgoers and businessmen showing varying degrees of charity, understanding and bigotry. Butler creates a setting wherein all are hyper-aware of racial issues, whose impact on interpersonal and social relations are everywhere palpable. Both blacks and whites harbor at least some level of anger regarding matters of race, leading some characters to acts of surprising kindness, and others to tragedy.

Amidst all of this is the central character, Roger Wing. Wing is a young, lonely recent high school graduate, a white martial artist belted in two traditions, whose mean-spirited father's death led his mother to marry a modestly successful man indifferent to both life and Roger, facts which weighed heavily on the young man. Wanting more for himself, "karate became more and more important to him, [and] he began to form an image of his future. It was an image of noble deeds, the deeds of a warrior-saint in the cause of justice."[48] The particular direction this calling would take was

2. Cultural Reflections on Fight Sports and the Church 61

revealed through visits to a Bible Club and, later, Youth for Christ (YFC) meetings, the initial draw being less of a spiritual yearning than one associated with Patsy, a young woman who (as Butler frankly writes) got Roger "seriously horny."[49] After hearing testimony at a YFC meeting, Roger once stands up and declares that he is saved, and decides to use the talents God has given him in martial arts to offer witness through a studio he intends to open called Jujitsu for Christ. He would train members of YFC and the Bible Club for free, and lead attendees in prayer and a Christian approach to martial arts. With this goal in mind, he buys a laundromat in a predominantly black neighborhood, the man who sells it to him almost (though not actually) warning him about there being "a lot of colored" folks about. As he begins living in his studio and preparing it to open for lessons, Roger is befriended by a black child named Marcus, who insists that this white young man come to dinner at his family's home. Initially shocked when they see who is coming to dinner (the mother drops a bowl of mashed potatoes upon first sight of Roger), the family nonetheless comes to regularly welcome Roger to the household and their dinner table.

The relation of Roger's religious convictions (such as they are) and his devotion to martial arts is explored throughout the novel. Asked to serve as a supply preacher, Roger is uncertain about the request until he asks if he can do jujitsu in the sermons. "Sure you can," his friend tells him. "You can do anything in a sermon, just so long as you do it to the glory of God." Advising Roger to go ahead and tie-in martial arts demonstrations with discussions of scripture, his friend further observes that Roger can "go around and witness for the Lord and help pay for [his] studio."[50] When asked by a parishioner what subject he typically preaches on, Roger exclaims, "Self-defense and Jesus, mostly." When the churchgoer questions the need for this, saying "Jesus is our shield," Roger responds, observing, "But unto them that hath it shall it be given, too, and from them that hath it not shall it be taken away. And that goes for defending yourself, too." The congregant shares the story of a "colored" boxer who prayed before fights, and of whom she once inquired as to what would happen if he turned the other cheek in the ring, to which the man (comically) replied that he would not need to do that in order to be a true Christian because, if he did, he would be knocked out and unable to take care of his children—and God would not want that. Roger then explains to the woman his own philosophy on Christianity and self-defense, in a somewhat simplistic fashion that would later be explained more seriously by another character; for now, Roger explains his approach to nonviolent self-defense by saying:

> If you have two equal people, the aggressor, the mean one, is supposed to lose. Because he's not clear. He's mad, and he wants things. He don't have the peace that passeth understanding. See, in jujitsu, a man comes at you, and you don't fight, you just grab

him how he's coming and help him along with it a little more until he is doing too much of it and he begins to see the error of his ways. It's just like when Jesus said heaping coals of fire on his head. You don't hate back, you just love, and they keep coming, and, and, and you flip them, and [...] you can make Christians out of them.[51]

Further evincing the strong-but-peaceful fighter model, Roger later explains that through love (expressed, according to him, by "flipping" combatants), one may change enemies into friends.

Roger's simplistic commitments are nonetheless tested on several occasions. Coming to the realization that when faced with evil one's only moral option is to "keep bad things from happening" because once they do happen all innocence is lost,[52] Roger once finds himself faced with needing to decide if he will train a black man who clearly wants to know how to fight in order to express his anger and hatred. When in one training session this would-be student attacks Roger, the instructor throws him down and, finding himself filled with hatred and thinking in racist terms, consciously clears his mind, engaging in "the most introspection he had ever done," ultimately deciding to choose not to respond to another's hate with his own.[53] His belief is further tested when, while working as a security guard at a bank, he encounters this same young man trying to rob the place, and he fires a gun a Roger. Instead of returning fire with his own pistol, Roger strikes the robber with it and, when the police enter, begs them not to shoot the robber. Uncertain how those in his black neighborhood will react to his "hero" status, since his opponent was black, Roger is pleasantly surprised at the supportive reaction he receives. Attending his surrogate black family's church, he finds the pastor approving of the congregation's "visiting friend's" actions in Christian terms; as Butler writes, "he had held a gun in his hand and had not fired it, even when he himself was being fired on," which was "a truly Christian act, not because it was passive, which it was not—Roger had subdued the robber—but because it was a refusal of anger." As the pastor says, Roger had "found another way, the way that is the way of Jesus."[54]

Ultimately, when tragedy strikes Roger's adopted family and a white crowd kills their oldest son, the martial arts evangelist takes flight with their youngest child, Marcus—the boy who had wandered into Roger's martial arts studio to invite him to dinner—doing so with the father's blessing, in order to save him from the fallout. It is Marcus that is the fictional writer of the book, the reader learns in the novel's last sentence. His point in writing the book (the novel says) is to invite reflection upon how, as one character says towards the story's end, virtue has less to do with skin color than "the blackness and the whiteness of our hearts."[55] Reflecting upon how Roger had cared for him (Marcus) as long as he could, even with bumps along the way, the young charge ultimately realizes that, in doing so, Roger did the right thing, and that he did it as he did most things in life, even martial arts, out of love. As one reviewer observes of the role jujitsu plays in the novel, quoting a line from the work itself, "karate isn't something you *know*, it's something you *practice*," concluding that "its function in the book is to provide a model for a method of cultivating the truth"[56]; that amidst confusion and uncertainty, as when one is being "flipped" by matters of racial tension, or by an opponent on a martial arts mat, one must work actively to master one's responses according to one's commitments, Christian or otherwise. Here, Roger, like previous literary fighters of the muscular Christian movement before him, embodies the careful, self-conscious balance of Christian commitment with that of having a warrior's heart. That said, one contrast with previous writings of the muscular Christian library, given perhaps the more recent date of the novel, is that the protagonist is less concerned with personifying traditional manliness and more (like the films and television fighters we will soon consider) with balancing the strength he derives from training in fight sports with his commitment to live peaceably.

To wit, just as the muscular Christianity movement found fictional, narrative support for its philosophy and practice from writers such as Kingsley, Hughes and Dickens, and from American novels such as *The Fighting Parson of Barbary Coast* and *JuJitsu for Christ*, so too do we find cinema providing popular cultural images of boxing and ministry. The earliest of these is significant both for its being a box office hit (even winning an Oscar for its lead actor, Spencer Tracy) and a respected title in film history. Based on the true story of Father Edward J. Flanagan, *Boys Town* (1938) follows the efforts of a strong-willed priest to establish a home for troubled youth. Evincing the tough-but-caring balance between the worlds of boxing and the church, Father Flanagan's philosophy is that boys respond to discipline if it is doled out with love. Referencing the patriotism of the muscular Christian movement, the priest plans to use the home to make boys into good Americans.[57] Showing that boxing has a place in church ministries with youth, a pivotal scene finds Father Flanagan telling two quarreling boys that they should settle their dispute in the ring. Flanagan's struggling institution, we learn, has a regulation-sized boxing ring in a room with chairs enough for all, and from where Boys Town residents cheer on young pugilists. Not only does this depict a church-based boxing program and a reverence for the ring as a place to settle arguments with physical dominance, but also some expertise on the part of clergy in the practice of boxing, as Father Flanagan himself referees the fight.

Another beloved film about a clergyman who ministers to boys is the musical classic *Going My Way* (1944), starring Bing Crosby as the athletic Father O'Malley. This movie only hints at boxing as a sport practiced by the boys of O'Malley's parish, as several of them wear boxing gloves while

Spencer Tracy as Father Flanagan, in the ring refereeing a boxing match between Mickey Rooney (left) as Whitey Marsh and Frank Thomas as Freddie Fuller, aiming to settle a dispute. From *Boys Town* (1938).

they rehearse for the boys' choir O'Malley directs. Nonetheless, the film's sequel, *The Bells of St. Mary's* (1945), prominently features a boxing storyline. This film stars Ingrid Bergman as Sister Superior Mary Benedict, a nun who heads an inner-city parochial school badly in need of repair, and Crosby, reprising his role as Father O'Malley, now reassigned to help the struggling church school.

The story finds the nun and priest sparring in more ways than one. After the two observe one boy beating up another in a playground fight, O'Malley compliments the fighting skills of the winner; Sister Benedict is more impressed with the boy who tries to avoid fighting and takes a beating. She notes that they do not tolerate fighting at the school, whereupon Father O'Malley explains, "naturally I like to see a lad who can take care of himself. On the outside, it's a man's world." Sister Benedict smiles and asks how these men are doing at running the world, to which O'Malley is nonplussed, adding, "you know what I mean—sometimes a man has to fight his way through." "Wouldn't it be better," Benedict retorts, "to think your way through?" O'Malley then raises concerns for a feminized church and society, asking, "Don't you think sometimes in raising boys, that a woman's influence can be carried too far?" "You mean," the nun replies, "they may

2. Cultural Reflections on Fight Sports and the Church

Father Flanagan (Spencer Tracy) calls a ten count to downed *Boys Town* pugilist Whitey Marsh (Mickey Rooney).

become sissies, Father?" After he says yes, Sister Benedict reveals that the boy who lost the fight did so because of her influence, as she told him fighting is wrong.[58]

Alone with the boy in her office, Sister Benedict shares how proud she is of him for turning the other cheek, and that it is he who is the "better man." When the boy confides that he doesn't feel proud, the nun sets off on a mission. She buys a book about boxing at a sporting goods store (much to the shop owner's surprise) and, after reading it, offers a private lesson in her office to her youthful trainee. Wearing her full habit, she demonstrates jabs, crosses, hooks, bobbing and weaving, fancy footwork, and how to throw a "pay off" punch. The scene lasts more than five minutes and ends as the nun herself takes a punch to the chin when her pupil hits her as they spar, staggering her. When her pugilistic protégé later successfully defends himself against the other boy (with subtle tips offered from the sidelines by the nun), Benedict is pleased—especially when he knocks the other boy down. Perhaps having learned to balance the somewhat contradictory advice he received from Sister Benedict, the victor apologizes to the other boy, shakes his hand, and offers to buy him an ice cream cone. When O'Malley knowingly inquires how the boy could have learned such skills in so little time,

Sister Mary Benedict, played by Ingrid Bergman, breezes past Father Chuck O'Malley, played by Bing Crosby—the priest reading the Bible, the nun studying *The Art of Boxing*. From *The Bells of St. Mary's* (1945).

the Sister replies with sarcasm: "Oh, we try to do our best to raise masculine little men—with our limited knowledge of the outside world." Reflecting the history of debates about the role of athletics, boxing, and "masculine" pursuits in the church, this film is noteworthy for how its tunic-clad protagonist compromises what might be considered a "feminized" approach to religion in order to remain relevant and speak to the needs and concerns of the church's young men.

Another film of this era that focuses on a boxing ministry and uses boxing to show how one can be both tough and genteel is *Kid Monk Baroni* (1952). Featuring Leonard Nimoy (*Star Trek*'s "Spock") in his first starring role, as Paul "Monk" Baroni, the film centers on a young thug (Baroni) with a misshapen face (what one character calls "primitive") and no direction in life. Baroni belongs to a local gang that commits petty crimes, until local priest Father Callahan invites him and the other gang members to the basement of St. Dominick's Church to learn how to box. Although the parish hopes to expand its modest facilities and programs, it reaches out to local youth in the best ways it can, to keep them off the streets. When giving Baroni his first lesson, Father Callahan explains that the boxing program

Sister May Benedict (Ingrid Bergman) teaches a bullied schoolboy, Eddie Breen (Richard "Dickie" Tyler) from St. Mary's parochial school, how to defend himself by giving a boxing lesson in her office. From *The Bells of St. Mary's* (1945).

is an alternative to street violence: "we're trying to prove that a human being can protect himself without killing his opponent." Upon downing the youngster, the priest explains to the suddenly intrigued teenager that the technique he used is an "extracurricular part of my religious training, better known as a left jab. It has a definite value convincing certain kinds of unbelievers."[59] It surely convinces "Monk," who trains with the priest and learns how to channel the anger he faces when people treat him badly for his less-than-handsome features. Counseling the young man, Father Callahan observes that Baroni is smarter than he lets on, noting that the young man actually shows refinement. Baroni confirms this, sharing that he loves church vocal music and would like to join the church choir. When members of his old gang (which he has by now renounced) see him in his choir robe, they emasculate him; they ask if he is a girl, if they might date him, where he got his "skirt," and call him "Callahan's sissy." Baroni handily beats his former gang associates—and when Father Callahan tries to intervene, accidentally knocks the priest out cold with a left hook. Thinking he is no longer welcome at the parish, and now on the run from police, Baroni starts boxing for money.

He finds a manager who wants to capitalize on "Monk" Baroni's "prehistoric" looks and savage, angry boxing style, thereby giving audiences a pug they can hate. Baroni thus begins a successful boxing career, applying the techniques he learned from the priest. Nonetheless, he maintains his interest in church choir music, listening to records in private. When he takes the advice of a girlfriend and gets plastic surgery to make him more comfortable with his looks, it changes his fighting style, as he begins to fight defensively, to protect his face—and he begins losing. Reestablishing his relationship with the priest, Baroni says of his left jab, "every time I connect with it, I say, here's a message from Father Callahan." But the young Baroni confesses he is unhappy fighting, whereupon the priest reassures him, saying, "You'll be alright, if not as a fighter, as a man." In the end, the manager makes a deal with Baroni, that if he fights in his old style one more time, the boxer's purse will go to build St. Dominick's much needed recreation center. It is a way to make things up to the priest and members of the parish, the manager suggests, adding, "This is bigger than penance." Baroni fights with all his heart and takes serious blows to his face in the process, sacrificing his newfound good looks. Although he loses, the money he makes still finances the church recreation center. Father Callahan consoles the young man, saying, "This was not defeat. You're a bigger man for the trying, for the sacrifice. The way you fight carries its own victories." Thus with shades of muscular Christianity's character building focus, and anticipating the ethical debates forthcoming in the next chapter, Kid Monk Baroni depicts a winning boxing ministry—one that successfully evangelizes young urban men, helps the church and its programs to grow, and (with its focus on a pugilist-chorister) provides a way to mitigate, if not resolve, concerns with maintaining masculine identity amidst interest in more refined, perhaps feminine, aspects of church life.

Some films may not portray a boxing ministry but do depict a religious figure who boxes for the church's cause, sometimes in support of church ministries. Along these lines, *The Leather Saint* (1956) finds a priest who secretly moonlights as a prizefighter in order to raise money to buy much needed equipment for a children's hospital. To balance the ethics of a priest who boxes, the "saint" punches his opponents as little as possible, and always expresses concern for their well-being in the locker room—*after* he knocks them out. *Tennessee Champ* (1954) depicts a simple, Bible-quoting son of an evangelical preacher who turns to prizefighting to have a platform from which to spread the Gospel and raise money on behalf of a church. The utility of boxing for both of these goals trumps any ethical concerns he may have about fighting. John Wayne stars in *The Quiet Man* (1952) as an American boxer who hangs up his gloves and moves to Ireland after killing a man in the ring; protecting his identity is a principled-but-frail

2. Cultural Reflections on Fight Sports and the Church

Elmer Gantry, played by Burt Lancaster, as a salesman-turned-preacher, giving a fiery sermon against evil and his own opponents from the center of a boxing ring, while members of the audience cheer him on as if they are watching a fight. From *Elmer Gantry* (1960).

local priest who once was a lightweight boxer. The satirical classic *Elmer Gantry* (1960) channels Hughes' philosophy and Sunday's imagery, and shows a fire-and-brimstone preacher using the symbolism of the boxing ring as a setting from which to preach a sermon on fighting for "true" religion against its opponents. Summoning the spirit of the Christian warrior, Gantry stands center canvas, riling the crowd in pugilistic fashion as he sermonizes against social evils, vowing to fight all who oppose him, while members of the crowd respond in kind, ironically yelling, "smack 'em down, preacher!" and "hit 'em! murder 'em!"[60]

Even television gets in on the act, as the cast of the long-running Korean War set series *M*A*S*H* (1972–1983) includes William Christopher as Father John Francis Patrick Mulcahy (whose name was changed during the series to Francis John Patrick Mulcahy), a Jesuit priest whose frequent remarks about the evils of war and his desire for peace is balanced by his past as a champion amateur boxer. He is, therefore, both peace loving and a strong fighter. In the final episode, he shares his post-war plans to serve a parish and be a boxing coach for the Catholic Youth Organization, as he had before the war—until an explosion leaves him deaf. In the penultimate episode, the members of the M*A*S*H unit create a time capsule, into which Mulcahy places his boxing gloves; he remarks upon doing so that perhaps in the future nations can settle their differences using only these, instead of warring.[61]

This balance, of the peace-loving fighter, is established throughout the series, as individual episodes focus on Mulcahy's boxing in relation to his values and character. One such occasion arises in the episode "Heroes," in which Mulcahy's favorite childhood boxer arrives in camp as part of a tour to uplift the spirits of injured soldiers in M*A*S*H units. Not as kindly in private as when he is on display before the troops, the boxer nonetheless matters to cheer up the bed-ridden soldiers, as well as to inspire Mulcahy. Alas, the pugilist has a stroke and is given no hope of recovering. Sitting bedside to comfort the unconscious man, Father Mulcahy confides that the boxer had been a childhood hero of his—one of two, he explains. The first was Plato, whose writings on the "ideal plane" impressed him. In a monologue that speaks to various matters heretofore addressed and several to come, the priest confides that his attraction to this abstract ideal was probably due to the fact that "my real life was less than ideal. I was small and wore thick glasses, probably from reading too much Plato, and I was an easy target for the neighborhood kids. I didn't even try to fight back. I didn't think that fisticuffs were very Platonic." The turning point for him came when his father took him to see a boxing match—one featuring the man now lying unconscious before him. Mulcahy recalls being impressed when, after easily getting the better of his opponent (much to the delight of the crowd and his father, who were calling for more punishment), the boxer refused to continue, and asked the referee to stop the fight because his opponent was too hurt to continue. Mulcahy then shares the life-changing insight that overtook him in that moment, when "I realized, for the first time, that it was possible to defend myself and still maintain my principles." Observing that had Plato been a boxer he would have fought like that—like his boxing hero—the Father goes on to share that "that was when I made up my mind to keep one foot in the ideal plane and the other in the real world."[62] With that, he thanks the boxer and leaves. Hence, *M*A*S*H* presents a minister who balances ethics and fighting, idealism and realism, maintaining manly and peaceable principles, even as he fights hard for his convictions, including those in the service of peace.

Another episode likewise shows Father Mulcahy ruminating over the use of his boxing skills. In "Dear Sis," the priest writes a letter to his sister, a nun, about how ineffective he feels to serve the needs of the doctors, nurses and wounded in camp. Amidst so much physical suffering, where medical expertise is what saves the lives of the soldiers, the priest confronts a crisis of purpose. He contemplates his crisis while throwing punches at a speed bag hung in his tent. One evening, as wounded men are being triaged on the ground about the camp, a panicked soldier resists the efforts of the head nurse to help him and hurls her across the ground. Stepping in at the nurse's request to try to hold him down, Mulcahy is stunned when the soldier punches him. Mulcahy responds by throwing a hook that sends the man rolling several feet away. Immediately filled with remorse, the priest later tries to apologize to the soldier whom he hit, but the young man refuses to forgive the priest, adding to his guilt by asking, "Where were you ordained, Father—Stillman's Gym?"

So troubled is Mulcahy that he confides in one of the surgeons. Suggesting that he failed to live up to the ideals he once taught to others, the priest explains, "I used to coach boxing for the CYO. I told my boys it built character!" He explains that as Christ's representative, he is not only supposed to believe in certain principles, but also live them. Humorously resisting the surgeon's sympathetic observation that if another man had come to the priest for counseling, having failed while trying to do his best, that the priest would let him "off the hook," Mulcahy retorts, "Sure I would. And if the hook didn't work, I'd probably land an uppercut." In the end, the doctors and nurses of the unit honor the Father by raising a toast to him for how his modest decency among them gives them strength. They all then sing a round of the song "Dona Nobis Pace," which is Latin for "give us

Father John Mulcahy, played by William Christopher in the long-running TV series *M*A*S*H*, takes out his frustrations on a speed bag mounted in his tent, as the former Catholic Youth Organization coach serves patients and doctors of a mobile army surgical hospital unit during the Korean War.

peace," the priest sharing that he prays those words every night. The episode ends with Mulcahy concluding his letter to his sister by observing that whether or not one feels useful is beside the point when moving from crisis to crisis; the point is simply to "keep moving."[63] Balancing again his conscientious pursuit of ideals with pragmatism, the series here once again depicts this priest, a former leader of a boxing ministry, as a man of character, who will fight (literally or figuratively) if necessary, while remaining dedicated to the ideal of peace.

Another television character with a religious background who heads a fight sport program, this time at a martial arts dojo, is Trent Malloy, originally of the *Walker, Texas Ranger* (1993–2001) series, and later the central figure of a short-lived spin-off series, *Sons of Thunder* (1999). Malloy is a pastor's son, who disappointed his father by leaving the seminary to enter the army. Now a sergeant with the army rangers, Malloy uses the martial arts skills once taught to him by Texas Ranger Cordell Walker (Chuck Norris) to serve as a hand-to-hand combat instructor. He learned these skills when, after a childhood incident in which Malloy accidentally killed another boy while playing with a gun, he swore off the use of firearms. Malloy returns home when his father, the Rev. Thunder Malloy, from whom he has been estranged since his decision to leave the seminary and enlist in the army, suffers a heart attack and dies. After the Reverend Malloy's death, Trent decides to stay near home, in part to reconsider the direction of his life. While serving as a security guard at a local mall, where he is not required to use a gun, he uses his martial arts expertise to thwart various illegal activities. During this time he also seeks the counsel of his father's replacement pastor about his search for meaning and a new vocation. So familiar with scripture is Trent that he correctly identifies Luke as the source of a Bible verse the pastor recites to him, that "to who much is given, much is expected." The two discuss Trent's "gifts" (such as his martial arts skills, and his religious training), as well as his "burdens" (his need to stay near his birth family and help them, and to reconsider his vocation and how he might serve others).

The two-part *Walker* episode in which Trent is introduced (itself titled "Sons of Thunder," and which originally aired in 1997) finds him helping his younger, high school aged brother stand up to neighborhood bullies, who misuse martial arts they are being taught by an unscrupulous local trainer (here clearly referencing a similar scenario from the film *The Karate Kid*). He also reconnects with a childhood friend, now on the police force, and works with him and Walker to bring a criminal to justice, all with the use of his martial arts skills, and no gun. One day, while sparring with Walker, Trent shares how he would like to give back to the community and help others with his "gifts," Trent sharing that he thinks this may best be done by becoming a private investigator, while Walker simultaneously says Trent should become a karate teacher. In the end, Trent becomes both, opening a martial arts dojo, "Thunder Karate School," from which he also runs a private investigator's business. While discussing his decision to open the school in the establishment's office, his police officer friend compliments his choice, saying "There's a lot of people out there that need the martial arts." Trent, at that moment unpacking and holding up his father's Bible to place on his new desk, replies, "That's not all they need." The end of the episode finds the Reverend Thunder, in flashback, preaching the Beatitudes from his church's pulpit; he catalogs all who are "blessed," from the poor in spirit, to those who mourn, who hunger and thirst for righteousness, are meek or merciful, and have pure hearts, as the faces of various characters who embody these traits flash on the screen. When the pastor finally lists the peacemakers as also blessed, and who will be called children of God, it is his son Trent's face that appears on screen, before the episode finally ends with an image of a cross atop a church, and a shot of the heavens.

With Trent Malloy established as a former seminarian who is an expert in martial arts, refuses to take up fire arms, and keeps the Bible handy in the office of the dojo where he teaches neighborhood children karate, the series uses fight sports to establish a religious figure, as with similar characters in popular culture, who is a just "peacemaker" but not a pushover. The spin-off series continues this balance, its title (*Sons of Thunder*) not only referencing Trent's father's name, but also alluding to a usage of the term in the Bible, from Mark 3:17, where Jesus uses this nickname for two brothers (James and John) who are among his closest disciples, perhaps in reference to the zealousness of their faith and witness. To wit, the short-lived series finds Trent and his partner, his childhood friend turned cop (hence, the "sons"), helping others via Thunders Investigations, while Trent also teaches at the dojo, Thunders Karate. Notably, quite in keeping with the spirit of the muscular Christianity movement and the stated purpose of many fight sports ministries, Trent once tells the mother of one of his students, whose life has been turned around since he began training with the former seminarian, that "martial arts can be a turning point for a lot of kids. It can give them a sense of discipline, focus, and a new way of looking at the world."[64] Thus, Trent, the zealous peacemaker who refuses to carry guns but uses martial arts to defend others and pursue justice, instills character in the youth who train with him, leading by example to show that a believer can love peace, shun firearms, and still remain "manly" and faithful, with the judicious, ethical use of martial arts.

In same year that the original "Sons of Thunder" episode of *Walker, Texas Ranger* aired, the film *The Boxer* (1997) premiered. It starred Daniel Day-Lewis as a former Irish Republican Army operative and pugilist named Danny Flynn, and is set during the tail end of "the Troubles" in Northern Ireland. Upon his release from prison for his role in a bombing, Flynn resurrects The Holy Family Boxing Club, a nonsectarian boxing gym that invites members of all faiths to participate, Protestants and Catholics. Depicted as a peacemaker, his skill as a boxer ensures that he is not seen as what Sister Benedict and Kid Baroni's gang mates called a "sissy." Flynn's principal enemy is an IRA lieutenant who is committed to continued resistance with acts of terrorism. When Flynn discovers that the lieutenant is hiding explosives in the community center he has turned into the boxing gym, Flynn disposes of these, throwing them in a river. Their antagonism comes to a head when the terrorist kills a Protestant police chief with a car bomb, right outside a venue where an exhibition boxing match Flynn organized between himself, a Catholic, and a Protestant boxer was intended to raise good will and build bridges. To show the strength of the protagonist's character, Flynn once refuses to continue boxing when a referee will not end a fight Flynn clearly is winning, his opponent beaten down and unable to defend himself. Balancing his peacemaking role with a strong, ethical character, the film is as significant as a modern example of a "manly" but peace-loving Christian fighter, as it is a depiction of a boxing ministry in popular culture.[65]

Pop culture's reflection on church leaders who fight and fight sports ministries is not, however, restricted to the realm of fiction. No less relevant is the documentary *Fight Church* (2014), which looks at mixed martial arts ministries and MMA fighter-preachers, who explain how their fighting is not only compatible with their faith but is also an integral part of their calling. For balance, the film includes perspectives of other religious leaders who oppose the sport, to say nothing of its place in ministry. It follows efforts by these various religious leaders to oppose or support a bill that would legalize professional mixed martial arts fights in New York State—the last state to do so. The film is a treasure trove of perspectives and quotations, particularly from MMA's clerical proponents about their views on how martial arts and the church are compatible, in a manner reminiscent of the rhetoric of Billy Sunday, Bendigo, and Thomas Hughes.

Hence, Paul Buress, a pastor and head of an MMA ministry at Victory Church in Rochester, speaks of how one learns to surrender through fighting, as one must to God, and of the love of others that comes from training with them. He opines that meekness means having strength to destroy but choosing not to, adding that he finds "nowhere in scripture where He says I just want you to be people's punching bag forever." Buress later declares that it is possible to love Jesus "and have a warrior's spirit," harkening back to the warrior archetype previously discussed. Another preacher shares a similar thought, explicitly complaining about the "feminized" church, and how men are taught "never to respond with aggression and force, almost like women"; he asserts that we have a problem in society because "[men] don't have a warrior ethos, we have a bunch of cowards."

Another pastor-fighter, Preston Hocker (whose cage name is "the Pastor of Disaster"), says he uses fighting to bring glory to Jesus. Bespeaking an awareness of a feminized church and the need for men's ministries, he declares, "Tough guys need Jesus too." At one point, Hocker says of a Christian professional MMA fighter that he admires him because "every time they put a camera in his face, he's thanking Jesus, he's representing Christ to the fullest. I try to model myself after him," adding just after this, "He's malicious!" Hocker's characterization of his training and fighting as a form of ministry is offered as the filmmakers show slow motion images of the pastor in a martial arts fight, his opponent beneath him, Hocker punching downwards. The documentary follows him and another MMA-pastor as they train to fight each other. The film also shows Pastor Buress fighting on Easter Eve and remarking upon this fight in his Easter sermon, proclaiming, "All of these wins and all of these losses are temporary. The real win has already been won 2000 years ago. Jesus never tapped, and if you surrender to him you can have real power and real strength." The film depicts various pastors leading mixed martial arts ministries with adults and children, sharing fellowship and training, preparing for fights and fighting, and offering their support to legalize professional mixed martial arts in New York.

For balance, the documentary includes remarks by a Catholic priest who opposes the MMA legislation and lobbies congressional leaders to uphold the ban in New York. It also includes remarks by one martial artist, Scott Sullivan, who began to perceive a conflict between his fighting and his commitment to Christian ideals. Eventually, Sullivan says he found himself unable to reconcile his Christian commitment to love his neighbor with a sport where the goal is to inflict damage upon another. Notably, the legislation the priest and others sought to oppose ultimately passed the legislature, not in the documentary, nor in the period it depicts, but more recently, in April of 2016. Professional mixed martial arts fights are now legal in New York. Several of the fighter-preachers in the film indicated a desire, if the legislation passed, to fight on a professional card, so as to bring attention to Jesus and their ministry, and to reach MMA fans. As John Renken, a former professional MMA fighter turned born again preacher, and head of Extreme Ministries in Tennessee, says in the film: the Gospel calls him to reach out to lost souls, "and lost people are watching MMA."[66]

Clearly, there are many who see no contradiction between fight sports and Christianity, and openly integrate the image of the fighter or warrior with their Christian identity and ministry. This perspective is further attested to in contemporary popular culture in a number of ways. For example, one online apparel maker offers t-shirts printed with the words "Jesus Army Jiu-jitsu Soldier," to identify the wearer as a fighter for Jesus. Depicting Jesus as a "scrapper," another illustrates Christ in a white jiu-jitsu robe, known as a gi, on the ground and holding Satan, who is robed in black, from behind in a choke hold; it features the words "Jesus has your back" beneath the image. "Jesus loves knockouts" is the text for another t-shirt, the words appearing beneath a clenched fist set against a brick wall, where the shadow of a cross is cast in the corner, itself small in relation to the more prominently sized bare knuckles. The outline of the famed Brazilian "Christ the Redeemer" statue, showing Jesus with his arms outstretched, serves as the "T" on a t-shirt bearing the words "Jiu Jitsu." Another line of athletic and casual wear named "Jesus Didn't Tap" offers t-shirts, hoodies, shorts, caps and other merchandise bearing the company's slogan. (Notably, the "T" in "Tap" is a cross.) Describing itself as one of the first "Christian-based MMA clothing companies," the business was founded by Jason David Frank, a martial arts champion and actor, who played one of the characters in the children's television series *Power Rangers*. The company website explains the meaning behind the slogan for which it is named: "in the sport of Mixed Martial Arts, to 'tap' is to quit or give up. The message of the Jesus Didn't Tap line is that Jesus didn't quit after going through unimaginable suffering and pain when he was crucified on the cross."[67]

Expressing a similar sentiment are popular memes (in this case, popular, shared images posted on users' internet sites and social media pages) depicting a muscular, long-curly-haired and bearded Jesus, standing in athletic shorts in the corner of a boxing ring, holding boxing gloves in his tape-wrapped hands. Here is the visualization of Billy Sunday's scrapper Jesus—a savior who is a manly fighter, as further attested to by Hughes. Unbeknownst to many who circulate these memes is the identity of the artist who created the images of a boxing Christ, Stephen Sawyer, whose website is Art4God. Although cropped from many versions of the circulating memes, Sawyer includes on the original of one of these images the word "Undefeated" underneath boxer Jesus.[68] On this particular image, the word "savior" appears along the ring's corner post. A page devoted to "Undefeated" at Sawyer's website explains its message that "Jesus willingly fights and intercedes on our behalf," and suggests that Christians should "choose to be in the ring, to fight the good fight of faith, and be grateful that we are in the same corner with the Undefeated one."[69] The image even appeared in *The New York Times* in conjunction with an article discussing how a more "macho," warrior image of Christ has become popular in some religious circles, particularly in regards to how Christ will appear in the Second Coming, and is intended to counter what some see as a more effeminate portrayal of Jesus that exists in culture.[70]

These and other products of modern pop culture channel the values of the muscular Christianity movement, expressed in contemporary tropes. They reflect one sensibility of the age, and powerfully bring into stark relief what some see as resolutions, and others see as prevalent anxieties, to matters concerning the relationship of Christianity, fight sports, and masculinity.

Ritualized Combat, Masculinity and the Church

These mediated images, like arguments concerning gendered ecclesiology and men's ministries books, reflect on some modern anxieties concerning masculinity, including as it relates to the church and religious expression. Some call this a crisis of masculinity—a need by men and broader society to come to terms with what it means to "be a man" in a world with greater gender equality, changing expectations and opportunities for men and women, and the evolution of societal understandings of gender and gender roles in a postmodern era. These anxieties have been the subject of considerable popular writing and media reflection. *Time* magazine, for example, recently published an essay by Jack Myers, author of *The Future of Men: Masculinity in the Twenty-First Century* (San Francisco: Inkshares, 2016), reflecting on the place of men in the 2016 political election year, and noting that both Donald Trump's and Bernie Sanders' styles (combative and emphasizing the rhetoric of fighting, aimed at restoring one's dignity and place in the world) aptly appealed to a "generation of young, discouraged and angry men—men who are feeling abandoned by the thousands of years of history that defined what it meant to be a real man: to be strong; to be a provider; to be in authority; to be the ultimate decision maker; and to be economically, educationally, physically and politically dominant."[71] This fight for control and dominance, and the relation of these to masculinity, resonates with the basic appeals, to many, of fight sports.

More directly applied to fight sports, writer Jonathan Gottschall, an English professor turned MMA practitioner, builds upon the observations of Jesuit scholar Walter Ong, from the latter's book *Fighting for Life: Contest, Sexuality, and Consciousness* (1981), as he writes that opportunities for modern men to test themselves with the hallmarks of "traditional masculinity—bravery, toughness, stoicism" are less common nowadays, and that absent these opportunities, men will follow the example of literary character Don Quixote and "invent their own dragons" to fight; that is, modern men will "[find] a way to be men in a post-masculine world."[72] Ong himself addresses a pervasive "male combativeness," writing that the

[need] for adversaries is common to all human beings, male and female. But by and large through the entire animal kingdom, among infrahuman as well as human species, conspicuous or expressed adversativeness [sic] is a larger element in the lives of males than females, for reasons relating both to the development of individual males and to the evolution of the species.[73]

Part of what defines a man, then, is that he has challenges to face—something, or someone—an opponent—to fight, to prove his grit.

Writers from Hughes to Ong suggest that a masculine model for Christians looking to follow is found in no less a figure than Jesus Christ himself. Indeed, evocative of men's posited need for conflict and opponents, Ong says of Christ's followers that their faithful discipleship is itself a "high-risk undertaking, involving struggle"; further, he notes that their model is found in a man who did not have to invent opposition (like Quixote) but who faced real opponents in an idyllic "manly" manner. Thus, echoing many of Hughes' themes, Ong characterizes Christ in terms that resonate with the ideals of modern "masculinity," saying:

if he is not entirely like a dragon slayer, Jesus' work is still that of a male fighter. He had to go it alone. Though he has male followers and also a large number of close and more reliable women followers, when the time comes for the agony in the Garden of Olives and for the trial, torture, and death that follow, he has to fight the fight by himself, the male loner, destined for high-risk combat.[74]

Hughes, that nineteenth century founding figure of the muscular Christianity movement, provides a historical bookend to the same themes Ong (as well as Gottschall and Myers) raises. When writing about what constitutes "being a man," ideally illustrated for him in the example of Christ, Hughes states that it comes in part from having powerful enemies against which to struggle.[75] Such conflicts test manliness, and provide opportunities to evince it.[76] A man must be able to show courage, Hughes writes, which involves not only the "animal," "brute" qualities of "persistency," the "contempt for safety and ease" and the "readiness to risk pain for death," but also the more manly willingness to do this as an act of "self-sacrifice for the welfare of another."[77] Although athletic tests may be meritorious and able to hone courage, Hughes says they are nonetheless not definitive of manly courage, which may be shown even by the weak.[78]

Nonetheless, using words like "battlefield" and "soldier," Hughes speaks of a man's journey through life, and that he must rise to the occasion even amidst the ordinariness of the everyday world. That is, even in the thick of mundane existence, men should aspire to higher ideals, Hughes says, for ideals fade over time and need rekindling; men rightly long for the need to witness acts of valor, Hughes writes, as a reminder of those ideals.[79] Indeed, Hughes recognizes an inner tension held in the hearts of men when they perceive "the difference between the man God meant him to be

[...] and the man he and the world have together managed to make of him"; happy is the man who can withstand the doubts cast by the awareness of this chasm and nonetheless, "take [his] stand resolutely" for the ideals of manliness even in his ordinary life.[80]

Hughes here writes of the same crisis of masculinity still spoken of a century and a half later by Myers, Gottschall and others. To witness or participate in acts of valor—standing up to an opponent and giving your all, especially when this involves self-sacrifice for another's benefit—would provide a balm for what ails men's suffering, to mitigate, as Hughes writes, the tensions arising from the awareness of the space between the ideal manly life and the everyday life of most men. In terms of popular culture, this may account for the popularity of action films, particularly among men, wherein a lone protagonist often stands up to overwhelming opposition with bravery, acts of violence, a "readiness to risk pain for death," and a willingness to sacrifice oneself for the benefit of others, befitting Hughes' discussion. The experience of watching such films provides a cathartic experience for men perceiving the difference between their own opportunities to evince ideal manliness in their own lives and clear acts of emblematic manliness in popular cinematic fiction, particularly when the hero is an ordinary man caught up in extraordinary circumstances and provided with the opportunity to combat evil, show courage, and fight for others.[81]

Something similar may be said of being a witness to or participant in acts of ritualized combat, such as in the ring or octagon. Witnessing a struggle between opponents may permit men to "participate," even vicariously, and at the more "animal" level (that is, without the "sacrifice for others" Hughes says lies behind acts that more fully constitute manliness), in a therapeutic experience that relieves some of this tension. Thus, acts of ritualized combat, such as that of the ring or cage, may purge some of that tension by allowing men to witness acts of courage that place on display an idealization of such virtue, beyond that of one's own ordinary life. Indeed, this evinces aspects of philosopher Rene Girard's thought concerning the function of ritualized violence. Hence, Kasia Boddy, in her magnum opus on boxing and culture *Boxing: A Cultural History* (2008), uses Girard to observe that competitors are "substitutes for all the members of the community," and that by witnessing ritual combat, observers are "vaccinated" against the "evil of violence" by witnessing an act of that very violence; symbolically the winner "lives," the loser "dies," and the community goes on, having beheld an act that portrays the very worst life may offer (challenge, defeat, death [here, symbolic]) and after which life endures, that tension relieved.[82] That it is the most "manly" of men who are the combatants in these rituals serves to show that even such men as these are subject to tests of survival and "manliness," which they face with bravery and

Hughes' readiness to risk it all. In this sense, even the losers, while symbolically "dead," have proven their manliness.

Thus, the ritual combat serves, in part, to attest to one's grit, albeit amidst carefully crafted rules and regulations that actually minimize risk. Noting that men throughout history have faced ritualized combat as ways to maintain honor, Gottschall (like Ong) observes that such behavior is found even in the animal kingdom, and that for men the test in such ritual acts is of one's "strength and bravery"[83]—the "courage" to face opponents that Hughes argues lies at the heart of Christ-like manliness. Even so, the use of a carefully delineated space (a ring, octagon, or simply observers forming a circle), "seconds" in a fighter's corner, padded gloves, time limits, a referee, rules that permit time for recovery, and the ritual surrounding entrance into the arena, preparation (the handshake or touching of gloves) and endgame (where combatants step to the center of the ritual "world" to hear the verdict, judges announce a victor, combatants shake hands or hug, and the victors strut in a display of prowess) together make such ritual combat set apart from what actual life-or-death combat would entail.[84] Nonetheless, these tests of honor, courage or manhood facilitate participants' ability, with safety measures in place, to ritually face "risking it all," and thereby demonstrate their masculine merits. For those who tout fight sports for their place in showcasing or developing manly traits, these points are pertinent.

Not only do the participants have something to gain from the experience of such ritualized combat, but so too do the witnesses. The meaning of the event comes through ritualized participation for the combatants, or vicariousness for the audience. This is not to minimize the actual courage of the combatants and the real dangers they face. For all the safety measures and rituals surrounding such battles, fighters face real risks and must show bravery. For professional boxing, and even more so for mixed martial arts, the stakes make of these events a form of what philosopher Jeremy Bentham has termed "deep play."[85] Geertz applies this concept to Balinese cockfighting in his famous essay, and cultural critics, such as Boddy, extend his analysis to boxing and other combat sports. As such, deep play

> is a game whose stakes are so high that, from a utilitarian point of view, it is irrational to play; this does not make the game unplayable, however, but elevates it. Instead of merely demanding the calculation of odds, the game works symbolically to represent the uncertain gamble that is life itself.[86]

To "risk it all" in such ritual combat is thereby what proves participants' courage and manhood, while witnessing this event permits audiences to participate vicariously in an elevated struggle, where there is a test, an opponent to face, and a winner and loser, but life goes on—and seeing this helps the audience face their own mundane, everyday struggles. To wit, "fight pastors" interviewed for *Fight Church* talk of gathering with congregants at their church to watch live UFC broadcasts, or attend fights as audience members.

Thus audiences may be inspired both by witnessing ritualized combat, and by reading about or watching acts of "manly" courage in popular media. As regards the latter, it is noteworthy, as film historian Leger Grindon observes in *Knockout: The Boxer and Boxing in American Cinema* (2011), that the boxer "stands alongside the cowboy, the gangster, and the detective as a figure that has shaped America's idea of manhood," be that in works of literature or cinema.[87] Just as pertinent an observation is that the vast majority of boxing films have been produced in the United States,[88] highlighting something of an American fixation on cultural representations of this "purely masculine" sport. Perhaps, given the much-posited and discussed crisis of masculinity facing modern American men (in the church and elsewhere), this makes sense, as does the fact that no sport has received more cinematic representation than boxing.[89] In a time period—discussed by Ann Douglas, and writers concerned with a feminized church—that saw economic changes shift from favoring the local "self-made man" to the all-powerful corporation, men became more dependent on others, challenging the myth of the rugged, lone individual; the cinematic boxer, usually self-made and combating gloved opponents as much as the establishment, portrays a mythic image that soothes modern man's masculine dilemmas.[90] Hence the portrayal of ritual combat in fictional cinema itself presents the same cathartic experience to address modern men's "crisis" of masculinity. Indeed, professional fights often are couched in terms of some personal gripe between combatants, whether these are real or manufactured by promoters, the staged fictionality of which is often sensed yet accepted by fans. Further, these interpersonal conflicts often have to do with an affront to a fighter's masculine pride, making the resulting fight itself very realistic—even as it falls into the pattern of a "familiar ritual," that "all too *masculine* ritual—of competitive disputation, where the point is less to be right than to win the fight."[91]

Looking ahead, this is not the case in many actual fight sports ministries, where concern for what is right is part and parcel of the training—and, perhaps surprisingly, what is right is often being willing to walk away from conflict, or being willing to retreat from an act of self-defense at the appropriate opportunity, even if this might call into question (as some would see it) one's courage (or, perhaps, "manliness") to stand and fight an opponent to the end. The courage, taught in many of these ministries, is to do the ethical thing by engaging in conflict only when necessary, doing so not to prove one's grit, but to protect one's or someone else's well-being, and then leave the conflict by whatever means necessary, even if this means retreating from it at the first sensible opportunity. The appropriate image here may be more of the *reluctant* warrior—one not set on proving one's bravery or dominance so much as being willing to sacrifice for others (in a manner befitting, as we will later see, the model of the shepherd), and here further sacrificing one's ego by being willing to withdraw from an altercation. In this way one's sacrifice—of ego, perhaps, or a clear cut "win"—may even be for the sake of the wellbeing of one's fellow combatant, perhaps even in an act of love, if not mercy. Thus in practice, some fight sports ministries are apt to present an alternative to the view of "masculine" discipleship constructed by the muscular Christianity movement and channeled in some modern men's ministries literature, to say nothing of some constructions of masculinity in the broader popular culture—although, notably, in keeping with the peace-seeking fighter at the heart of many pop cultural films, TV shows and novels focused on fight sports ministries. In fact, despite the history of fight sports ministries being demonstrably concerned with masculinity, and some modern fight sports ministries receiving more national media attention, many contemporary boxing and martial arts ministries count other concerns as more central than those related to issues of bolstering masculine identity in the church, being concerned more so with providing fitness-focused activity, fellowship, opportunities for formation, and a safe place for youth to gather and avoid dangers of the streets. While we will examine how this is put into practice in modern fight sports ministries ahead, the ethical reasoning underlying these ministries' practices is the subject we will next explore.

3

Ethical Issues Regarding Fight Sports and the Church

In her book *On Boxing*, Oates observes, "No American sport or activity has been so consistently and so passionately under attack as boxing, for 'moral' as we'll as other reasons."[1] As we have seen in Chapter 1, church leaders' opposition to boxing has history. So, too, does church leaders' support for boxing, expressed by institutional, rhetorical and fictional means. The entry of mixed martial arts onto the scene has only expanded the discussion. What, then, are the ethical issues of concern to the church as it reflects upon fight sports, both in general and as regards ministries of the church? What are the particular arguments for and against such activities, and how do these relate to the church's broader values? If a theology of sport is applied to boxing and martial arts and their use in church ministries, what insights are gained as to how these may or may not ethically fit into the church's mission? And what guidelines might such ethical reflection provide for actual fight sports ministries? These are among the ethical matters we will explore in considering the relation of fight sports to the church.

One need not necessarily start within the church to find moral opposition to boxing and mixed martial arts. Indeed, those in the church raising opposition to fight sports often do so by citing non-ecclesiastic professional organizations that voice concerns. For example, ethical reflections on whether the church should support or oppose professional boxing and mixed martial arts cite the call for a ban on these sports by both the American Medical Association and the British Medical Association.[2] The list of harms suffered by those involved in these professional sports, which led these and other organizations (such as the American Academy of Neurology) to pursue their prohibitions, includes traumatic brain injuries, concussions, neurological problems, and even death. To be sure, other sports likewise lead to injuries—a counterpoint made by supportive ethicists, who also note that higher mortality rates for other sports (such as rugby, horse racing, and skydiving) are often unfairly overlooked by those opposing fight sports.³ However, given that the objective of professional fight sports is to hurt, injure or incapacitate an opponent, issues of intentionality arise. In other sports, while injuries may occur, these may be accidental, or (for sports where violence and injuries are also the norm, such as hockey and American football) the result of excessive (albeit expected and rewarded) force, and the infliction of these is not itself the basis of scoring, as in professional boxing and MMA.

Still, there are those who respond that boxing is an art of "controlled violence,"⁴ that professionals (unlike in other sports, such as football or rugby) are trained to defend themselves against attacks and to counter strike, and that those who engage in these sports do so willingly. Further, there is risk of injury in many activities that most would not consider unethical. One Christian sports ethicist notes there are considerable risks, injuries and deaths possible when engaging in such an everyday activity as driving a car, which goes without ethical question.⁵ Clearly, however, the public spectacle of boxing and MMA, their celebration of violence (controlled or otherwise), and their high-profile "role model" athletes and the rewards bestowed upon them, make these professional fight sports more deserving of ethical reflection and scrutiny than these other risk-involving activities. Indeed, all these concerns lead one Christian sports ethicist to conclude that high-risk sports, including boxing, "would be *least* on [his] list of sports to be encouraged in the Christian community."⁶ Even so, Christians do engage in such professional sports, as both participants and fans; have used fight sports programs for evangelism, character building, and to bolster the church's perceived gender identity; and do train in such sports, some for competition, while others for recreation, fitness, self-defense, and/or fun. A sense of play, in fact, underlies a theological approach to Christian sports participation advocated by many ethicists, as we will see by this chapter's end.

One important point to establish at the outset is that whatever ethical concerns are raised regarding one particular use of fight sports in ministry may or may not apply to other uses. Hence, given the range of objectives involved in fight sports ministry programs, outlined in the introduction and reviewed in the forthcoming case studies chapter, not all of the ethical issues applied to professionals need necessarily apply to fight sports ministry programs, just as concerns raised for one approach may not apply, strictly or even loosely, to others. Recalling that these ministries may be focused on the use of boxing, individual martial arts or mixed martial arts training for (1) fitness, (2) self-defense, (3) recreational sparring, or (4) competition complexifies the discussion. Indeed, even advocates of amateur boxing would have answers to many of the concerns raised for professional bouts, since amateur boxing uses protective headgear, focuses on out-pointing one's opponent (as opposed to injuring them), and tolerates a much lower threshold for harm before a referee stops a fight. Similarly, grappling forms, such as BJJ, involve the "tap-out"—an opportunity for one to concede before injury occurs. (One saying among martial arts practitioners, acknowledging the sensibility of concession, is "tap today, train tomorrow.") Further, martial arts themselves are sometimes taught for form more than engagement, as is demonstrated by solo martial arts form exhibitions, where individuals show mastery of moves and techniques, which are sometimes scored competitively. In short, what may arise as a concern applied to professional boxing, for example, may not strictly apply to learning to box for fitness or self-defense—albeit other issues may arise, such as how to ethically respond to violence one might encounter in everyday life. With this caution in mind, we turn now to examine various ethical matters regarding fight sports and the church, particularly as these might be engaged by the church, including: biblical rhetoric, imagery and themes; the concept of imago dei, and the understanding of the body as a temple; the role of character development; competition and Christianity; and theologies of play.

Biblical Rhetoric, Imagery and Themes

One natural place to begin a reflection on fight sports and the church is to look at the Bible for its rhetoric, imagery and message. Indeed, fight sports were known in the ancient world in the form of gladiatorial fights, wrestling, free-form grappling, and (sans its modern rules) boxing. References to such sports are in fact found in Pauline rhetoric, amidst Saint Paul's broader use of sports metaphors, to suggest something about what it means to be a good Christian: to, like an athlete, "endure hardships," strive for a goal, stick to a course of action, and follow rules to receive a reward.[7] Athletic games were prominent at the time and places where Paul preached and ministered, so his use of such rhetoric to appeal to followers, and allegorically instruct them, is not surprising.[8] Thus, among Paul's use of athletic metaphors, one finds reference to fight sports. Most prominent among these is 1 Corinthians 9:24–27:

> Do you not know that in a race the runners all compete, but only one receives the prize? Run in such a way that you may win it. Athletes exercise self-control in all things; they do it to receive a perishable wreath, but we an imperishable one. So I do not run aimlessly, *nor do I box as though beating the air*; but I punish my body and enslave it, so that after proclaiming to others I myself should not be disqualified.[9]

That Paul would use these particular athletic references in an epistle to the congregation at Corinth evinces his ability to appeal to the life experiences of his audience, as Corinth was long the site of the Isthmian Games; thus, his use of language in relation to a popular cultural event familiar to his intended readers would find resonance, as the apostle tries to explain the importance of "training practices, discipline, and goal-oriented attitudes," here relating an athlete's discipline and training in pursuit of a goal to that of a Christian.[10]

Two primary reasons Paul might use such athletic metaphors to discuss evangelistic activities or spiritual matters are that they reflect his recognition of his audience's commonplace knowledge of athletics, including its "imagery and terminology," and the established rhetorical tradition of "appropriating athletic metaphors"[11]—what Price would call the "conscription" of sports by religion. Given Paul's skill at adapting his message to his given audience's experiences, the evangelist may well be drawing on their assumed experience with and appreciation of sports, in order to make a connection with the everyday social realities of his readers.[12] Much in the fashion of Christ's parables, which draw upon the everyday experiences of his listeners in order to explain realities with which they have little or no direct experience, so too Paul may be capitalizing on his readers' routine lived experiences in order to explain matters new or foreign to them. Hence, the proliferation of organized games and opportunities for personal athletic training in places he visited make Paul's appeal to such experiences all the more natural and well-suited to his audience, who would readily understand the basis for the comparison.[13] So too would the regular use of athletic metaphors in contemporaneous literature make Paul's appropriation of such literary techniques rhetorically effective. In fact, one need not necessarily choose between these two reasons, as Paul may well have effectively employed athletic metaphors, such as those of 1 Corinthians 9, for reasons regarding both.[14]

Paul's use of such athletic references was for persuasion, to inspire his audience by allusion to an activity they would well know and appreciate. What is more, the 1 Corinthians reference, and others—such as Paul's appeal to having "fought the good fight," finished the race, and kept the faith in 2 Timothy 4:7—may have drawn upon common "athletic figures of speech" of the time, familiar expressions based upon "sporting language."[15] Thus, similar to how many nowadays use sporting idioms without necessarily following a particular sport, let alone advocating for its practice, Paul may have on occasion simply used popular idiomatic language when making sporting references. Hence, just as modern people off-handedly remark about "rolling with the punches," "throwing in the towel," "hitting below the belt," or being "saved by the bell," "in your corner," or "on the ropes," without necessarily knowing much about boxing, so too Pauline athletic references need not imply that he was a sports fan or participant, let alone an advocate of any particular sport. Indeed, such metaphors are "so general in their lack of concrete details," according to one biblical rhetorical critic, that it is easy to imagine that any "Hellenic Jew could have either written or understood them," without having firsthand knowledge of the games from which such language originated.[16] Thus, despite those who might suggest otherwise, Paul's use of such references does not necessarily mean he was an advocate for particular sports, nor should it necessarily serve as justification for those who pursue such sports today.[17] To wit, note that in the aforementioned quote from Corinthians, Paul makes a clear contrast between "we" Christians and "they" athletes; that while the latter strive for "perishable" rewards, "we" struggle for the "imperishable."[18]

However, simply because Pauline references to boxing and other sports may not strictly advocate for such activities, this does not necessarily mean that such activities are necessarily to be considered prohibited, either. Paul evidently thought athletic imagery inspiring and proper enough to merit metaphoric appropriation. Indeed, the status of the athlete as an "ideal type," to whom "ordinary" citizens might aspire, is precisely what Paul and others draw upon to appropriate such imagery for their own purposes. In fact, the first century Greek philosopher and historian Dio Chrysostom used the persona of the champion Olympic boxer Melancomas to inspire others by drawing a profile of him as an archetypal assembly of desirable traits ("brawn, beauty and brains," in addition to being a victor) that others might emulate.[19] In contrast, Paul himself may use similar imagery and the adulation it inspires for more nuanced, subversive purposes. Reflecting in particular upon Corinthians 9:27, where the boxer uses his skills to bring to bear an assault on his own body instead of another's, and hence bring it into submission, the intended reading may indeed be a victory, but not of the customary sort; instead, the apostle/boxer succeeds at submitting his own body in order to establish self-control, such that he may bring his body "into a higher service," one beyond satisfying simply his own personal, temporal desires. Indeed, here as elsewhere (Philippians 3:12–14) in place of earthly rewards, the "victor" achieves deferred ones, and in fact "wins" not earthly glory (the typical reward for athletic achievement), which to the apostle might even prove shameful (Philippians 3:14–19), but a heavenly one, thus subversively using the athletic ideals to serve Paul's own countercultural persuasive purpose.[20]

Such use of athletic imagery has also been taken up by modern preachers, particularly in the muscular Christian era, who have drawn upon biblical references to make metaphoric points, if not also to justify followers' pursuit of combat sports. Thus, in colonial era New England, preachers not only urged followers to "wrestle" with spiritual matters, but also to actually grapple, as Jacob had wrestled the angel—sometimes even exemplifying the practice in their own personal lives. Hence, long before the "fight pastors" of today, who participate in MMA tournaments (as documented in *Fight Church*), the Rev. John Wise, a colonial era Ivy League educated biblical scholar and celebrated athlete, gained renown for summarily manhandling a hooligan who dared challenge him, slamming the man to the ground "until [he] begged for mercy."[21] Indeed, wrestling at the time enjoyed favor, particularly over boxing, as a more "ethical" fight sport, due to its "constrained violence," which left it "free of the theological problems" facing pugilism; wrestling in this regard held at the time a "unique cultural space," "somewhere between the sacred and the fun."[22]

That the image and spiritual symbolism of Jacob wrestling the angel held power for church goers is demonstrated by its staying power, even as it also has held literal inspiration for athletes in particular; hence, sermons and hymns making reference to the feisty angelic encounter have continued into the modern era, reinforcing wrestling's "connection with the divine," as in twentieth century American army camps where ministers working with the YMCA "urged soldiers and sailors to wrestle as Jacob wrestled."[23] The biblical wrestling episode was sufficiently acceptable for inclusion in the aforementioned stained glass sports bay of St. John the Divine cathedral in New York City, as was the depiction of another famous physical contest between the young warrior David and the towering Goliath, whom David conquered with courage, skill and the aid of weaponry.[24]

Alongside these biblical images, which seem to affirm an ethically affirmative place for fighting in church iconography, are those at the end of the Christian scriptures, the New Testament, where we find the image of a "blood drenched" warrior Christ amidst much apocalyptic reference to retributive violence, here recalling the image of the Lord as a warrior, which arises from as far back in the biblical narrative as the Song of Moses, and Exodus 15:3.[25] Indeed, if one searches the Bible for evidence of acts of retributive violent to, say, justify the use of self-defense techniques in response to violence or evil, one will surely find passages that may be so used, just as surely as one will find passages that may be used to advocate against such action. At stake in this equation is the very model of God in Christ, which rightly forms the basis of the understanding and practice of discipleship. As one modern biblical ethicist notes reflecting on these matters, "Whether Jesus accepted, advocated or used nonviolent or violent resistance against the violence of oppression and injustice determines how we Christians are to imagine the very character of our God," and hence our own response in such circumstances where we find the same.[26] While not focused on the application of such deliberation to the ethics of fight

3. Ethical Issues Regarding Fight Sports and the Church 89

sports (particularly for self-defense, or the defense of others), something from scholarly reflections on violence, like that of John Dominic Crossan (and others), may provide context within which to explore how such issues might apply in these circumstances. Indeed, acknowledging the confusion created by the source material he examines, Crossan admits that "even a superficial reading of the Christian Bible reveals God and Christ to be both violent and nonviolent in a somewhat bipolar if not schizophrenic fashion."[27] Is the reigning model that of Christ astride the warhorse, as in Revelation, or that of Jesus on the "peace donkey" as he enters Jerusalem?[28]

At stake in this discussion is whether the Bible supports both an understanding of God as endorsing force under some circumstances and promoting radical nonviolence in pursuit of justice at the same time. Crossan argues that whereas the historical Jesus, John the Baptist and Paul advocated nonviolent approaches to justice, redactors reinterpreted their message along the lines of civilization's values and introduced support for "violent retributive justice."[29] In the present context, this point may relate to discussions of self-defense, which, as we have seen, is among the stated goals of some fight sports ministries. Is engagement of another by use of physical means appropriate for defending oneself or others? Indeed, provocative though the inquiry may be, is it showing love for another who is facing physical harm to allow them to suffer it without intervening? Biblical messages about the use of violence and nonviolence, and whether these are modeled in biblical figures' messages, particularly that of Christ, are surely more than instructive here.

Likewise relevant is Crossan's reflection on "escalatory violence," humankind's penchant for increasing the response to each new level of violence in a conflict, which harkens back to Ellul's position, raised in the Preface. Crossan calls escalatory violence "almost a seductive inevitability," but maintains that it is nonetheless a choice, calling it "our avoidable decision, not our unavoidable destiny."[30] Although Crossan is here discussing communal violence and how civilization's values obscure those of God, the concept may be aptly applied to responses on an individual level. Clearly, a use of violence to "get even" (as is part of the implication of "retributive" and "escalatory violence" in Crossan's and Ellul's discussions) would be unacceptable. However, is the same ethic applicable to individuals faced with preservation of life or well-being? Is it ethical to engage with another to defend oneself or others from physical harm, in an act of self-defense, on the individual (rather than societal) level?

One Christian response to this scenario might be that to permit oneself to be subject to violent attack would expose the hatred and abuse of power by another, and thereby serve a critical function. Relevant here is Christ's admonition to "turn the other cheek" if one strikes you on your right one, and whether this saying advocates a posture of nonresistance or has more nuanced meaning. Some scholars have suggested that this phrase has less to do with whether or not one may engage in physical self-defense than (given culturally specific meanings of the time) with restricting legal responses to a smite,[31] or with challenging the aggressor with a no-win response to the situation, when one's right cheek was backhandedly slapped by another using their right hand, and any further action would involve an open right hand or the left backhand, the cultural meanings of which were equally undesirable, and which, in any case, would be done to humiliate the other, not injure them or start a fight. The reason for this is that the assailant would need to use for the second strike either the left hand, which was reserved only for unclean tasks, or the open palm or fist of the right hand, which would signal that the opponent one was intending to humiliate with the original slap was actually of equal stature.[32] Further, since this discussion is in the context of elaborating upon the "eye for an eye" reference in Matthew, the meaning here might have more to do with refraining from vengeful responses than with circumstances of self-defense.

Given this, might a response to a physical attack that mindfully limits the engagement only to that which is necessary to diffuse the situation, or retreat, be acceptable within a Christian context? In keeping with this question, many leaders in the martial arts community do precisely this: advocate limiting one's engagement with violence to that which is necessary, even to promoting the retreat from a situation as soon as one is able.[33] Notably, this response provides an answer to those concerned with unchecked escalatory and/or retributive violence. Hence, it may arguably be a selfless show of love for one's neighbor, and a pursuit of justice, to use one's self-defense skills to aid another involved in physical conflict with an assailant. Indeed, the writings of Walter Wink, a theologian whose work reflects on violence and nonviolence, are relevant here. He himself makes note of abuses he sees in how others apply biblical passages about turning the other cheek and loving one's enemies, and how these have been applied in ways at odds with a proper understanding of the gospel message.[34] Critical of both passivity and violent opposition, Wink advocates a third response, when possible: that of militant nonviolence, observing that neutrality supports oppression, and that the pursuit of justice should be a Christian's goal; this, he observes, "may require an acceleration of conflict as a necessary stage" to resolve unjust conflict.[35] Again, although Wink is discussing larger, systemic conflicts and responses, the underlying philosophy may be applicable to individual circumstances of encountering and responding to unjust domination. Most tellingly, although he encourages creative nonviolent responses that expose and confront injustice, Wink nonetheless does recognize a place for counter-violence in response to unjust aggression.[36]

3. Ethical Issues Regarding Fight Sports and the Church

Applied to the present discussion, one may glean from such reasoning guidelines concerning the use of self-defense when confronted with aggression. Ideally, one's own use of aggression would avoid escalation, and seek to end the conflict as soon as possible with minimal harm to all involved, including the aggressor. Indeed, a willingness to sacrifice one's own well-being for another displays a love for them, just as one's willingness to disengage from the confrontation at the earliest point possible arguably shows love, or at least mercy, for an assailant. Being willing to diffuse a situation and then retreat from it focuses more on the commitment to avoid escalation and end conflict than to maintain one's pride with an assertion of dominance. To apply a quote from Crossan to this reflection, "Justice without love may end in brutality, but love without justice must end in banality." To love another and even one's opponent (the "enemy") enough to confront, and then seek to end unjust conflict responds to both parts of this equation, for timely disengagement shows love or mercy for an "enemy" (the goal not being brutality or domination, but justice), and to put oneself in harm's way to protect another rises above a banal limitation of love that stops short of having it sufficient enough to pursue justice on behalf of one who is being exploited and is in danger. As Crossan concludes, "Love empowers justice, and justice embodies love."[37]

This argument has clear implications when one is helping achieve justice (and well-being) for another, and in circumstances of a defense against unjust attack; more concerns are involved when considering defense of oneself, or the application of fighting techniques in the voluntary activity of fight sports for recreation or competition. In order to fully consider these circumstances and the ethical principles involved, we must introduce more concepts for theological reflection, beginning with the understanding of human beings as imago dei, and that of our bodies as temples.

Imago Dei and the Body as a Temple

A set of concepts raised by ethicists regarding Christian engagement in sports, particularly sports that are more likely to subject participants to injury and involve aggression aimed at another, are those of humankind as imago dei, and human bodies as temples wherein dwells God's spirit. Both bespeak a place of honor that should be afforded the human body. The first concept, imago dei, posits that humankind is created in God's image and hence due respect in all its created goodness and grandeur; this respect extends to all aspects of human existence, from our capacity to reason and exercise free will, to the created gift of the body in which such capacities are incarnate and through which we experience God and act in God's world, and applies both to others and ourselves. The second concept, that of the body as a temple, recognizes the body as the dwelling place of God's spirit, and thereby an entity that should be afforded respect, much as one would respect a temple, a place of worship.[38] Hence, the body is conceived as "a container for the soul," "a means of salvation," a "living expression of faith, a gift and gesture of love and divine creation," and "a sacred vessel."[39]

Indeed, given this, one may argue that defending one's body in self-defense, if one is under attack, is in fact protecting one's means of acting in the world with the means God gave people for this purpose, as a gift. The application of the concepts of imago dei and "body as a temple" to sports, however, is more multifaceted. Thus to some, any willful exposure of that sacred body to harm, when such is unnecessary to fulfill one's calling, is self-indulgent and contemptuous, failing to show due respect for God's gift of the body. It is a "sacking" of the temple.[40] In terms of a Christian ethic of sports, this is sometimes cited as a reason to avoid sports likely to lead to bodily injury, a diminishment of our capacities, or even death. Hence, boxing may be denounced on this basis alongside other sports, such as American football, hockey or rugby, for subjecting the body and mind to potential harm. Even so, boxing and mixed martial arts are often singled out for ethical critique above and beyond the scrutiny given other sports, and a question arises as to whether this level of scrutiny is justified.

One response to this approach is to examine statistics regarding various sports, to compare their rates of injury and death. In doing so, we learn (as previously noted) that other sports, such as fishing, equestrian sports, swimming, and motor sports, annually lead to more deaths than boxing, and that traumatic injuries (including those to the head) are more common in cycling, skiing, hockey, equestrian activities, and several other sports. One study that looks at the incidents of head injuries treated in hospitals ranked the top ten sports most often leading to potentially neurological problems, and while cycling, football and baseball led the list, boxing did not even merit mention.[41] The question arises: should these activities likewise be discouraged on ethical bases? Of course, one must weigh other factors as well, such as how many participants engage in various sports, which might affect interpretations of such statistical data. Then there is the matter of intentionality—that, as some argue, the point of boxing and mixed martial arts (particularly in their professional forms) is to inflict injury, whereas in other sports injury may be accidental or, as in football's tackle or hockey's check, the result of unsporting conduct (the use of excessive force), even though such behavior is common, expected and rewarded.

Michael Shafer, in his excellent consideration of Christian sports ethics (*Well Played*, 2015), acknowledges and then critiques some of these concerns. While he concedes that an activity's propensity for injury should be considered when reflecting upon the ethics of that activity, he nonetheless notes that life is full of daily risks we take, including driving a car, about which we show little moral concern when they are undertaken responsibly.[42] Even so, one does not typically drive one's car into another's in a competition to see who is the superior aggressive driver, or who can continue despite damage. Boxing and mixed martial arts involve a willful act wherein, at the professional level (and to a certain extent in amateur and recreational levels as well) one is in fact taking aim at another's "temple" and, according to some ethicists, thereby failing to respect other's and one's own existence as imago dei—that we should "value human bodily integrity," and "respect the bodies God has given to others," as well as ourselves.[43] Indeed, that which makes our ability to act in the world as imago dei—our brains—is at risk in such activities, at least in terms of the practice of professional and full-force competitive fighting, although usually through a lifetime of trauma leading to pugilistic dementia, and not via an individual event.

One interesting response to these concerns comes from former *Christianity Today* editor Mark Galli, who defends boxing for being an "art of controlled violence," a sport that operates within "tight constraints," with safety measures (such as gloves, timed rounds, recovery rules, and a referee's presence and intervention). Even so, to keep a match from becoming a free for all, those restraints must be honored, and boxers, Galli suggests, are to be admired for being "masters" of controlling the violent impulse (a suggestion related to the idea of fight sports as ritualized violence, as previously discussed). Galli cites as evidence a book by a priest-turned-boxer, who learned through boxing to confront personal fears and obstacles, and thus taught other men facing personal demons (from drug addiction to gang membership) to face and "fight" those challenges, not unlike (as we will see) the mission of many fight sports ministry programs offered for at-risk youth. Galli sees in these efforts the redemptive qualities of controlled violence. Indeed, reminiscent of the earlier discussion of biblical themes and Crossan's reflections, Galli notes that throughout biblical history—including "the Flood, the Exodus, the Exile, the Cross, or the final defeat of the Beast"—redemption often comes with violence.[44]

While this may be true, in his effort to thereby justify the violence of fight sports and relate it to God-like qualities, Galli might do well to consider that the violence in some of these biblical examples was imposed by God against sinners or oppressors in an act of retributive violence, or as part of a divine plan to achieve salvation through an act of loving sacrifice; the kind of redemptive violence Galli proposes in the ring is qualitatively different from these examples, in that one's opponent is no more or less a sinner than oneself, and the salvation of which Galli speaks is at least in part self-directed, not a loving act of sacrifice to save others. Notably, in Galli's example of the priest who uses boxing to help others overcome personal challenges, there is an element of loving outreach; even so, some might argue that the crux of the redemption found is not so much in an act of violence itself (although the physical challenge and/or danger may be part of the draw for some), so much as it is in the discipline applied to achieve a goal, the focused pursuit of excellence, and the satisfaction of accomplishment. Indeed, the threat of destructive violence may, as we have seen, raise significant ethical concerns for Christians in fight sports. In this light, Galli's emphasis on how boxers learn to control violence is instructive. For those iterations of fight sports ministries that do prepare participants for competition, this ability to control oneself may be a central concern. Without it, the dangers about which ethicists reviewed herein have warned would surely be applicable.

All of this is not to say that boxing, martial arts and other sports do not have their place in the lives of Christians, with other ethical supports. This is particularly so considering the various goals of sports ministry programs. If the body is a temple, caring for that temple by means of fitness training may be a good thing. If doing so makes one better able to pursue one's calling, and protect others or oneself from harm, all the better. With such positive ethical points in mind, one might use guidelines of Christian ethics to establish boundaries for such activities or anticipate potential areas of ethical concern. For example, while, historically, the "body as a temple" theologians sought to find Scriptural basis for promoting health and caring for the body as a gift from God, this can imply that those who are physically weak or not inclined towards this focus on the body are somehow not as righteous as others.[45] What is more, an excessive focus on the body can lead to a form of idolatry; that "for all its benefits," taken too far even health promoting programs "can be a singularly indulgent and selfish experience."[46] In such cases, trying to justify one's excesses with appeals to maintaining God's temple may be nothing but "false piety."[47]

That said, clearly there are precautions against taking devotion to the body too far. Ministry participants may well avoid being so focused on oneself that this becomes an indulgence and not an authentic gesture of honoring God's gift of the body and maintaining it to be better able to fulfill one's calling and do God's will in the world. Even so, some ethicists state this is not the best posture to take to defend Christian engagement in sport, let alone fight sports; that there are stronger theological supports, not as given to the potential problems of "false piety" and misplaced focus. This argument regards a theology of the created goodness of pure play, and indeed involves the conception of imago dei. Before moving on to discuss the theology of play, however, we must first consider other benefits cited by some

3. *Ethical Issues Regarding Fight Sports and the Church* 95

proponents of fight sports (and other sporting activities) for Christians, along with what others see as attendant cautions. Still, it is worth noting before leaving this discussion that, despite all the potential pitfalls, one ethicist declares that sports and other fitness activities can certainly teach a "respect for the human body," and an appreciation of it as God's gift, for all the feats it can achieve.[48]

Character Outcomes

From the beginnings of the muscular Christianity movement through today, many proponents of sports ministries, fight sports ministries included, have touted how their programs procure positive character traits in participants. Even so, while historians often cite "character development" as a goal of the muscular Christianity movement, few outline precisely what particular virtues these include. This may in part be due to a vague use of the term by many of the movement's original proponents. For example, the stated YMCA goals for its programming frequently mention the "social" benefits of their programs, alongside the physical, spiritual and intellectual—rather broad categories, these.[49] Others in the muscular Christian movement, however, do endeavor to outline specifically what they mean by "character." Charles Kingsley, one of the founders of the movement, himself wrote that "games conduce, not merely to physical, but also moral health"; that beyond daring and endurance, sports also teach "temper, self-restraint, fairness, honour, [and] unenvious approbation of another's success"—virtues, he claims, that could not be taught by reading books.[50]

Indeed, while character development is regularly cited in modern justifications for sports ministry programs as one of their raisons d'être, only some take time to elucidate precisely what traits this includes. One attempt at such elucidation by a Christian sports scholar uses biblical quotes to try to outline character benefits attained from sports ministries, to establish moral benefits for participants. One problem with this and similar cases is the authentic applicability of these quotes. Hence, some take references to suffering and persevering for the faith and apply these to the sacrifices necessary to attain athletic achievement. To wit, they cite James 1:2–4 (about facing trials and tests of faith by showing perseverance), 1 Peter 1:6–7 (about enduring suffering to attain praise, glory and honor), and Romans 5:3–5 (about glorying in suffering because it produces perseverance, character and hope) and apply these to athletic pursuits as activities likewise requiring suffering and perseverance, in a manner that takes these out of their spiritual context and that of more genuinely applied understandings of suffering for one's faith. The argument is that one learns by allegory: that one may "suffer" through athletic pursuits and thereby learn the benefits of showing resolve sufficient to achieve glory, and thereby learn to apply these traits to spiritual tests and challenges to one's faith.[51] Some might see the use of biblical material about the *spiritual* to justify the *athletic* as a misappropriation of such verses. Similarly, using other biblical references to portray Christians as "soldiers" engaged in "spiritual warfare" who must go through "boot camp" (note here the standard muscular Christian reference to the warrior archetype), one sports ministry advocate writes, "The fields of sports competition are the training ground in secular things so that the competitor might learn to succeed in spiritual battle."[52] While there may be some merit to this claim, the simple equation begs further engagement.

Shirl James Hoffman, in his now standard reflection on the history and ethics of Christian engagement with sports (*Good Game: Christianity and the Culture of Sports*, 2010), acknowledges this enduring claim, that sports may teach transferable skills that help shape Christian character and morality. Indeed, he identifies a "military model" of sports ministry character claims that directly befit application to the above assertions (of endurance and sacrifice), noting with some suspicion why such advocates ignore other biblical virtues that are perhaps less easily cited in seeking to justify the transferability of athletic skills to a Christian lifestyle, such as humility, compassion and mercy. The implication is that to herald the "heroic" qualities concerning the attainment of glory and understate other more "passive" characteristics of an authentic, well-formed Christian experience, reveals a gratuitousness underlying some enthusiasts' claims,[53] and supports a problematic view of Christian discipleship (as we will later discuss). Finally, while Hoffman recognizes that sports may indeed provide all sorts of benefits (lasting friendships, preparation to face challenges, and skills needed to succeed in a competitive world),[54] he also notes that lessons that may be learned from sports are not necessarily all good, or even Christian ones. Indeed, Hoffman notes there are plenty of examples of unsporting behavior, which may also be learned from engagement in athletic activity, and result in the development of unfavorable character traits, such as self-interest, arrogance, insensitivity and duplicity.[55] To support this point, Hoffman cites research that finds that, in addition to positive traits, sports also lead to higher levels of "aggression [and] irritability, and a lower valuation of honesty."[56] One solution to the character question, Hoffman suggests, is that Christians could just as easily learn positive traits through other pursuits—ones that are "less ethically complicated" than sports.[57]

One response to this perhaps somewhat excessive dismissal of sports as a character training ground is that sometimes it is necessary to meet people where their interests lie—that if sports, including fight sports, are a source of "common interest that people share," as Christian ethicist Michael Schafer states, then this "opens avenues" and may therefore be one platform by which to address issues of faith to followers, and to open others to evangelism.[58] This is certainly the case with inner city boxing ministries, outlined in the forthcoming case studies. Shafer likewise addresses the issue of character development, stressed so frequently in the history of the muscular Christianity movement and often by contemporary boxing and martial arts ministries (as we will see). Shafer in fact directly addresses Hoffman's points about the potential negative effects of involvement with sports on an athlete's moral character. He himself offers a list of positive traits that may be garnered through participation in athletics, including "teamwork, determination, fairness, commitment, and respect for rules."[59] Then, like Hoffman, he acknowledges these may also turn into negative qualities if misdirected, such as when an athlete's "determination" is directed towards the accumulation of accolades and wealth, or when its excess leads to an "unhealthy obsession." Hence, as Schafer elegantly cautions, one must consider the context and measure of these traits, and recognize that "simply because the potential exists for moral formation does not mean the development of an athlete's character is a foregone conclusion."[60] In the end, Schafer is more open than Hoffman to the potential positive contributions of sports to Christian formation, noting that if negative traits are revealed, this may actually provide an opportunity to correct them, while at the same time reinforcing an athlete's positive inclinations.[61]

As to how this relates specifically to fight sports ministries, the idea of catering to people's common interests and providing opportunities for Christian formation using such activities is instructive. If one is designing a boxing ministry for inner city youth who are drawn to boxing more than other pursuits, this may provide one avenue within which to build confidence, provide a positive outlet, and address matters of moral concern and appropriate Christian discipleship to participants. The same may be said for rural and suburban regions, where many are interested in martial arts. For all the concern with sports' potential to develop problematic as well as positive character traits, dismissing them simply because the same character formations could take place via other venues neglects that these alternatives may also have their own possible pitfalls, and that sport ministries may be thoughtfully engaged in a fashion that encourages more of the positive effects than the negative. There is no need to throw the fight sports ministry baby out with the challenging Christian formations bathwater. Yes, character and moral development may be pursued via other avenues, as Hoffman states, but simply because one area presents particular challenges does not necessarily mean this avenue of outreach is without merit; in fact, it is precisely via a program that might successfully respond to identified challenges that participants might become unusually well equipped to respond to the ethical and character issues raised.

Potential negative effects notwithstanding, sports ministries may, as ethicists acknowledge, help teach important character traits, particularly if these are undertaken under the guidance of well-studied leaders who are cognizant of the potential pitfalls and benefits of their program and the messages, explicit and implicit, these send, and who respond appropriately in their design and execution of such programs. Hence, in a Christian context, emphasis placed on appreciating God's gift of the body, while not turning it into an idol; teaching self-defense skills to build confidence enough to walk away from unnecessary encounters; teaching love of oneself, others, and even one's "enemies," with enough humility and well-honed control to leave a confrontation, even by retreating, at the first possible moment; and being able to engage in appreciative recreational play with others, or even a competitive challenge, in such a way that values the striving for excellence of all, whether or not "victory" is achieved; these come closest to engagements of fight sports ministries in such ways as to reflect Christian values and foster development of Christian character traits. More will be said on these latter matters in the coming sections of this chapter. Suffice it to say in the context of discussing character development as an ethical issue in terms of fight sports ministries that this has important challenges to recognize and consider in developing such programs, but that arguably, with forethought and proper program implementation, these may be addressed in sufficient, perhaps even surprising and uncommon ways, in order to mitigate problems and actually respond to these concerns in ways that produce positive outcomes.

Competition and Christianity

Competition provides another point of ethical consideration for Christian fight sports ministries. For those programs that do include competitive interaction or preparation for competition, an awareness of how pertinent ethical matters relate to issues of faith is important. Prominent American football player and coach Vince Lombardi's famous aphorism that "winning isn't everything, it's the only thing," while probably resonating with much of American culture, is a good place to start a reflection on Christian ethics and competition, as it is the antithesis, by most ethicists' accounts, of what Christian involvement in sports should entail. Designers and leaders of fight sports ministry programs would do well to reflect upon how their approach responds to these concerns (and others), and how best to construct a method and message that remains true to Christian principles.

3. Ethical Issues Regarding Fight Sports and the Church   99

One critique of the "win at all costs" mentality is that it sets oneself up as the locus of concern, with less (or even no) consideration of others. If the goal of competition is to do all one can to ensure one's own victory and the defeat of an opponent, then the focus on the "other" and what is good for community, so central to Christian teachings, is compromised. Among the problems with this mentality is the resulting perception that others are "obstacles" to one's own achievement, which can "objectify" an opponent as an enemy.[62] This approach divides interests and ultimately alienates competitors from one another.[63] This "self-centeredness," this "[pursuit of] one's own interests without sympathy for anyone else" is, for a Christian, one of the most "troublesome aspect[s]" of competitive sport, according to Hoffman. Hoffman goes on to note that

> Christians deliberately suspending concern for one another (even in this limited sense [of sports play]) and engaging in deception, cunning, and physical dominance in an effort to further their own interests is a very troubling one indeed. True, players only suspend mutual sympathy in an illusory sense as part of play, but even in pretending to be motivated by self-interest, they are pretending not to be the Christians they claim to be.[64]

Noting that the boundaries of sport play and the real world are "extraordinarily fragile," Hoffman finds a significant "dissonance" between the Christian faith and the unrestrained focus on competition.[65] Casting aside any claim that competition is part of human nature, Hoffman writes that competition may best be seen as a "distortion of the created essence of 'human relationship' or 'community,'" which, he says, *do* have claims of an inherent place in human nature. His quest is for a way to redeem sport play from its use of competition as anything other than a "simple organizing principle," so that in sport one may focus on more Christian ideals and relationships.[66]

Others disagree with the place of competition in the created order, albeit notably without disagreeing that its implementation in Christian sports play is in need of careful reconsideration. Seeing competition as "part of God's design for the world," with the example of trees competing for sunlight, root space, moisture and nutrients, Greg Linville argues that competition is "amoral," a force which "may bring out either the best or the worst in all who compete."[67] Nonetheless, he too concedes the need for a reassessment of a Christian approach to competitive sport—one that sees competition as part of "God's design," while at the same time reexamines how we approach it under the guidance of Christian principles.

Shaffer himself reviews the positions of both Hoffman and Linville, noting an apparent contradiction in Linville's argument, which at one point perceives competition as amoral or neutral and then suggests it is a created good, before considering the differing theological understandings of the role of competition between these ethicists. Shaffer writes, "Linville sees competition as a created good that can be corrupted, whereas Hoffman sees competition as a corruption or distortion of the created good of human relationships."[68] Despite varied understandings of the inherent good (or not) and particular challenges in their conceptions of the role of competition in human society and the created order, all three see a need for reformation of Christian approaches to sport play and competition in a manner that reflects Christian values and priorities. The heart of the matter for these and other ethicists reflecting upon the place of sports and competition in the life of Christians concerns a shift from an exclusive focus on self to one that focuses on relationships, others and community.

Thus, Linville proposes that the solution is to shift the understanding of those against whom one competes from "opponents" to "co-competitors." This, he argues, emphasizes that one should afford others "dignity and respect," and that all involved in sport should be "encouraged to excel" and "compete to their fullest." That this means encouraging one's opponents and may seem "ludicrous" (to some) is understandable, he writes, unless and until "church leaders, athletes and coaches examine their premise for competing."[69] If this is in keeping with what he calls "Christmanship" (a term he uses in contrast with "sportsmanship" and "gamesmanship"), then it will be to encourage participants to strive for victory, while also not prioritizing the need to be "number one" as the ultimate goal.[70] Indeed, Shafer agrees, saying that not competing as best as one can "insults a co-competitor" by not giving one's best. On the other hand, showing so much "zeal" for competition that one seeks to "humiliate" an opponent is also problematic; thus, both a "patronizing" and "arrogant" approach to competition fail to respect oneself, one's co-competitors, and the point of competition, from a Christian perspective.[71]

Others take Linville's basic premise, about the need as a Christian to reassess the "premise for competing," and develop it further. Hence, Hoffman argues that claims of competition's ability to help one achieve excellence misunderstand the essence of competition, which is not an internal struggle so much as a struggle against others; in this way, Hoffman perceives what is likely the most difficult journey for the Christian sports player. He nonetheless concedes that competitive sport can "enlighten" human beings about their own strengths and weaknesses (and this, we should take care to recognize in considering the range of fight sports ministry program objectives, may be attained even through non-competitive training), as well as their control of self and development of interpersonal abilities. Hence, Hoffman ultimately does see sport as a learning opportunity, a test of "Christian character"—albeit one which, given the hazards he perceives in engagement in sport, may be "costly."[72] Acknowledging that by its nature sport involves opposition and a striving to win, thus inherently invoking the very challenges he raises for finding a proper place for sport in a Christian life, Hoffman ultimately finds a potential solution in the emphasis in sport on the element of play.

He is not alone in finding redemption to the challenges faced by sport competition in conceiving of it principally as play. Writing not from an explicitly Christian perspective but nonetheless addressing many themes Christian ethicists raise, Drew Hyland proposes that the contrasting claims that human beings are "by nature" competitive and, alternately, "by nature" friendly and loving need not be mutually exclusive.[73] His argument is that there is a conception of the human situation that can accommodate both perspectives, and that "human play is just the theatre where that complex nature gets most visibly manifested," in a manner that makes these natures not merely "compatible" but "closely connected."[74] Examining the origins of the word "competition," he observes that it means "to question together, to strive together." Thus, the mutual pursuit of excellence is his conception of competition that allows co-competitors to remain truly "friendly." He notes the same is true for the word "con-test," which means a testing together. Such conceptions do not foster a sense of alienation between participants (an "opposition"), so much as a mutual striving towards excellence.[75] How do we judge whether or not that ideal of friendly competitive play has been achieved? By whether friendship, as opposed to alienation, has been achieved, for "all competitive play which fails to attain its highest possibility, that of friendship, must be understood as a 'deficient mode' of play."[76]

Shafer takes up many of the same themes, such as alienation and friendship, as well as love (which he notes is a central Christian virtue) and, like others, seeks to "re-evaluate [the] understanding of the purpose and goals of sport in a Christian context."[77] He agrees with Hyland on the importance of friendship, but differs with him on the importance of it in understanding competitive play in terms of the "social dimension" which, for Shafer, is an "outcome" of sport, not its "purpose."[78] Indeed, seen in this way, many other claims discussed throughout this examination of fight sports might well be so relegated, to "outcomes": the character development, so important to the muscular Christianity movement; the honing of ethical discernment; the evangelistic outreach made possible through sport; the honoring of the body as temple, to maintain it through physical activity, and respect it as imago dei; and, yes, even the pursuit of "friendly" fellowship; all these are outcomes, he argues, not purpose. The crux of the ethical discussion, he says, while not omitting these other matters, should rest on the *purpose* of sport play. Here, we reach a turning point, as what makes humans beings in God's image may well have as much to do with our understanding of *play* as anything else. Before systematically reflecting on the implications of all this specifically for fight sport ministries, this matter, then—of theologies of play—receives our final consideration.

Theologies of Play

Most Christian ethicists writing about Christian approaches to sports advocate the importance of experiencing these activities as play. They say that if one is in the mindset of play, this is the essential element that is the saving grace of participation in sport. Sport experienced as authentic play, they argue, more than settles many ethical concerns with Christian engagement in sport; it also provides an experience wherein participants may achieve, however ephemerally, a sense of the eternal freedom that awaits the faithful; the joy of creation; and, indeed, a sense of what it is to be divine. Before addressing these points and articulating how they relate to fight sports ministries, we must first briefly consider what philosophers and ethicists say about the nature of play itself.

Johan Huizinga (in *Homo Ludens*, 1950) provides the classic philosophical discussion of the nature of play. His definition of play, in fact, works its way into many Christian ethicists' reflections on their proposed solution of how best to balance all the ethical concerns facing Christian participation in sport. In sum, Huizinga defines play as

> a free activity standing quite consciously outside "ordinary" life as being "not serious," but at the same time absorbing the player intensely and utterly. It is an activity connected with no material interest, and no profit can be gained by it. It proceeds within its own proper boundaries of time and space according to fixed rules and in an orderly manner. It promotes the formation of social groupings which tend to surround themselves with secrecy and to stress their differences from the common world by disguise or other means.[79]

Although this definition is compact, it has proven fruitful for discussions of how the experience of play may correct potentially problematic aspects of Christian engagement in sport. While an exhaustive explication of Huizinga's definition is not possible here, there are important aspects of his definition worth highlighting. That play is free and results in no profit means it is a chosen activity done for no purpose other than its own enjoyment. (Coerced activity and professional sporting activities, therefore, are not truly "play.") It is an experience apart from the ordinary (not unlike sacred activity) that fully engrosses participants, as they enjoy an experience of being "apart together."[80] While play has its own rules, these are to create an order apart from the world's "usual norms," so that the resulting unique, fully enthralling experience, known only to its participants, provides a "magic" which they retain even afterwards.[81]

3. Ethical Issues Regarding Fight Sports and the Church

While Huizinga's is not the only philosophical consideration of play, his is foundational, and hence provides ethicists with fertile grounds on which to base their argument that understanding sport as play is key to overcoming most ethical challenges for Christians involved in sports.[82] Perhaps even on initial review, why this is so is apparent from Huizinga's themes: the ecstasy of the experience; its being set apart from ordinary time and experiences; its focus of creation; its sense of a community apart; the sense of play as its own reward; and the focus on delight and transcendence. All of these evoke the experience of the sacred (to say nothing of worship) and come into play in understanding the experience of sport-as-play as important correctives to many otherwise troublesome aspects of sport play—particularly those of competitive sport.

Hence, whereas Christian ethicists voice concern for sports' emphasis on personal victory and rewards, experiencing sport as play (for its own sake) provides an antidote for such self-centered thinking. This reorientation allows participants to focus more on performance than achievement, and less on personal victory than what is good for a community and its members. By thus shifting the focus from agon (competition) to arête (a striving for excellence), a participant is able to "diminish the importance of winning" and recognize instead individual efforts and the striving to achieve one's best.[83] Said otherwise, where we seek to emphasize grace in sports, we shift the focus from "the all-consuming desire for personal victory" by glorifying oneself, to a focus (in its emphasis on community, excellence and delight) that more truly glorifies God.[84] Part of the challenge is the stakes we are taught to place upon sports by well-publicized sporting events (such as professional and collegiate sports) where so much is at stake in terms of finances and public stature. Thus, Hoffman suggests a first step in understanding sport in an authentically Christian way, "will come when Christians appreciate the death-grip that big-time sports have on sports played at any level and when they recognize how this can snuff out the spiritual potential of sports."[85]

Play, then, is best understood as its own reward. It is thus "autotelic," something to be appreciated for its own sake and not what it may confer. This not only answers concerns about the "win at all costs" mentality (as something to confer status and dominance over others), but also provides a corrective attitude towards Christian use of sport, which is sought by ethically concerned proponents. Thus, instead of emphasizing the role participation in sports may play for other ends (that is, its "outcomes"), Christians should emphasize the appreciation of sport play as a means of enjoying God's creation, apart from other benefits, such as on the body (fitness), social life (character traits), or anything else.[86] As Hoffman writes, in a customarily sharp tone, "reimagining sport as an autotelic, leisure-based experience means shunning flaccid rhetoric about the sports field as a training ground for character, as a way of building strong bones and muscles, or as a fertile field for evangelism, or realizing any other practical benefits. [...] In the end, it is the experience that counts, and this alone is sufficient reason for Christian involvement."[87]

The shift, therefore, is from understanding sport as *instrumental* (that is, as an instrument for producing ends outside itself) to one with *intrinsic* worth, for our ability, in play, to create (in the image of God), to help others appreciate the good in themselves (in the spirit of friendship), and to "simply delight in God's creation," one part of which is the gift of play itself.[88] This is not to say that those instrumental, outside benefits (character building, fitness, evangelism, etc.) are not worth considering when devising church-based sports programs, so much as to say that the primary focus of engaging in sports play in the Christian context should be what autotelic play has to offer participants.

In pure play, we experience joy. That joy provides an experience of transcendence and, in stepping outside of this ordinary world, *homo ludens* experiences some of the freedom and joy of the eternal.[89] We are released from the bounds of the physical body to be connected to something beyond the physical, something more spiritual.[90] Authentic play allows participants in childlike manner to "anticipate the eschaton," "when sin will not corrupt the goodness of which we are to delight," when "Christ reigns over all."[91] As a part of God's world, and "part and parcel of the created order," experiencing play in the spirit of thanksgiving and gratitude for this God-given grace, a manifestation of God's goodness, permits participants to reorient their relation to sports play, from one focused on victory and gains, to one of worship for the blessing of this gift.[92] In play we experience something analogous to being divine and the act of creation. Poetically stated by one theorist:

> Play could be considered an invitation, passing back and forth between the energy of God and the energy here in this world's creation; then, when the urge to play comes upon us, we, like children, respond to it in glee—and then it is gone for a time. The response, the communion, is returned and exchanged with and to the Creator until the next time. [...] Play is an archetype of goodness and joy, a cluster of energy mirroring the last memories of the perfect human state and union with God—the Garden of Eden.[93]

In our ability to imagine and enter another experience outside our own world, in freedom, for the purpose of taking pleasure in that act of creation, we experience something akin to divine creation, the definitive activity of God, in whose image we are created.[94] Accordingly, in the end, "play is, therefore, an indication of transcendence; but it is more. For the believer, it is the human person's fleeting imitation of God"; "[thus] *homo ludens* is most profoundly imago dei."[95]

Ethics of Fight Sports Ministries

Fight sports ministries face ethical challenges. The preceding assembly of concerns and guidelines sets parameters to which leaders and participants of boxing and martial arts ministries should be mindful and responsive. Responding responsibly to these guidelines will help ensure such programs operate in a way that not only may be acceptable to all concerned but may even help participants confront real challenges facing the faithful, as they consider how best to respond to the ethical issues involved. Taking up one by one the various goals of fight sports ministry programs already discussed—for fitness, self-defense, recreation and competition—will allow us to consider how these guidelines pertain to all types of fight sports ministries we will discuss.

As for those focused mainly or partly on fitness, one positive ethical consideration these programs manifest is to respect the body as a temple—a gift from God, to be honored and cared for. Making the most of this gift by being a good minister of it, just as all of God's gifts, is one way to honor it. Recognizing the benefits a well-working body affords us, and helping make the most of it by maximizing the body's potential is one way people have, in freedom, to thankfully respond to the gift of the body, by looking after it. Participants in such ministries are, in that sense, good stewards of the gift of their bodies and, in offering help and encouragement, facilitators of others' stewardship of their bodies. If this makes participants better prepared to pursue their calling, all the better. Better still is the fellowship involved in the joint pursuit of fitness, involving mutual support and enjoyment.

A concern would be that participants not go too far and turn appreciation into excessive pride, to "overvalue the human body" and make the pursuit of physical perfection a form of idolatry.[96] Nor should participants see as any less worthy others' pursuit of different ways of developing and caring for God's additional gifts (such as the intellect), who may not place as much emphasis on care of the body. To overplay the connection of the physical with the spiritual as somehow superior to other avenues towards spirituality and moral awareness (as was a tendency with some in the muscular Christianity movement) suggests the more athletic have greater powers of discernment, and this too is idolatrous.[97] If one is authentically concerned with maintaining the gift of the "temple" by pursuing good health for oneself and supporting that pursuit by others, while also experiencing joyful play amidst fellowship, the use of fitness oriented fight sports ministries need not be a "singularly indulgent and selfish experience," as Hoffmann cautions.[98] A Christian boxing or martial arts program may well have means to respond to these considerations. One way, in the Christian context, may be to offer an opening or closing prayer, thanking God for the body, while also being thankful for other gifts; thanking God for fellowship and the opportunity to support others; and reminding participants of the need to appreciate God as the source of all blessings. In the end, fitness-oriented boxing and martial arts ministry programs (as with those that offer fitness as one component of a program along with other goals) may reasonably respond to outlined ethical concerns and provide a program that offers enjoyment, play, fellowship, gratitude and care for one aspect of God's creation—their own and others' bodies.

Those ministries focused on self-defense must respond to other concerns. These include ethical issues concerning violence, love of others, and the body as an entity due respect, as regards the concepts of imago dei and the "body as a temple," that the body is a place of spiritual dwelling. Acknowledging at the outset that there is a range of ethical positions as to whether any use of violence is justified for Christians, a fight sport ministry program would do well to responsibly and explicitly consider how its approach acknowledges and responds to these concerns. The sense of self confidence and control that comes from training in a martial arts or boxing program might, as it reportedly has in many circumstances, help participants feel less of a need to prove themselves in everyday situations. This confidence may lead them not to even engage in altercations, or to limit these to only that which is necessary in any physical confrontation that arises. This, in fact, is the message of many fight sports programs—to avoid conflict and end any altercation as quickly and mercifully as possible—and clearly more in keeping with established ethical boundaries than programs that might advocate a different, more aggressive approach. To teach participants to avoid conflict, based upon biblical and ethical principles; to teach precepts for engaging in conflict, if necessary, only as necessary to protect others and oneself, and to disengage, even retreat, once a situation has been adequately handled; indeed, to teach love, mercy and concern for an attacker (what some might call, with previously acknowledged concern, an "enemy") in addition to those being attacked; and to base these decisions on Christian principles, taught during training; these would be the most ideal circumstances within which to develop and offer a Christian sports ministry program with a focus on self-defense.

In fact, as we will see, many fight sports ministry programs that do exist and have an emphasis on self-defense take this very approach. In this way, they are in keeping with counterparts in secular schools, which happen to teach the same approach, albeit not explicitly related to a set of Christian guidelines with concerns for evincing a life of Christian discipleship. Such an exemplary instructive approach may be found, in fact, in the Gracie Jiu-Jitsu Academy, a secular institution and leading martial arts school. While what one learns in training at their facilities may one day be useful in defending oneself or others, the Gracie philosophy also states, "we don't just teach people how to fight, we give people the confidence so they never need to."[99] Knowing one has skills to defend oneself may lead some to choose not to fight, if provoked. Further, many self-defense schools advocate leaving a confrontation at the earliest possible opportunity once a conflict has been adequately handled and a situation sufficiently diffused, so as not to unnecessarily prolong confrontation. If staying might lead to more conflict, retreating—even precipitously, by running, no matter how "cowardly" doing so might be perceived by others—is, they say, an honorable way to avoid escalation. Given the Christian precepts discussed, this approach is one that arguably may respond to the theological and ethical concerns outlined herein: that is, to teach the use of defense techniques sufficient only enough to save oneself and/or another, and to encourage disengagement from conflict with an "opponent" as soon as possible. In Christian terms, this is arguably one way to show love for all involved, maintain the dignity of all as much as is possible, and honor God's gift of the body by protecting it from undue harm.

Turning next to programs that emphasize recreational engagement in fight sports, these too have their own ethical considerations. So long as such programs maintain a focus on friendships, a mutual striving together towards excellence, and an authentic sense of "play," as discussed, these may be an acceptable experience, even a blessing, for participants. Responding to other concerns, recreational boxing is often practiced without full force behind a boxer's punches and, as long as those sparring are fairly matched in terms of skill and weight, and they are well-practiced at defensive techniques (such as slipping or blocking punches), these safeguards may help mitigate concerns about subjecting the body to undue damage. In martial arts, such as BJJ, as long as participants are likewise fairly matched or taught how to work well with those of other belt levels (higher and lower) and are closely watched by instructors, concerns with sustaining undue damage may be minimized. They may be additionally mitigated by the fail-safe mechanism of "tapping out"—the act of tapping an opponent (a "co-competitor") anywhere on their body, or just saying "tap," to concede to a no-win situation and be released from a hold. Significantly, often those training together in such forms share camaraderie, and engage in sparring in the very spirit of "striving together" advocated above as a hallmark of friendly competitive play, where a focus is on helping others improve.

Indeed, helping others to learn and achieve, even if this means placing oneself in a compromised or submissive position, involves a further Christian grace. Here again, church-based fight sports ministry programs may learn from the successful, commercial approach of the Gracie Jiu-Jitsu Academy, which operates under the philosophy "keep it playful." By this, they mean that winning or losing, or proving who is better, should not be the sole focus of training, so much as should enjoyment and being willing to place oneself in submissive positions to learn how to handle them, and help a partner who is not as advanced to grow.[100] The goal of helping others to improve and experience achievement, and to be encouraged by others for one's own achievements, is an approach to Christian fight sports ministry programs that appropriately responds to the ethical concerns outlined, while emphasizing the positive attributes of celebration, fellowship, grace and gratitude,[101] instead of a singular focus on dominance and achieving personal glory.

Practiced in this spirit of thanksgiving and gratitude, as Shafer says of genuine Christian play, where the aim is to enjoy the activity and the reoriented sense of space and time without excessive focus on winning or rewards, recreational fight sports ministries may provide a way to experience play as "a manifestation of God's goodness."[102] To experience delight in creation and the joy that may come from this form of autotelic play (that is, recreational sparring), while enacting practices that minimize both the risk of bodily injury and a focus on domination, may thus be recognized as one blessing in life among others via a martial arts form that appeals to many. As we will see in discussing actual fight sports ministry programs, the appeal of fight sports for fitness, self-defense or recreational play draws many participants of various sorts into such ministries. In some cases, such as in inner city programs, these ministries provide an important outlet for participants, as well as a chance to influence, perhaps in surprising ways, those participants' religious formation. Their attraction to such programs provides one avenue within which to receive support from program leaders and enjoy creation. Though character and moral development, as well as physical fitness and social benefits, are (according to theologies of play) best understood as of secondary importance (part of the *instrumental* understanding of sports programs), such graces, though ancillary, are nonetheless appreciable, and many fight sports ministry programs do publicly count these as among their benefits. With a focus on play and recognizing individual achievements, such as in bag work, sparring, mastering a technique, or "finding an opening," as opposed to doing whatever is necessary to be victorious, these ministries may take an approach appropriate for an ethical Christian engagement in fight sports.

Competitively focused programs have the most challenging ethical concerns to face from a Christian perspective. As ethicists discuss, so much pressure is brought to bear in secular society on winning, often at all costs, that to maintain an appropriate balance in such program—one that delights both in the experience as a gift, and in others' achievements as much as one's own—is appreciably difficult. Even so, as one writer about

3. Ethical Issues Regarding Fight Sports and the Church 109

martial arts notes while defending the potentially more rough-and-tumble approaches to the sport, "rough play" may occur "more in the spirit of fun than of anger."[103]

Further, as Hyland writes, recognizing a "teleological" relation between competition and friendship by approaching competition as a "striving or questioning together towards excellence" will allow sport play to avoid the alienation between participants that might otherwise arise if the focus on competition is not properly focused on play and mutual striving; indeed, seen in this way, fulfillment is not possible without friendly-focused competition, which requires all participants to be similarly aligned.[104] "Reimagining sport in the Christian life," writes Hoffman, "will require readjusting old views and taking steps to bring the way sports are organized and played into harmony with the new vision."[105] To avoid "competition's corrosive effects on human relationships," one needs to engage in competitive sports play in a carefully designed context, one that encourages playful co-competitors who approach competition with a sense of humility.[106] As some sports ethicists suggest, contrary to what the broader society encourages in calling people to be heroes, God instead calls them to be saints—to see their actions in the broader context of God's plan for the world and its people.[107] The creation of a program capable of doing just this takes intentional, mindful planning. This, in fact, leads some Christian ethicists to suggest that "the best (and perhaps only) chances for this to happen will be in precincts over which Christians exert direct control," such as in church sports ministry programs.[108]

Many commercial fight sports clubs do promote such mutual striving and respect, albeit the secular setting would not permit basing such practice on Christian principles. Even so, many secular programs just as often value victory above all else, encouraging members to focus on personal gain more than a graceful, humble approach to "co-competitors." Thus, ministry programs with a clear understanding of how their approach employs Christian values, however different these may be from the larger society's focus on achieving personal glory and domination in competition, would be best for Christian practitioners. In fact, as we will see, many fight sports ministry programs are conscious of the challenges they face and their need to adequately respond to them. Their mindfulness is worth noting. Because of the challenges, some ethicists reviewed herein are not fans of fight sports pursued in Christian contexts, to say nothing of secular ones. Hoffman, for example, cites boxing alongside football and hockey as an example of "high-risk collision sport[s]" that, because of the physical confrontations involved and the "mental states" necessary to engage in such acts, make these "last" on his list of sports "to be encouraged in the Christian community."[109] Other writers reviewed, such as Galli, recognize that these sports do indeed have their virtues and appeals in Christian contexts.

There is a recognized need for leaders of Christian sports programs, inclusive of fight sports ministries, to be well-versed in the theological and ethical issues underlying their practice. Particularly if they see these activities as being compatible with the Christian faith, they have an obligation to consider how the particulars of their program relate to broader Christian principles and values. One scholarly analyst, James Mathisen, has referred to what results when sports ministry practitioners try to explain the relation of their sports programs to Christian theology, without adequate understanding of the latter, as a "hermeneutical disaster"; while acknowledging they may be "passionate" and "well-meaning," those not cognizant of the relation of faith to practice, he says, fail to fully appreciate the relationship of Christian values to their sports programs.[110] Christian sports ministry leaders should, in other words, understand the relationship of their programs to tenets of Christian theology and ethics. Correspondingly, Mathisen suggests that those of a more academic inclination should be mindful of the need to engage in dialogue with practitioners, to understand what appeals draw participants and be able to appreciate these. Thus, while often "there is a disparity between practitioners and scholars," what all those involved should pursue is "a more unified approach" and dialogue between the two sides.[111] This book itself is one effort to foster that dialogue and inform Christian ministry leaders' practice with a discussion how Christian ethics and theological reflection may enlighten approaches to fight sports ministry programs. This much is academic. To engage the other half of the dialogue, befitting Mathisen's counsel, we must now look to case studies of practitioners, those leading actual church-based fight sports ministry programs, to consider the challenges and benefits these leaders perceive and how they respond to these, before finally reflecting on what we may learn from all of the matters addressed.

4

Case Studies of Fight Sports Ministries

Speaking with the leaders of boxing and martial arts ministries, one immediately is struck by the diversity of such programs. Some are urban and cater to youngsters "at-risk"; others are rural and provide "family oriented" activities. Some feature religious activities such as prayer and Bible study; others do not. Some are housed in a church; others are in church-owned buildings, or in separate commercial spaces. Some train students for tournaments, while others are aimed at training for personal enrichment. Some draw mostly existing congregation members, while others draw more participants from the community, adding evangelism to their aspirations. The goals of these ministries range from those emphasizing fitness and self-defense, to those focused upon recreational sparring and training for competition. The forms taught range from Western boxing and kickboxing to grappling, jiu-jitsu, taekwondo, and karate, including various specific martial arts traditions and forms. Some are independent and have no church affiliation, while others are sponsored and supported by churches whose traditions range from Catholic to mainline Protestant and Evangelical.

That said, the Christian identity of these programs does, in various ways, guide their approach to their ministries. As we will observe, the national media's focus on more sensational fight sports ministries and their leaders may obscure the more conventional and modest reality of many ministries—perhaps even the majority of them. As Oates observes, "[it] should be understood that 'boxing' and 'fighting' [...] can be entirely different and even unrelated activities,"[1] and many fight sports ministries, in fact, try to keep these separate. These programs either teach fight sports for fitness, or offer controlled, recreational sparring for fun, and many that train at-risk youth do so to channel their behavior in humbling ways, away from the need to fight in the street and instead to build the self-confidence and grounding in Christian principles that leads participants to walk away from conflict. This is to say, many do not glorify "fighting," and in fact advocate the avoidance of hostility; along these lines, many focus more the use of fight sports training for character or confidence building (that is, in Oates' terms, boxing apart from "fighting"), or if they are geared towards self-defense, advocate avoiding engagement if possible, and otherwise leaving an altercation at the earliest possible opportunity (that is, fighting as a last resort, without concern for "winning," as in boxing). Indeed, the same applies to martial arts ministries. As essayist Jonathan Gottschall observes, drawing a somewhat different dichotomy from Oates, "MMA is really, really bad for you," referring to the injuries that may occur with more aggressive training or competitions, before adding, "MMA is also really, really good for you," citing the fitness and social benefits, as well as the way the sport may strengthen one's character.[2] As these observations both draw on elements of ethical dimensions of fight sports ministries, this is an appropriate place to begin a consideration of the practice of these fight sports ministry programs, to consider how these practical ministries relate to Christian ethics, values and practices.

Ethical Issues in the Practice of Fight Sports Ministries

Many of the ethical considerations addressed in the previous chapters arise regularly in discussions with fight sports ministry leaders. These include everything from reflections on violence in a Christian context to the treatment of the body as a temple (either by the care of it, or by the avoidance of harming it), and from reflections on character development to issues of competition, the striving together for excellence, and the focus on play. While the ministries reviewed reflect a range from faith traditions, locales and styles, there is a consistently striking mindfulness to how the leaders approach their ministries, not only in their relationship to Christian faith and mission broadly considered, but also how their practice relates to matters of ethics.[3]

For example, one Lutheran minister, Pastor Jarrod Lanning, who heads a martial arts ministry at his parish, Trinity Lutheran Church in Landis, North Carolina, discusses the relationship of his ministry to the "stewardship of the physical body." His program focuses mostly on fitness and self-defense, as the particular form he teaches, Chayou-Ryu, is based upon natural body movements drawn from other parent styles, such as taekwondo and hopkido. In reflecting upon the application of his teaching to self-defense situations, he asks, "Is it a faithful act to stop violence from happening to your body if you are capable of doing so? My answer to that is yes." Noting that even well-known pacifists acknowledge a place for "nonviolent martial arts" in self-defense, Lanning admits to some frustration with those who see the use of nonlethal forms of self-defense as violence. "From a theological standpoint, and from a practical standpoint, people who understand it as violence are really missing the point," he says, explaining that people have a responsibility to be good stewards of their own and others' bodies. "If you have the ability and training to [stop an attack], I don't see it in terms of violence. You could take it even further and see it as stopping evil," he added. Sharing the scenario of someone attacking another with a knife in a back alley, when the intended victim can either allow their body to be injured or apply nonlethal techniques to defend themselves, Lanning says, "I don't know that there's a real big context for Christian witness in that particular situation."[4]

In fact, Lanning describes the form he teaches as a lifestyle martial art that emphasizes harmony of the body, mind and spirit. He notes the personal benefits to his student-practitioners for the fitness benefits they reap from training. Lanning humorously explains that while not everyone will have to face an attacker, everyone will at some time "be attacked by the ground" and have to come to terms with a fall. Sharing that what many take away from his training is the proper way to handle a fall without sustaining injury, he shares that this particular skill has been helpful for the farmers and field workers who come to his classes, among others.[5] This, too, is part of the stewardship of the human body—learning how to care for and protect it from injury. Thus, the martial arts form he teaches puts into practice matters supportive of the ethical concepts underlying the "body as a temple" theology. One student even shared how, after months of training with the ministry, his blood pressure problems came under control, and he enjoyed more quality of life with increased energy.[6] Hence, Pastor Lanning's non-competitive martial arts ministry is helping people with personal fitness, as well as preparing them to face situations where they may need to engage in self-defense. In teaching students involved with the ministry, he is guided by principles of proper stewardship of the body, and the teaching of nonlethal uses of self-defense.

Expressing a similar sentiment is an associate pastor of a church in Idaho and the founder and chief instructor of the Christian Karate Association, the Rev. Steve Wilson. Heading an organization with fifteen locations around the world, Wilson's organization combines Christian discipleship with martial arts training. In addition to including statements of Christian beliefs and the steps to salvation, the organization's website stresses a code of ethics, which outlines members' responsibilities to themselves, their family, and their community.[7] It also provides thoughts on self-defense. Wilson himself says, "I believe [it is] a biblical calling, that we should be able to protect ourselves or our loved ones if there are no other options." Thus, after trying to run away, escape, or call the police, he teaches that only then is the use of martial arts an appropriate form of "self-preservation."[8] Indeed, Wilson sees this as part of the created order, observing that God gave means of self-protection to animals such as the porcupine, viper and skunk. He also finds biblical support for the use of martial arts techniques in the Psalms, where David writes of God training his hands for war.[9] "That's martial arts right there," Wilson says, "King David quotes it in the Psalms, saying that the Lord was his martial arts instructor." Beyond instruction in karate, his organization also stresses Christian character qualities, some of which suggest fighting is not always the answer, as the organization's website suggests by quoting Proverbs 24:5, "A wise man is mightier than a strong man. Wisdom is mightier than strength," and Proverbs 25:15, "A soft tongue can break hard bones." Thus, Wilson's response to ethical concerns applies biblical principles to defend self-defense techniques, while also suggesting they should be applied only as a last resort.

Other ministry leaders express similar sentiments, drawing upon ethical arguments outlined above. For example, Pastor Thomas Richards of Saint Paul's Lutheran Church in Tannersville, Pennsylvania, leads a karate club ministry where he says the emphasis is on "controlled contact" while

Steve Wilson, founder and chief instructor of the Christian Karate Association.

sparring, in order to maximize safety while also teaching effective self-defense techniques. Thus, his approach answers the concerns of those troubled about mistreatment of the human body (the "temple") in training. Even so, Richards stresses principles of nonviolence, saying "we tell people we're going to build up your confidence so you don't have to fight. We tell them your first obligation is to walk away, your second obligation is to run away; you only [use the skills we teach] as a very, very last resort." In fact, this ethical concern is institutionalized in his ministry, as any member who does get into an altercation is required to appear before a black belt review panel to justify their use of their skills. Harkening back to the discussion of Ellul (among others) regarding the escalation of violence, Richards notes that there is a progression of effectiveness, and that students should always take the path of least violence, saying, "you are liable to the level that you're going to take things." In fact, he shares the axiom, "On the street, you should retreat," and only use those skills necessary to defend yourself or others from harm.[10]

Similarly, another karate ministry, offered as one of several fight sports ministries associated with the Rock Church in San Diego, applies similar reason, where leader Michael Birch says he teaches students that one should use the techniques he teaches to "diffuse violence" and not let it increase. He speaks in particular of working with bullied kids and how he teaches them to avoid being hit, to block blows and get away; thus, this once again is an effort to protect of the body (the "temple"), here with the principle of minimizing escalation applied. The leader of another Rock Church program, Andrew Truong of the "Trinity MMA" ministry, shares a similar sentiment, saying he teaches students to "use just enough force to stop someone" if they come under assault.[11] In many of these ministries, the fact that these guidelines are taught in the context of classes that involve religious activity and instruction in Christian character traits (as we will soon discuss) helps relate these ethical positions about violence and protecting the "temple" to broader Christian ideals and practice.

Some ministries take a slightly different approach to ethical issues, due in part to their locale and those to whom they are aimed. Thus, boxing ministries involving urban youth may defend the use of contact sports for what these may provide to those adolescents participating in the programs. One such program is the Fist of God boxing ministry in Cherry Hill, outside of Baltimore, where Mike Mosley coaches young people who live in rough neighborhoods. The program began as Cross for Christ Boxing Gym under the leadership of Charles Clark, who for licensing purposes kept that name when he moved his ministry to the True Foundations Outreach Center in Columbus, Mississippi, leading the Cherry Hill program to adopt a new name. Thus, Fist of God (as Cross for Christ) began as a prison ministry, where Clark taught boxing and mentored inmates. The hope was to get them interested in boxing, so that when they were released from prison they might join a program like the boxing ministry he later began, in order to keep the former convicts out of trouble. Originally catering to only a handful of participants, the program has grown to what it is today, with about 40 students now training under Mosley.[12]

Reflecting on Christianity and violence, Mosley notes all of the "warriors of God" and bloodshed he finds in the Bible, but quickly moves to a contrasting defense of his boxing program in the context of the streets where he offers his ministry, as a program associated with the Created for So Much More Worship Center. "We're teaching these kids to put down the guns and pick up the gloves," he says, suggesting that the aggressive sport taught in the ministry is better than, and may replace the type of aggression that uses weapons on the street. He continues, saying, "In an area where people are shooting each other, we're teaching them how to fight, how to defend themselves, but also, if they get beat up, it's not the end of the world; you shake the guy's hand and you keep moving, considering the alternative."[13] Thus he says an urban boxing program like his builds confidence and an alternative mindset to the one participants may have grown up with on the street, while also noting that he believes there is a place for self-defense in the lives of believers.

The head of a boxing ministry in Omaha, Nebraska, the Rev. Servando Perales of Victory Boxing Club, expresses similar sentiments. While his program trains students for self-defense and competition in tournaments, outside of that he explains that his gym has a "zero tolerance" policy for "fighting outside the ring, because," he stresses, "we're a *faith-based* boxing club. It doesn't mean we're better, it means we're different. When you honor the cross of Christ," he continues, "there's absolutely no reason you should be fighting on the streets, especially if you belong to Victory Boxing Club." He offers as a point of contrast his own experience as a youth, when as someone involved with gangs, violence and drugs he regularly engaged in street fighting. "We don't tolerate that kind of behavior," he continues, noting that his ministry teaches different values, such as "self-control, discipline, patience—all things you can apply in your everyday life, from boxing." These values, he says, help lead his young boxers away from a life of crime, based upon the biblical values he teaches, alongside the virtues gained from training in boxing.[14]

Another boxing ministry whose grounding in Christian principles led to unique practices is the Christian Boxing Academy in Jersey City, New Jersey—a program which ran from 2014 until 2019, when its founder and president, Cristino Felix, moved to Texas, where he hopes to begin the program anew. Felix explains that he very carefully selects coaches for the boxing ministry, so as to expose the program's youthful participants to the best role models. Intentionally using Christian language to bespeak a conscious Christian identity, he explains why he chooses trainers who embody Christian ideals, in order to help make "disciples" of his young boxers, saying the trainers "disciple" the young boxers, "so they can disciple other children."[15] In its Jersey City location where kids might otherwise have become involved with gangs or drugs, Felix envisioned his boxing academy as a refuge from bad influences, where he helped channel what might be aggressive behavior by teaching sportsmanship. "I don't teach them to fight," he explains, "I teach them to compete" in a goal-oriented, wholesome setting. His approach leads to different practices and, he hopes, a different mindset. Felix uses the example of how he teaches his boxers to end boxing matches, saying, "When the bell [rings], you stop. When the competition is over, you *hug*." He emphasizes the difference in practice from other boxing programs, saying, "I don't teach them to shake hands, I teach them to *hug*." Finding this a more conciliatory gesture, he notes that other clubs' boxers sometimes are wary of this gesture, but he nonetheless explains to his own boxers that "it's okay, they weren't taught the way you were taught." Felix wants his boxers to carry themselves differently in the world, in a Christian manner, he says, maintaining their own dignity while also showing compassion.[16]

Program Aims and Activities, Both Physical and Religious

Considering the stated purpose of their ministries and how this incorporates religious ideals, Mosley notes that the particular outreach of his Fist of God ministry is to offer kids in the program a positive self-understanding, expressed in love. Explaining that the emphasis is on mentoring, he notes that the kids involved have had a rough upbringing. "If they've been beaten down by life," he says, "they don't need to be beaten down anymore." Hence, he emphasizes the positive in his coaching, in a fashion reminiscent of the earlier discussion of seeking excellence together, to build each other up. Drawing 15–20 participants on a good night, students begin each session with conditioning for fitness, and then box for the second hour. On each night, the program involves religious activity. Mosley prays with his boxers at the beginning of each session. Also, the pastor of Created for So Much More will attend every once in a while, and Mosley encourages his boxers to go to Bible study classes provided by the church. The very fact that this ministry is housed in the church itself expresses something of the concern the church has for people of the local community, via this outreach ministry.

In fact, the church's pastor, Bishop Willard Saunders, articulates how the boxing program is very much a part of the broader ministry, saying:

> The boxing program has become a medium that is a part of our ministry to help children, young men and women, to be able to reach their own potential through an activity that creates discipline. [...] And it really helps us to be able to minister to them. It's not even separate from our ministry. It is our ministry. [...] Boxing doesn't just teach you respect for your ability, but respect for your opponent. You can be defeated. They learn what it feels like to fail in the boxing gym, but they [also] learn how much harder they have got to go back [...] and be successful and be able to work at it. That gives you a respect for life. It also gives you a respect for death. And it gives you, more importantly, a respect for yourself and other human beings.[17]

Here, the pastor not only articulates how the program is successful as an outreach ministry, but also how it reflects the ethical concern for helping participants appreciate their own and other's best efforts. One student in the program not only reiterates these points, but also supports the idea that boxing is not always about fighting, saying, "Boxing is not about aggression at all. It made me humble as a young teen. It kind of took me away from the immaturity [...] outside of the gym, and kind of [brought] me closer to [...] different people. And it [...] made me see the world a different way."[18]

Another boxing ministry geared toward at-risk youth is the Rock Ministry of Calvary Chapel in Kensington, Pennsylvania. Begun in 2003, the "Rock's" goal is to reach kids before they get into trouble on the streets, or to stop existing juvenile offenders from returning to trouble. In fact, the ministry's co-founder, Golden Gloves champion Buddy Osborne, spent time in prison and came to "strongly believe in the power of the Bible and the gospel to change lives."[19] He realized (not unlike boxing history's "Fighting Parson" the Rev. Frederick Wedge, discussed earlier) that he needed to reach out to help those headed for trouble *before* they became incarcerated. "How can I be more effective in the community?" Osborne says he asked himself after seeing a boy he had once trained arrive at the Philadelphia House of Corrections, where Osborne worked with juvenile offenders; Osborne continues, explaining that he asked himself, "How can I reach kids on the street block as opposed to coming in and giving a Bible study on the prison block?"[20] To this end, he developed the Rock Ministry boxing program. Originally making do with decidedly humble facilities, with a clothesline wrapped around posts to demark a ring, the ministry now features a proper ring, heavy bags and other boxing equipment. Offered in an area known more for drug deals, gang violence and crime, the boxing program, with its volunteer staff, has become a popular local outlet. "We basically opened the doors and they came in," said Paul Orr, the ministry's co-founder, adding, "The word of mouth in the hood is faster than the internet."[21]

One pastor who works with the program, the Rev. Craig Cerrito, defends the idea that a boxing ministry can be a successful way to reach out to young inner-city men, observing that "more kids than we can count have given their lives to Christ. Kids have been kept out of prison, had their lives changed. So the idea that God can't use boxing to reach these kids is empirically false." He adds, making a distinction not uncommon among leaders of fight sports ministries, "there is nothing unbiblical about training for combat, but there is about aggressive violence."[22] Their approach is to reach boys and young men from the ages of 10 to 22 who love sports, and to make sure they find a connection with the church's broader ministry. Hence, the coaches lead a Bible study once a week. The program therefore partly serves as evangelistic outreach, as it has brought members to the church; it also provides mentoring, a chance for the trainers to minister directly to the youthful boxers. "They come in rough around the edges, but in order to function here you have to take instructions and listen," Orr says.[23] The program is free, run by volunteers, and is certified by USA Boxing, the national amateur boxing organization. In fact, Rock Ministry boxing offers its young participants a chance to train and qualify for its competitive team, and their program has produced Golden Gloves champions, as well as Junior Olympics boxing qualifiers. An average night may see 60–70 boys and young men come not only to box, but also to finish homework or read the Bible. True to the spirit of the theologies of play advocated by ethicists as the best approach for Christian sports ministries, the young boxers reportedly "laugh, act silly and genuinely seem at ease."[24]

As to how the Rock relates to other broad issues in fight sports ministries, noteworthy is the fact that they have also developed a boxing program for girls. Admitting that they had not at first expected to develop a girl's boxing ministry, the leaders nonetheless responded to interest in such a program and now not only train girls and young women aged 12–22 but also have female trainers. Unconcerned with issues of gendered ecclesiology or providing strictly "men's ministries," Cerrito observes, "our emphasis is on saving kids from the dangers of the streets, rather than concerns with gender."[25] The ministry made other changes over the years. In addition to the boxing ministry, participants may now also choose to train in grappling (jiu-jitsu) and kickboxing. These programs not only teach tools of self-defense, Cerrito says, but also character: "Martial arts and boxing give a person a sense of confidence," he says, adding that this is important for young people growing up in the surrounding neighborhood."[26] The ministry's impact has been significant; having started with five boys and modest equipment, the Rock Ministry is now housed in a new facility, and has served more than 6,000 youngsters.[27]

Another program similar to this one had been run at the Teen Center at St. Peter's Church in Dorchester, part of Catholic Charities of Boston, until the Center discontinued the boxing program in recent years. After this, the boxing program (under some of the same leadership) has been absorbed into another area Catholic outreach program, as one component of the Colonel Marr Boys & Girls Club of Dorchester. In its time, the purpose of the Teen Center, which offered various activities, was to provide a "safe haven for adolescents living in Dorchester's most troubled areas [...] during after school hours and throughout the summer months"; it existed, according to the Catholic Charities website, to promote self-esteem, academic success, personal growth and involvement in community. Noting that those who live in the area are "disproportionately involved in teen violence," the Center was developed as an outreach, providing mentoring and other types of support to "interrupt the rapidly expanding cycle of violence."[28] Indeed, the Dorchester area is the highest crime district in Boston, with significant rates of gang violence, and more killings and drugs than anywhere else in the city.[29] Opened in 2003, the Center added boxing to its programming in 2010 as another means to involve young people, offer support, and increase trust between the young participants and police officers, who serve as trainers.[30]

The driving forces behind the boxing ministry had been Paul Doyle, a retired Drug Enforcement Agency agent and former heavyweight boxing champ, and Father Richard Conway, a priest at St. Peter's. Conway himself came up with the idea for the boxing program and enlisted the help of a fellow priest to convince actor and producer Mark Wahlberg (who himself grew up in Boston, and filmed the boxing movie *The Fighter*, a biopic about light welterweight champ Micky Ward, nearby) to donate money for the equipment.[31] Conway then reached out to Doyle to lead the effort and work with the teenagers. Doyle, who had been an orphan and grew up in Boston's housing projects, first started boxing in his youth, and says it taught him "confidence, discipline, and how to read and evaluate people."[32] Doyle agreed to the proposal, saying that once he saw the kids involved it tugged at his heart.[33] With modest facilities and equipment, including several heavy bags, pads for training, gloves and headgear, Doyle opened the program to area youth. Along the way, others joined him in the program's leadership, including amateur and professional boxers, and police officers working with a Safe Street program, who also serve as coaches.[34] That the kids got to work with police is particularly significant, as it helped them build trust between police and residents in an area where this is crucial. Thus, two nights a week the teens, mostly boys and a few girls, gathered to train and interact with their coach-mentors.

4. Case Studies of Fight Sports Ministries 121

Paul Doyle, a former Drug Enforcement Agency agent and heavyweight boxer, with Father Richard Conway, founders of the boxing program formerly of the Teen Center at St. Peter's Church in Dorchester, posing in the Colonel Marr Boys & Girls Club of Dorchester, where they continue their boxing program.

That it is boxing that they taught was not accidental. Doyle observes, "These are inner city kids. They can have a hard time melding into team sports, but they need something that's going to challenge them and lead to discipline."[35] Thus, though they trained for fitness and recreation, the broader purpose of the boxing program was to provide an opportunity for police and others in the community to interact with the kids and help them grow. Doyle notes that while wrapping the young boxers' hands, he and the other coaches talked, listened, connected with the youngsters, and helped them with their problems, both to forge strong relationships and to help individual youth. "The kids who come here want someone to teach them the right way," he says, "not just in sports, but in life."[36] Sharing that he did in fact see some students who have the potential to pursue boxing as amateurs or even professionals, he nonetheless adds that this was not his objective. Harkening back to the history of boxing program goals, including those in the Catholic tradition, Doyle notes, "It's the best character building there is."[37] Thus, while participants did learn to hit the bags and engage in very "controlled sparring" (thus, limiting concern with injuring the "temple"), the focus had been on developing their strength, confidence and discipline. In fact, reminiscent of Oates' observation that boxing doesn't always involve fighting, Doyle shares that the boxing coaches would teach the kids that "good boxers don't waste their fighting skills outside the ring."[38] Thus, self-defense is not an emphasis, nor is competition.

Neither was the emphasis on overt expressions of religion. Mike Joyce, who was in charge of programming at the Teen Center, notes that there had been no actual religious activity that takes place in the boxing program. Unlike in some other inner-city ministries, there was no prayer or Bible study. The focus of the ministry had been on building relationships with those in the community, keeping the teens safe and helping them grow, and not on overtly religious matters.[39] Doyle himself reiterates this last point, saying, "In real life, things can get desperate, but no matter what, don't quit. Boxing teaches you that. No matter what, you have to keep moving and keep punching."[40] As an observer wrote about the ministry, the coaches would help the kids "recognize the resilience they have developed to survive adversity and channel it toward higher ambitions. Especially in boxing, the kids who can benefit from it do so because it gives purpose and focus to the grit they already have."[41]

While the program leaders had hoped to expand the program in the future to involve young adults, the outreach ministry for the period it existed achieved its goals. Noteworthy for its lack of focus on self-defense or competition, the boxing program not only worked for the Center's purposes but also, given its focus, circumvented some of the ethical concerns with boxing ministries already mentioned; it did so while emphasizing positive aspects previously discussed, such as recognizing participants' achievements and supporting their pursuit of excellence, all while simultaneously being successful at building bridges in the community and mentoring youth. That the boxing program at the Teen Center at St. Peter's in fact accomplished its ambitions is reflected in the remarks of one young female participant, who says, "I like the sport, but I also like the guys who work here. They encourage me to go to college and they show you, all the time, that they care."[42]

Like the Teen Center, the Christian Boxing Academy (introduced above) has been led by a police officer—a lieutenant in the Jersey City Police Department and former amateur boxer, Cristino Felix. Having served on the force for almost 30 years, Felix was motivated to begin the boxing academy while working on the evening tour. Witnessing the aftermath of robberies, shootings and homicides, many of the victims of which were young African Americans, beckoned him to get involved. The turning point came one evening when he found himself kneeling over the body of a 13-year-old boy who had been killed, and he sensed God telling him to do more. "That was the beginning of it," he recalls, "that's what sparked it." Not satisfied with an existing boxing club with which he had been affiliated, because they tolerated playing rap music that used profanity and promoted violence, Felix began plans to open his own boxing ministry—one that was explicitly based upon Christian values. He organized a fund-raising event called Fisticuffs, where police officers and firefighters boxed each other in an exhibition and raised enough money to start a boxing-based outreach ministry. (Efforts to apply for federal grants were thwarted by the planned Christian focus of the program.) In the end, their efforts raised enough money to rent a small facility and, with donated equipment and volunteers helping with construction, created a gym with boxing equipment and (because a ring would not fit in the space) a makeshift ring constructed of buckets, posts, felt and rope. Felix humorously notes he had to regularly remind the young athletes not to lean upon the rickety, improvised ring. The result was the founding of the Christian Boxing Academy.[43]

The academy's stated purpose is "to teach and encourage the youth of Jersey City the importance of personal self-control and peaceful resolution through the disciplines of boxing and teach the importance of academics and sportsmanship."[44] Its mission is to provide a boxing-after-school program that will "enable the youths to learn the importance of foundation building in terms of their character, diligence, perseverance, and responsibility."[45] While basing itself on Christian principles and values, the academy nonetheless has welcomed those of all faiths. Felix notes, for example, that a Muslim child participated

The logo of the Christian Boxing Academy, founded by police officer Lieutenant Cristino Felix, formerly of New Jersey, now of Texas, where he hopes to begin his program anew.

in the program at the Jersey City location and was welcomed. "It's a Christian boxing academy because I'm going to stand on those Christian values and principles," Felix explains. "I'm not hitting anyone over the head with the Holy Bible. I'm teaching those values and principles that we're supposed to live by." Nonetheless, he would write scriptural verses on an erasable board, along with other, secular sayings intended to inspire his students. He has also prayed with his boxers at the end of training, when all the participants hold hands. Further, the academy in New Jersey had an "informal association" with Cityline Church, a non-denominational, multi-cultural Christian congregation. Felix notes that he invited interested boxers to come to church on Sunday and encouraged congregants to become involved with the academy.[46]

The academy's program had been USA Boxing affiliated, and typically drew 15–20 youths, aged seven to their early twenties, exclusively male. Felix explains that the academy had at one time permitted girls to train but changed its policy, to protect the program. He explains his relationship with the academy's participants as being "their minister, their confidant, their comforter, and their teacher," as well as a father figure for many. Explaining that the academy was a "refuge" for most boxers from gang and drug violence, and that the boxing program changed the lives of its participants, Felix shares his own appreciation for what his boxers give him, saying, "it's a euphoria to see them smiling." While still at the Jersey City location, Felix had hoped to find a larger facility for the program, where they might erect an actual boxing ring. He also envisioned using the ring as a location from which to minister to the kids by having them work on skits that would "help them learn how to carry themselves" in the world, with dignity and compassion. The curriculum, he explained, would come from the Cityline pastor, and Felix himself would lead the role-playing exercises aimed at helping his boxers learn to abide by scriptural principles in their everyday interactions and conduct.[47]

Plans changed, however, after Felix's son, Ramon Torres, committed suicide in March of 2018. Ramon had been a police officer for one year and, with his father, served as a coach for the young participants in the Christian Boxing Academy. In Ramon's memory, the Academy held a boxing event as a suicide awareness and prevention fundraiser, the proceeds of which went to children of New Jersey first responders who died from suicide. Drawing a huge crowd, the fundraiser was a success, and served as the closing event for the Academy, at least for its New Jersey location. Felix, who retired from the Jersey City police force, has since moved to Texas, where he currently keeps all of the gym's equipment in storage, and hopes to open the doors for a similar boxing program in the very near future.[48]

In some ways providing a contrast to the above police officer led ministries is that of Victory Boxing Club of Omaha, Nebraska, as this program is run not by a police officer but by a former gang member, the Rev. Servando Perales, who served time in a federal prison for drug-related offenses. While not being affiliated with a church, as in Boston and Jersey City, the program is nonetheless explicitly "faith based" in its approach and program offerings. The Reverend Perales' own life story factors centrally in how the boxing ministry came about and is run. In many ways a culmination of his journey, the program's aim is to reach young people and save them before they succumb to bad influences, such as those of gangs and drugs, and wind up in jail. In fact, despite his own background and because of it, parents are eager to have their children work with this reformed gang member, ex-convict turned pastor and engaged citizen, because, as Servando himself explains referring to reputation, "they know this guy is real."[49]

Growing up in the very neighborhood where he now runs Victory Boxing Club, Perales' family had moved there from Mexico in search of work. Perales' dad was reportedly alcoholic and abusive to his mother and some of his siblings. Eventually abandoned by his father, Perales turned to a local boxing club for a sense of purpose and belonging. "Boxing was definitely something good in my life," he says in a published biography, titled *The Cry of a Warrior* (2013). "The boxing world was the place I belonged."[50] Perales began entering and winning tournaments, until the lure of drugs and a gang he helped to found drew him in a different direction. "Boxing was my outlet, a release," he observes, "but there was still a big empty hole I was trying to fill with all of these different things."[51] Involved in drug dealing, stabbings, terrorizing his neighborhood and issuing threats to a teacher at his high school, Perales was ultimately expelled, and found himself in and out of prison.[52] The last straw came when officers from the police gang control unit came to arrest him, finding him with a gun; after a heated pursuit as Perales tried to escape, he was caught and ultimately sent to a federal prison. There he ran into a friend he knew from his days as a wayward youth. This friend was no longer the hoodlum he had once been; he was, instead, a committed Christian who played guitar for the prison chapel. He told Perales "God loves you and has a plan and purpose for your life."[53] That was the turning point for Perales, who became "born again."

Wanting to clean up his life, he decided to start boxing again, because it had been such a positive outlet for him earlier in his life. He trained with his friend while in prison and when he was released tried to pursue a professional career in Las Vegas, Nevada. Fighting on the undercard of the second Evander Holyfield versus Lenox Lewis fight, he was downed in the sixth round and came to terms with the fact that he was past his prime boxing years. This led to another change in his life: "That's when I began to

The Rev. Servando Perales in his Victory Boxing Club of Omaha, Nebraska, a faith-based boxing program.

realize it wasn't about me anymore," he confides. "After crying out to God and whining, not wanting to come home to Omaha as a failure, God said, 'No, I've got a bigger fight for you.'"[54] Perales returned to his hometown and took classes at a Bible college, ultimately becoming a minister. As he pursued this calling, he also felt a related one, to start a boxing club. He wanted to provide a place for youth in Omaha to pursue something positive and avoid drugs and the other troublesome temptations that had drawn him in as a youth. The difference with his boxing club, as he notes, is that it would be faith based. "It was ultimately God calling me to a greater fight," he says, "something bigger than myself, giving back to my community. The same streets that I once terrorized are the same streets God wanted me to rescue kids from, and share His love with them, through the art of boxing, through this gift God gave me."[55]

Understandably skeptical at first, his community slowly began to realize Perales' change was authentic, and they began to help. In fact, one of the very police officers who had helped to arrest him and send him to prison became his first financial backer and offered him a check to support his growing boxing ministry. With community help, Perales' Victory Boxing Club moved from his garage to a renovated warehouse, where one of their rings was donated by a former police officer who would also work as a coach at the Center. Adding facilities for a game room and computer lab, Perales has led his ministry beyond boxing, as it has become the Victory Boxing Club and Community Center, with a board of directors and much community support.[56] There, they not only train boxers but also, as a USA Boxing certified club, also host tournaments and travel to compete in other gyms. Having started with seven or eight boys, 10 years old and up, training in Perales' garage, the Center now attracts about 25 boxers every night, with perhaps 30 active members, 12 years old and up, and includes both boys and girls.[57] Victory's boxers have been successful in competition. Seeing this has attracted new members, as has the club's presence at community events, such as in parades and other forms of neighborhood outreach. Also helpful in this regard has been the Reverend Perales' speaking engagements at places like schools, where he addresses young people and shares the lessons he learned from his own life, turning from "gang leader to Reverend,"[58] and the roles that boxing and faith have played in transforming his life. This transformation is based in part on the character-building traits he gained from boxing, including self-control, discipline and patience, which he now emphasizes for those training at his center.

As to religious activity, while the boxing nights themselves do not necessarily explicitly involve religion, Perales notes that the program's approach is "faith based." As a community center not affiliated with a church, the program nonetheless emphasizes Christian values in its approach. Beyond that, Victory Boxing does offer a Bible study several times a month right in the gym, when training ends early and all who are interested are invited to participate. Further, the Reverend Perales will offer prayer with individual youngsters who need it, particularly if he knows a boxer is going through some difficult life event, such as the death of a loved one. Such opportunities may arise from the general mentoring and ministry he is able to provide, especially when he has one-on-one time with his participants. He gives the example of going on runs with young boxers, when they have time to talk, or other opportunities before or after training when he can engage his boxers alone and they can confide in him. "There's often times when a boxer won't say what's going on in front of everybody," he explains, "but they'll pull you in the office and say, 'Can I talk to you?'" This is when he is able to minister to kids' needs individually. Thus, boxing provides the opportunity both to engage with the participants individually and to train them in values that will lead them along in their life. In this way, Perales says boxing is "a tool to get them through the door and lead them closer to Christ." Recalling his own experiences, he adds that, while this in part involves learning to box and compete, "more importantly, I want them to fight and be victorious outside of the ring. We all have choices to make in life, and those choices can ruin you…." To help keep young people on the right track, he offers them a place to learn wholesome values and disciplines in his program, saying, "so for us, it's more than just boxing."[59]

Similar in mission to this boxing ministry is a program at Escape Ministries in Holland, Michigan, called West Side Boxing and Fitness. A program that has emphasized boxing, with some martial arts, the ministry is led by boxing coaches Ruben Silvas and Trinidad Morin. Escape Ministries describes itself and its affiliated programs as "an urban teen and young adult leadership program" whose mission is "to inspire, equip and empower children or promise, young adults and their families in at-risk environments, through faith in Jesus Christ, to be tomorrow's positive leaders in our community."[60] Silvas reiterates that commitment, noting that he works closely with parole and probation officers to try to encourage youngsters who are in trouble to join the boxing program and "change their entire mindset." He states that the boxing ministry, which is USA Boxing affiliated, provides a platform through which to change the lives of at-risk youth, and to "teach them more about God, and that there are other things [to do] than being in the street with their buddies." Thus, he volunteers as a coach with the program because, as he says, "it saves lives."[61]

The boxing club started humbly enough in 2010 as a neighborhood effort by Silvas and Morin, offered at their homes. Over the course of one summer, they attracted so many kids that their program came to the attention of the local pastor of a Reformed church, who offered them a room in the church basement for their program. The program continued to grow and ultimately partnered with Escape ministries, which offers a range of services, including career counseling, job placement services, a mentoring and tutoring service, and an alternative schooling program for those expelled or suspended, in addition to the boxing club. The boxing program now has 20–25 young people training on any particular day, and is open throughout the week (and Saturday) as an after school program. Attracting members from ages four to 35, most of the participants are teenaged boys and girls, although the vast majority are boys and young men. Silvas, himself a former amateur boxer, estimates that over the years the program has touched the lives of as many as one thousand participants.[62]

The program works, Silvas observes, because it teaches self-discipline and respect. He is not only a mentor to those participating in the program, he shares, but has also become a father figure to many of the boxers, as quite a number come from broken homes. He notes that the program does not consider boxing as something violent but rather a sport that helps the ministry reach at-risk youth, to teach them about character and allow the staff to intervene for youth in the program who are in need. He offers the example of one troubled young man who had been enrolled in an Escape program that caters to suspended or expelled students and allows them to continue their schoolwork under Escape's supervision, noting that this young man also became devoted to the boxing program and is now "a straight arrow with a job and all." Silvas also shares the story of a young man who once hugged the staff members and thanked them and the boxing program for having kept him from doing something he should not have done, Silvas speculating that this means they may well have saved the young man from attempted suicide. He adds that by getting to know the kids involved he is able to tell when one of them is having problems, and to intervene by talking and praying with them, noting that his boxers may "walk in frowning" but "leave smiling."[63]

Additionally, he recounts stories of the youth saved from gangs and the juvenile detention system, noting that the program teaches participants to be humble. When he first started, he recalls, his goal was to build champions, with a champion's attitude and mindset; but, he confides, that changed over time, as he realized that what his boxers needed most was humility, saying the boxing program gives participants an "opportunity to change their lives" by teaching them "to be humble and submit their life to God." Silvas says that is when their program becomes "so much more than a boxing club," because instead of building champions, "I wanted to build disciples for God." Part of the approach involves religious activity. He may offer a prayer for all or take students aside and counsel and pray with them, as needed. Additionally, a pastor comes once a week to talk about the Bible from the center of the ring and offer a short homily. Thus, the program's emphasis, rather than being on winning competitions, is upon submitting one's life to God; "That" Silvas concludes, "was more of a prize to me than some trophy."[64]

Somewhat similar to the preceding ministry programs, but distinct in one important way among those included herein, is a boxing program aimed largely towards at-risk youth in San Jacinto, California, called "Boxing for Christ." The similarities are in the target membership, motivation and approach. What makes this non-profit ministry unique is that it was founded, and is overseen by a female president and CEO, Sonia Ramos. Ramos herself had at one time been involved in selling drugs, but it was when her son got caught up in such activity that she felt called to provide a program geared towards keeping area youth on the straight and narrow path. She explains that when her family lived in San Diego, her son David was involved in a boxing program, and that helped keep him away from bad influences. When the family moved to San Jacinto, however, there were no clubs that would take him in, because he was soon to turn eighteen and was too old for existing programs. Thus, as she reflects, "there's nothing to do here. It's a small little valley. And so he started hanging out on the streets." When Ramos became sick battling a pituitary tumor, her son made a bad choice to try to help the family, she explains, and was caught transporting 17 kilograms of cocaine. Facing the possibility that he could be sentenced to 17 years in prison, Ramos says, "right there, I made a promise to the Lord, and I said, 'Save my son!'" In what she sees as a response to both her and her son's prayers, he was ultimately sentenced to serve five years, and was released in half that time. This led directly to her sense of calling to begin the boxing ministry: "So I opened up the program Boxing for Christ because that was the only thing that kept [the kids] away from the streets, and anything that I wanted to do from here on, I wanted to do it for the Lord. Well," she concludes, reflecting on the gym's success, "I didn't expect the outcome of this program!"[65]

With the motto "Change Your Life with Us," and a club logo of a pair of boxing gloves hanging from a cross, the organization's stated mission is to support the local community by using boxing to

> promote and provide a safe haven and healthy environment for our youth and young adults. Along with teaching our students self defense, discipline and self esteem, Boxing for Christ provides an outlet for our youth to release aggression in a healthy way along with life skills to help in their future to be productive members of the community.[66]

Begun in January of 2012, the program, Ramos says, has over the years reached more than 700 youth, and sees 35–40 students participate daily. USA Boxing certified, the program has four coaches, including two of

4. Case Studies of Fight Sports Ministries 131

Ramos' sons, one of whom is the very son whose troubles led Sonia to begin the program. Motivated by her past awareness of the need to provide a program for youth of all ages, Ramos does not put a cap on the age range of those who can be involved and says that the program involves kids from age seven through their late twenties. This provides guidance for even the older boxers, because, as she observes, "sometimes these kids think they know, but they're not fully mentally grown."[67]

The program is open to both boys and girls and involves about 20 percent of the latter. In fact, one of Ramos' daughters won the Golden Gloves competition in Pasadena. As to how running a program such as this differs because it is led by a woman, Ramos notes that the challenges began from her very efforts to found Boxing for Christ. "When I first started,

Sonia Ramos' son David, whose experiences inspired her to found Boxing for Christ. David now coaches participants at the boxing gym.

because I'm Hispanic and I'm a woman," and wanted to found a boxing program, she shares, "there wasn't a lot of faith." Not a boxer herself, Ramos notes that some in the community questioned, "Why boxing? Christ never boxed." Facing doubts of her own from all the criticism, she nonetheless persevered, saying that God told her not to worry about pleasing everybody, but only to focus on pleasing Him. She notes that she sold some of her own possessions to start the ministry and continues to live in a one-bedroom trailer, and that once the city started seeing the outcome of the program, they got on board. The success of Boxing for Christ, in fact, has led to recognition of her efforts involved in running such a program, including receiving a commendation as a "woman of distinction" from her state senator, and a letter from the U.S. president praising her program. Not only has Boxing for Christ reached many kids, but its success in competitions has led those from neighboring communities to come to San Jacinto to spar with Ramos' boxers.[68]

The program is very community oriented. They receive referrals from local probation officers to help get at-risk youth into the program. Boxing for Christ also expects its participants to do community service. In the past, this has involved working with the local school district to help unload donations for an annual toy drive, cleaning up local parks, and other efforts. "Wherever the community needs volunteers," she says, "we try to be there." This helps broaden the aim of the program beyond boxing, to build an awareness in area youth of the need to provide service, and to create a sense of good will on behalf of the local community towards the ministry. Ramos notes this relates to broad goals of the program, which not only include getting kids off the streets but also preparing them physically, mentally and spiritually to live wholesome lives.[69]

As to religious activity in the program, Ramos says she prefers to take a subtle approach. Harkening back to her own past when she rebelled against religion, she fears taking too heavy handed of an approach to religious involvement might drive some would-be participants away. While her own mother is a successful preacher in the area, Ramos herself stirs interest in religion at Boxing for Christ with quotes written on the walls of the gym, including the gym's primary inspiration, Philippians 4:13 ("I can do all things through Christ who strengthens me") and other sayings, such as "Exercise daily with the Lord." Seeing the scriptures and quotations, she says, leads some participating youth to start asking questions. She shares the story of one young boxer who came to her to confide that he had never before known who God was, because no one ever introduced him to God, but that Boxing for Christ provided him with an appreciation of God and who He is. Other than that, the religious appeal comes from an awareness of how the program began, and God's efforts, as Ramos recalls it, to help

4. Case Studies of Fight Sports Ministries 133

Sonia Ramos, founder and president of Boxing for Christ in San Jacinto, California, with her youngest son Danny, a USA Boxing certified coach.

establish Boxing for Christ and lead it to success. She notes that somehow the religious message gets through, as it is not uncommon for her fighters to kneel and pray before they go into competition. Still, one not need be religious or even Christian to participate in the program. "God told me to make this for everybody," she explains, adding, "We're one big family here."[70]

The participants come with a range of challenges to face, from reestablishing themselves after incarceration, to those facing anger control problems, obesity, or who come from broken homes. Noting that the boxers involved in the program do well in life because of the influence of the gym, Ramos shares that her future plans are to build the program into an academy, one where participants could dorm, especially if life at home is among the sources of their problems. This would also help keep youth away from gangs, drugs and the bad influences of the streets, she says. Currently the facility consists of a gym which she pays the city to use, and includes a ring, bags and other boxing equipment. The program does charge a modest fee for classes ($20 a month) but provides means for even those who cannot pay to be involved through grants and by asking those who have trouble with payments to help clean the gym. "To me, it's not about the money, it's about changing lives," Ramos adds. The academy she envisions would provide life skills training and tutoring, to help participants succeed. This, Ramos says, is what makes her most happy, to see "the lives that are changed," that "these kids have a safe haven to go to," one they find in Boxing for Christ.[71]

While several of the fight sports ministries already mentioned incorporate informal religious activity in their programs, sometimes even in the ring, one ministry actually includes a worship space right next to the boxing rings and training areas; this is SonRise Church of Salem, Oregon, and its Church Street Boxing program. Although the ministry has moved about over the years and somewhat shifted its focus, SonRise has been in its current facility since 2016, a site boasting signs for Church Street Boxing along its big, long windows, and a sign bearing an image of Christ crowned with thorns and the words "SonRise Church" above its central doors. The ministry is the creation of Pastor Mark Morrow. He describes himself as a domestic missionary whose mission is to reach the unchurched—those to whom a traditional church might not appeal. This constituency may include the homeless, the addicted, the disenfranchised, gang members, or simply youth who need a place for fellowship, mentoring and character building. "Our objective is to meet them on the street block instead of the prison block," Morrow says. Inviting any and all, the ministry's motto is "Come as you are"—although one thing the outreach ministry does expect of participants is active engagement. Pastor Morrow explains, "you've got to have some determination and drive in life, and boxing is a great avenue to teach those principles." Even so, the boxing program is what Morrow describes as a "tool," one by which to reach people on more than one level. Thus, he explains, "the most difficult thing for me as a pastor is to see the gym full of people working, working, working to excel in the physical realm. Bottom line as a pastor: God is not going to care about your right hook or jab. He's going to care about what's inside." Hence, the relationships built among fighters, coaches and the pastor give the program an avenue to go beyond just training, and "to speak truth into people's lives."[72]

The program welcomes those eight years old and up, and uses a "safety first" approach, where boxers are always supervised and must wear protective gear. The members include some all the way into their fifties, but it consists mostly of teens and young adults, mainly though not exclusively boys and men. The boxing program runs weekdays with about ten volunteer coaches helping the 25–40 participants they might have join in training on any given day. In all, Church Street currently enrolls about 200 members and, while there is a monthly fee to participate, the ministry offers scholarships to those who cannot afford the fee. Financial support comes from two local churches, as well as from other sponsors and individuals. While they may pray at the end of training, and members may find signs with inspirational messages about, Morrow says his approach is not to "shove Jesus" at participants; instead he seeks to use the boxing program to build relationships and "start a conversation."[73] Thus the facility strives to be "a faith-based place for people to come and receive training in boxing and in life." Morrow sees the athletic and spiritual goals as interrelated, as they involve many of the same virtues and disciplines.[74] As for activities on the weekends, SonRise offers nondenominational worship on Sunday mornings, when Pastor Morrow offers a sermon. Some of the boxers may participate, while others not; and not all worshipers box. Pastor Morrow emphasizes, however, that even for those boxers who do not worship at SonRise, the boxing program still offers an opportunity to bring people to Christ. "Ultimately," he says of the program and the relationships it builds, "the goal is change and salvation." Although a non-traditional means of reaching people with a religious connection, Morrow accentuates that that is the entire point—to minister to those who might not otherwise have Christian guidance in their lives.[75]

While the ministries discussed thus far have largely been run by amateurs, police officers, and ministers, one urban fight sports ministry, Victory Ministry and Sports Complex in Joplin, Missouri, is run by a professional mixed martial artist. A not-for-profit organization that provides programming in various areas (including the arts) as well as worship opportunities, a major focus of Victory is on athletics, including its boxing and MMA programs. Describing itself as a "Christ-Centered community center for all ages, accommodating participants with many different interests,"[76] the considerably well-appointed facility includes a gym and fitness center, and is directed by Teejay Britton, a professional MMA fighter and one of the instructors of the fight sports classes. These classes include, separately, adult and youth boxing (which includes some kickboxing and muay thai), and MMA/Brazilian jiu-jitsu classes; these classes are open to men and women, boys and girls, as Britton notes there is no concern with gender issues at Victory. The facility has a cage (for MMA), boxing ring, bags, and mats for grappling. Classes may draw anywhere from ten to 25 participants. While Victory does charge for classes, Britton says he hopes they will be able to pay off the debt on the facility and be able to allow people to train without cost, as well as be open 24 hours a day.[77]

Classes take a somewhat cautious approach to training, not unlike other fight sports ministries. Commenting on how some facilities encourage students to go "all out" and train at "110%," Britton cautions, "We don't do that here. You've got to take care of your body." He adds, explicitly acknowledging an awareness that the body is God's gift, that the physical self is necessary to do service. Much of the class instruction is devoted to traditional training and sparring, or "rolling." True to their commitment to keep students healthy, the program's rules do not allow beginning boxers to spar, only permitting this as they learn more skills, so they can avoid getting hurt. Meanwhile, new students in the MMA class may grapple, but only slowly. As to religious activity, Britton shares that he begins and ends sessions by praying, asking beforehand if anyone has particular prayer requests they would like included. Trainers will also stop for counseling and individual prayer if during training someone quietly indicates a need for it; as Britton says, "you'd be surprised how many people, even during training, or during water breaks, may come over and say, 'Hey, man, I'm struggling with this, would you maybe have a prayer with me real fast.'" Similarly, although Victory is not itself a church, they do provide worship services and prayer sessions, and allow new local churches, or those in transition, to use their facility. They also train area pastors in boxing and MMA and will refer students to those ministers or other churches in the area, if the leaders at Victory think there might be a good fit between a particular church and an interested student. Sharing that he just put a student in touch with a pastor at a local congregation, Britton says, "You get them plugged in, and let God be God."[78]

Britton not only directs the gym programs and leads classes, but also speaks to groups outside of Victory. Using his notoriety as an MMA fighter, he preaches at high schools, colleges and church conferences as part of Victory's "Messengers of Victory" ministry. Coming from humble beginnings himself (his family lived in poverty, his mother was paralyzed for a while during his childhood, and his father abused alcohol, before reforming), Britton learned the hard way of the need for discipline in his life, as he notes he was often in trouble. Athletics gave him opportunities, and he traveled the world as a professional basketball player before taking up boxing and MMA.[79] Now, at six-foot-four-inches, he is the world's tallest 135-pound professional fighter. He speaks to audiences of the need for Christians to sacrifice, and of God's word and love. Admitting that he is often asked about the compatibility of being a youth minister, preacher and martial arts fighter, he says, "I don't look at BJJ and MMA as violence, I look at it as a sport." That and the controlled, cautious approach he teaches at the Victory complex are how he responds to concerns with doing violence to the human body in his training ministry. He also observes with irony (recalling the above discussion of sports ethics) that he more often became

4. Case Studies of Fight Sports Ministries

injured playing professional basketball than he does now as an MMA fighter.

As to his role as a professional in the MMA world and how this affects how he ministers and preaches on behalf of Victory, he says:

> We just want to be a blessing to people. We're blessed and we can bless people. And we want to be a light in a dark world. MMA is a very dark world, and we're called to be a light. We're made different, not to fit in. That's one of my prayers: I don't want to be a regular MMA fighter. I want people to say, "Man, something is different about you"—not just my fighting, "something is different about you."[80]

Thus, reminiscent of remarks made by some Christian ethicists reviewed, Britton sees the role of the Christian athlete as one who is known for taking a different approach to sports—one that reflects Christian values.

Another urban ministry (already introduced above) which likewise caters to adults is the Rock Church's Trinity MMA program. As to its goals, the emphasis in training is on learning strikes, moving, and stimulating the brain, with a focus on safety. Thus, Trinity MMA's approach emphasizes fitness, self-defense and recreation, without competition. As the leader, Andrew Truong says the approach of the class is not to take things too seriously—the emphasis is on having fun. Here again (as with several programs discussed above), we find a ministry in tune with theologies of play. As to religious activity, Truong says he begins and ends sessions by praying, asking for prayer requests from participants, and often shares a verse from the Bible while the students are stretching: "something that gives a connection between the Bible and martial arts," he says, adding that when one trains in fight sports, "it requires focus and [pushing] yourself. [...] It's all about digging in deep and giving it all you've got." Thus invoking character building and the striving for excellence, he concludes by saying that after the Bible reading, he will offer a devotion, explaining what the verse means to him, before the class moves on to drills.[81] Meanwhile, the other Rock ministry introduced earlier, the karate program geared towards both kids and adults, likewise involves religious activity, although it adds training for competitive tournaments to the fitness, self-defense and recreational focus of its sister program. Michael Birch, the leader, says the class always starts and ends with prayer, and that he specifically has the kids lead the prayers, so they learn to "grow with that." Further relating to character training, and invoking something of the warrior archetype, Birch notes that he shares religious commentary throughout the class. So, for example, when the students stand in line, he relates this to how one must stand "in the Lord," to "put on armor, how we're righteous in him, how we represent truth." In this way, Birch adds, religious reference is "woven into everything I do" in the karate ministry.[82]

Andrew Truong, instructor for the Rock Church's Trinity Mixed Martial Arts program near San Diego, California, uses an approach that emphasizes fun and finding connections between Christianity and martial arts.

While some of the character training in these ministries is somewhat informal, there are programs that take a more formal approach to this aspect of training, and more systematically involve character development. Thus, Steve Wilson, chief instructor of Christian Karate, notes that his program teaches students a "character quality of the month," with a definition and Bible verse attached to it. Students are expected to know these character qualities, as much as they are expected to know the karate techniques they study. For example, students might learn about "determination" (the antithesis, they teach, of "faintheartedness") and that this means "purposing to accomplish God's Will in God's time regardless of the opposition"; supporting this is a quote from II Timothy 4:7, "I have fought the good fight, I have finished the race, and I have remained faithful."[83] Additionally, the classes begin and end with prayer.

Regarding another religious commitment, Wilson notes that, as martial arts are receiving lots of cultural attention these days with growing exposure in the media, more and more new students are drawn to participate in the various congregational programs in his ministry. Thus, both evangelism and the principles of discipleship are among the religious activities associated with this fight sports ministry. Overall, the aim of Christian Karate, according to Wilson, is to "get people interested, and then lead them to the Lord and help them to grow in their spiritual walks." Through evangelism and instruction in character and discipleship, the ministry thus involves a "twofold process." This is all accomplished, Wilson says, while teaching "real deal" martial arts, including everything from fitness and teaching self-defense, to preparing students for karate competitions.[84]

Like this one, other suburban or rural fight sport ministries involve similar activities used by their urban counterparts, without the focus on reaching "at-risk" youth. Nonetheless, they do promote similar principles, using martial arts as a means to teach discipline and a commitment to self-improvement. For example, Trinity Martial Arts Club of Praise Lutheran Church in Fort Wayne, Indiana, and the Concord Karate Club of Concordia Lutheran Church in Fort Wayne, both started and led by Pastor J. Brown (the first begun in 2008, the second in 2012), involve similar purposes. Teaching karate to all ages, in two groups (one kindergarten through 2nd grade, and another 3rd grade through adults), these classes involve everything from fitness to self-defense and preparation for competitions and tournaments. They also emphasize character building, such as developing self-control and discipline.[85] Brown shares that the programs have made clear differences in students' lives, helping them to better focus and achieve success, such as at schoolwork. His approach includes Bible study, prayer, devotions and scripture memorization, to complement the physical training with spiritual and personal growth. Inasmuch as these ministries have proven themselves as a draw to people who might not otherwise have come to church, the programs also involve evangelism. Brown observes that the clubs provide a "ministry of reaching people that maybe the normal church would not." He thereby adds outreach to the ministries' other purposes.[86]

The Rev. J. Brown, the founder of various church-based karate and martial arts programs, which have included Bible study, prayer, and devotions, alongside training.

Finally, we look at the aims of two other church programs already mentioned, beginning with the karate club at St. Paul's Lutheran Church in Pennsylvania, led by Pastor Richards. This is likewise an outreach ministry, drawing people from the surrounding community for free lessons. The program caters to young and old, men and women alike, and Richards shares that the club has brought new members to the church; further, even though not all newcomers to the class join the congregation, the program still provides opportunities to minister to participants, as Richards explains:

> It's a great outreach program. We find that it's a great opportunity for ministry, even among unchurched people. Being a pastor, they'll bring their concerns to me, and we try to work with them, support them, with counseling and things like that. And it gives them a taste of the church that they may not be getting on a normal basis. The church is a place where they can come if they have problems. I take off the belt and put on the collar and do the best I can to help them.[87]

The fact that the program is run by a minister is the only real religious focus of the classes; although Richards does occasionally reference the Bible, this is not a part of the regimen, nor is prayer. The involvement of religion is solely provided by the building in which the classes are held, a church, and the vocation of the instructor, a pastor.

What St. Paul's program does provide is opportunity for character

4. Case Studies of Fight Sports Ministries

development. Thus, the students learn a five-point code: loyalty to your master; respect for parents and elders; honor friendships; no retreat in battle (that is, do your best at all times), and; in fighting, choose a sense of honor. Noting that this code dates back millennia, Richards also observes that it happens to parallel, in many ways, the Ten Commandments. The overall goal of the training, Richards says, is to make students more confident and help them become good citizens. In the program's promotion of personal achievement, Richards adds that he sees people's whole attitude change—that students develop a commitment to excellence and set high standards for themselves no matter what they do, as they are encouraged to do in their training. With its emphasis on controlled contact, the program strives to keep its participants healthy, as it teaches students to have a "sound body, mind and spirit," while also teaching them self-defense techniques and preparing interested students for tournaments.[88]

In contrast, the program at Trinity Lutheran in North Carolina, headed by Pastor Lanning, does not prepare students for competitions, but does focus on fitness, self-defense and a "martial arts lifestyle"; this means the aim of the program is to train one's mind, body and spirit, which Lanning explains involves Eastern concepts more than religious practices, and is thus compatible with the Christian faith. In this way, the emphasis is on "techniques of the human body and how to use them for self-defense,"[89] as well as helping students achieve "focus, respect, discipline, confidence."[90] Inviting people of all ages, both men and women, the program, while including church members, also draws people from the community. Started in 2011, the class now averages 15 participants at a time, with as many as 25 involved overall. While Lanning does occasionally pray in class, "especially at times of need," the overall approach is otherwise traditional martial arts instruction. Even so, Lanning sees the martial arts ministry as an outreach program.

In fact, Lanning neatly addresses a number of issues related to church fight sports ministries by offering the following remarks about his program: "I think it is outreach. It's something that is a kind of a unique blend of gifts that I've been fortunate enough to be given, and I see it as an extension of my own ministry. [As to the] principles that are involved, I really see that as work on stewardship of the human body...." Regarding the non-competitive nature of the program, he observes that competition is not always a good thing, nor is it necessarily something he prefers to promote, adding that it is his wish for his students to develop their own skills at their own pace, and that the focus of his class is on recognizing individual achievement.[91] Thus nicely and succinctly addressing a number of theological and ethical matters related to his practice, Lanning's remarks provide an apt conclusion to the discussion of actual fight sports ministries.

Media Distortions of Fight Sports Ministries Practice

For all the challenges fight sports ministry leaders face in designing their programs, discussions with them reveal a keen awareness of the ethical concerns outlined in the previous chapter, and an admirable effort to respond to these on their own. On the whole, these leaders conscientiously avoid injurious-level sparring or grappling in favor of training for fitness, self-defense, and recreational play. Concern for the well-being of the body, in terms explicitly related to caring for God's creation, is everywhere apparent, as is an admonition to avoid violence whenever possible and restrict physical altercations for self-defense to the minimum, even to disengage and retreat if necessary to avoid escalation. That several ministries specifically welcome a playful attitude, by design or in practice, is encouraging as a mindful response to theologies of play. Most programs involve character development as a goal, true to the history of fight sports ministries. Finally, most involve biblical foundations in one way or another, either in the use of biblical references during training, or in the leader's articulation of the relationship of fight sports to Christian foundations.

Where these ministries differ from those receiving more high-profile media attention is in their lack of defending or even glorifying violence, and their understanding of the role of fight sports in relation to gender issues and the church. Whereas matters of gender are a nonissue for those ministries contributing to this study, they are a factor for many fight sports ministries receiving national attention, either in making these ministries part of an effort to reclaim a masculine identity for a "feminized" church and reach out to men via sports ministries, or by undergirding a theologically-based essentialist understanding of gender. This is true of some of the MMA programs covered in the documentary *Fight Church*, as it is of more sensational ministries and church leaders receiving national exposure. To be sure, media covering these ministries may exaggerate sensational aspects of these programs for their own needs, and yet those aspects of these ministries lending themselves to such portrayal may be what led the media to examine these programs in the first place.

For example, ABC News broadcast a story about fight sports ministries and the controversies surrounding them, opening with the following "lead in" by the reporter: "A controversial trend is taking hold in a place in America you might least expect: church. Christian ministers with a passion for fighting are bringing the brutal sport of mixed martial arts to their congregations. They believe there is a time to pray and a time to strike your fellow believer square in the mouth."[92] The segment features the Reverend Hocker, seen in the *Fight Church* film, who is proudly caught on camera smiling and declaring, "my nickname is the Pastor of Disaster," as the segment juxtaposes images of him in church with those of him in a fight cage. It contextualizes him as "one of a growing number of pastors who believe the brutal sport of mixed martial arts has a place not only in the cage but in the church."[93] The segment includes lots of footage from *Fight Church*, adding freshly produced interviews with those appearing in the documentary, and involves mostly support from those interviewed for the phenomenon, with some against. Bearing the title "Prayers for Punches," the national news piece (perhaps even unfairly exaggerating some aspects of the program) focused only on sensational depictions of a fight sports ministry.

Similarly, the *New York Times* covered several ministries and their founders included in *Fight Church*, as well as other nationally prominent evangelical leaders, to highlight the selective focus of some fight sports ministries on the very matters addressed above—defending or glorifying violence, and relating fight sports ministries to gender issues. An article titled "Flock Is Now a Fight Team in Some Ministries" (prominently appearing on the front page of the *New York Times*[94]) includes interviews with John Renken of Xtreme Ministries near Nashville, and Paul Burress of Victory Baptist Church's MMA program (both of whom appear in *Fight Church*), as well as Washington-based Brandon "Fight Pastor" Beals of Canyon Creek's Fight Church ministry; it also includes Ryan Dobson, pastor and son of James C. Dobson, the founder of the conservative evangelical organization Focus on the Family. The article presents in contrast a pastor's prayer raised just before a cage fight, that he and his fighters represent the Lord well, with his subsequent call for one of his fighters to throw hard punches to an opponent's head to finish the fight. It includes another pastor observing that Jesus was a "fighter," and presents the fight sports ministry as part of a broader effort to combat a feminized church. It also quotes another pastor who provides a defense of the church's need to provide ministries that draw more men, and to do so in ways that support traditional masculinity. Dobson shares his own criticism of the church, saying, "We've raised a generation of little boys."[95] While the article devotes a few paragraphs to critics who are concerned with the use of MMA in the church, its focus on fight sports ministries with more sensational aims, perhaps, than those discussed above elevates these in the public's mind, at the expense of more moderate ministries.

Likewise, a *New York Times Magazine* article titled "Who Would Jesus Smack Down?" focuses on a prominent, some would say controversial evangelical pastor, Mark Driscoll, who has been publicly supportive of MMA and the UFC. Driscoll led Mars Hill Church in Seattle, a megachurch ministry (now dissolved), from which Driscoll—who has been known by some critics as "the cussing pastor"—proclaimed messages filled with, according to the article, "hellfire theology and the insistence that women submit to their husbands."[96] (Driscoll has since become pastor at The Trinity Church in Scottsdale, Arizona, which he helped found in 2016.) Boasting the "coolest style and foulest mouth of any preacher you've ever seen,"[97] according to the *New York Times Magazine* profile, Driscoll once wrote on his blog (an event itself covered by the media) in defense of combat sports' compatibility with Christianity, criticizing those whose "picture of Jesus is basically a guy in a dress with fabulous hair, drinking decaf and in touch with his feelings, who would never hurt anybody," in favor of his image of Jesus as a short-haired man who "was in good shape from a labor job and lots of walking across rugged terrain, and upon his return will come again not in humility but rather in glory."[98] In a documentary titled *Fighting Politics*, Driscoll appears, saying that "as a Pastor and a Bible teacher, I think God made men masculine"; that "men are made for combat, men are made for conflict, men are made for dominion"; and that men will either fight in inappropriate ways or do so in a legitimate sport like MMA, where he says society may "let men be men and do what men do" to "see which man is better," and "let the other fat, lazy men sit around and criticize them while watching."[99] The *Times* article references Driscoll's concerns with a feminized church, and notes his "hypermasculinity" and intolerance of dissent from followers (which reportedly led, in part, to his later departure from Mars Hill), quoting Driscoll as saying he appreciated the advice of one congregant, a UFC fighter, to control one's critics by threatening to break their nose.[100]

Print articles like these, and a host of reviews of the film *Fight Church*, together with the film itself, may promulgate a certain public impression of fight sports ministries, obscuring others. Indeed, one reflection on the phenomenon of "Christians and Cage Fighting" appearing in *Religion Dispatches* directly compares the approach to fight sports documented in *Fight Church* with the style and message of Driscoll, as it states, "In the brutality within the cage and online, *Fight Church* and Driscoll enact what it means to be 'authentic' men—pre-emptively on the attack and cynical in their assessment of opponents as they wage violence against them."[101] Similarly, the prominence of professional MMA fighters who proclaim their Christian faith and say they fight for God's glory, several of whom appear in *Fight Church*, provide one particular image of fight sports and the church, as do the earlier mentioned historic boxers who proclaimed their Christian identity. Some of this may be media exaggeration for sensationalism, while some of it may indeed reflect what some might see as sensational approaches to the relationship of fight sports and the church. Nonetheless, they reflect a particular depiction of fight sports ministers and their advocates.

4. Case Studies of Fight Sports Ministries   145

Lost in this may be the approach to faith and fight sports of more workaday ministries, with different emphases, aims and methods. Most do not glorify violence for the sake of Christian witness or evangelism. Most focus on fitness, self-defense or recreational uses of fight sports, while those that focus on competition are typically geared towards controlled, well-refereed amateur bouts. Several specifically say they strive to teach their fighters humility. Most include women and men among their participants with no articulated concern with drawing one gender or the other, or of using fight sports ministries to reclaim a feminized church. Of course, the presence of women in training does not necessarily mean that by employing boxing and martial arts as church-sponsored activities they are nonetheless still efforts to re-masculinize the church. Even so, none of those interviewed about their ministries conceived of their program as a way to counter ecclesiastic feminization. Several programs, in their focus on at-risk youth in troubled inner city areas, may have originally been geared towards men, yet this was because men were more often than women incarcerated, or more likely to get in trouble with law enforcement; yet even some of these ministries later expanded to include women, and many have since their beginnings invited both men and women to participate—again, with an explicit notation that their approach is unconcerned with gender issues in the church.

Indeed, the outreach ministries which are designed to help urban youth most often receive local media coverage, as opposed to national, and if in national media are more likely covered on public broadcasting outlets.[102] One example of this is the PBS piece about the boxing ministry in Baltimore, previously mentioned. Another example of programs receiving local coverage is Omaha's Victory Boxing Club, which has been covered several times in the local *Omaha World-Herald*, and on Nebraska's public broadcasting station, NET.[103] This is even so of rural and suburban fight sports ministry programs, which are also more likely to receive local rather than national media coverage.[104] As discussed, the approach, focus and goals of these programs often differs not only from contemporaneous programs receiving more prominent media attention (at least in the way the media covers these), but also from that of fight sports ministries of history. Whereas programs of the past catered only to boys and young men, seeking to provide ministries to attract men to the church, and sought both to combat with more "manly" activities what leaders perceived as a feminized church, many of the programs of today are unconcerned with these issues. To be sure, there are those programs that are so focused, and the prominence of popular men's ministries advocates that focus on the warrior archetype support the ethos underlying these ministries; however, the attention afforded to more sensational portrayals of fight sports programs and their proponents obscures other, differently focused approaches to fight sports and the church by many ministries. It is to the matter of how these various approaches to fight sports and the church relate to broader issues of theology and discipleship that we finally turn our attention.

Conclusion

Fight sports and the church might at first seem an odd combination, even discordant; yet on closer examination we have found they share substantial bonds. They share a considerable history, traced back to the age of muscular Christianity, since when they have found both institutional practice, such as in YMCA and CYO programs, and intellectual and rhetorical support from church leaders ranging from Thomas Hughes and Billy Sunday to modern day pastors. Even in debates about their compatibility, from the beginnings of commercial boxing in the United States to efforts to legalize professional MMA in the modern age, the two have been bound in church discussions. They likewise share a cultural history that reflects upon the relation of fight sports and the church, from their role in theoretical debates about gendered ecclesiology and efforts to "re-masculinize" a "feminized" church, to popular religious books about men's ministries and evangelizing men, which often appeal to their audience by employing the warrior archetype and the rhetoric and imagery of fighters and fighting. Even film and television programs, while using the juxtaposition of fight sports and the church to present sensational images or presenting church leaders as "fighters" for their faith and beliefs to balance their pursuit of peace, have regularly depicted the two in relationship.

In reviewing Christian ethics, we find substantial reflection on the compatibility of fight sports with Christian ideals, and reasonable concerns balanced by sensible supports, particularly when considering ethical responses to the range of goals pursued in fight sports ministries: for fitness, self-defense, recreation, and competition. While involvement with or viewership of professional fighting has its own particular ethical considerations, the issues raised in local ministries or amateur boxing, martial arts, or mixed martial arts programs differ considerably from these. Many fight sports ministry programs do considerable good, with outreach to those likely to respond favorably to such programs, and who report benefitting greatly from them. From urban outreach ministries aimed at at-risk youth, to those in suburbs and rural areas geared towards congregations and their communities, the range of practices includes demonstrably ethical, respectable, faith-based approaches to fight sports ministry programs. The modern practice of boxing and martial arts ministries, documented in statistics, media coverage and case studies, demonstrates not only a remarkable practice of fight sports in church ministries, but typically also a studied, thoughtful response to their relationship with Christian ideals and their role in relation to the church's mission. How these fight sports ministries relate to the overall message of the church and to broader Christian values and ideals is a matter that invites explicitly theological reflection. It is to this matter that we finally turn.

At the outset, it is helpful to note that theological deliberation requires reference to theological terms and concepts, such as faith, discipleship, grace and (in the Christian context) a discussion of the life and purpose of Christ. The current chapter will differ somewhat from those that have preceded it, therefore, in its use of terminology and style of reflection, but this is necessary for a full consideration on the relationship of fight sports and the church. Among the matters appropriate for theological engagement are: the place of boxing and martial arts in the life of the church and believers; how this aspect of one's life or ministry relates to one's life of faith and style of discipleship; and how one's manner of pursuing fight sports or fight sports ministry may be informed by broader theological discussions, such as those that contrast a life lived for glory versus that of sacrifice and grace. Thus, we will review these matters, discussing relevant theological concepts and theologians as these apply. Ultimately, while outlining various approaches for contrast, I will argue for one as more fitting for a Christian tradition and consider how this approach relates to the practice of fight sports and fight sports ministries already introduced. While developing its own perspective and acknowledging others, thus proceeding in a manner that is explicitly open to dialogue, the conclusion will nonetheless present a case for a theological approach in keeping with many of the ministries discussed, particularly those that are less well-covered in the national media spotlight.

Fight Sports as Adiaphora

One helpful place to begin a reflection of fight sports ministries in relation to the church is to consider the general role of sports themselves, and hence by extension ministries that involve them, in the life of believers, and which theological concepts pertain to this reflection. Many would say, applying a notion derived from Protestant theology, that these ministries are best considered "adiaphora"—that is, among the "indifferent things," which are neither required nor condemned. As that which is neither necessary nor prohibited, the place of these "indifferent things" in a believer's life is generally acceptable, so long as they are not raised in practice or perception to the level of the essential, and do not otherwise conflict with Christian values and strictures. The concept, in part, has historically been applied to suggest that Christians are free to enjoy everyday pleasures, such as sports, so long as these are not given to abuses.[1] Among the possible abuses, discussed in the introduction, are those outlined by Price. Thus, if sports "supplant" religion by raising such activity to the level of devotedness one should reserve for religion; or, if one sees an athletic victory as a reflection of God's favor, and thus "co-opts" sports to purportedly express religious authority; or, if those involved with sports "conscript" the values associated with sports in a manner that allows those values to take precedence over those of one's faith; these would be reasons to be concerned with such uses of fight sports or their associated ministries, as not in keeping with broader Christian values. If such engagements with fight sports and their associated ministries do not raise these objections, then, as adiaphora, believers are free to pursue these activities in the context of a faithful life.

This point raises ethical and theological issues. While sports, particularly as involved in ministries, can be a gratifying part of Christian life, concerns arise if these run afoul of ethical guidelines, or otherwise challenge God's intent for humanity. This, in part, is why boxing and martial arts ministries, or any Christian athletics program, should be practiced with a consideration as to how these ministries relate to ethics and theology. Already considered are many ethical guidelines, discussed in their own right in Chapter 3, and explored in terms of how actual fight sports ministries respond to them in Chapter 4. While abuses may occur, one should note that pathways to appropriate engagements in fight sports ministries certainly exist. These pathways lead to programs that befit Price's category of sports "commingling" with religion, wherein attention is paid to balancing faith and sport in a manner that comports with the notion of adiaphora. As that which is neither required nor condemned, so long as programs respond faithfully to ethical and theological concerns, many of these ministries might actually be commended for the considerable good they do. In their successful outreach to city youth; in their mission to help maintain healthful bodies (the "temples") and minds; in their emphasis on building constructive, Christian character traits ("formation"); in their providing an opportunity for fellowship and play; and in their evangelical capacity to bring people to the church; in these and other ways, fight sports ministries, as adiaphora, may be appreciated and accepted.

Should such programs or their advocates be given to misuses, however, these should be identified and subject to correction, with the goal of reformation in mind. To use religious language, if such ministries pursue an idolatrous goal, one apart from the heart of Christianity, such as by presenting as *essential* things that are adiaphora, problems arise. Depending on one's viewpoint, one might find such idolatry in some practices of fight sports in ministry. As we have seen in the history of fight sports ministries and cultural appropriations therefore, one tendency in the association of fight sports and the church has been to use such programs to bolster a perceived "masculine" identity for the church and its leaders or members, often presenting that identity as fundamental to the church's proper fulfillment of its mission. The model of God in Christ presented is therefore singularly in keeping with that of Sunday's "scrapper" Christ, or Hughes' and others' encouraging modern-day adherents of the faith to perceive as *essential* a vision of the church that reflects this character. Boxing and martial arts ministries have been part of some churches' commitment to advancing this notion, one that Price would call a conscripting of religion by sports, to advance their own agenda. In response, some might respond in keeping with the concept of adiaphora that to idolize a particularly gendered identity for the church, masculine or otherwise, or even (harkening back to Gelfer's and Pyle's point) one particular way of being masculine for Christian men may impose unnecessary strictures on Christian identity; if these are tied to fight sports programs as a means of imposing a strictly gendered experience of the church where such an experience should not be understood essential, this may result in an abuse of such programs.

Similarly, to focus more on one's identity as a fighter above one's commitment to Christianity is likewise problematic, as overplaying the importance of engagement in fight sports or any other nonessential activity risks idolizing it. Given a review of the priorities and behavior of some Christians engaged in fight sports, this too is a concern worth addressing. In this vein, the pursuit of glory in the ring or octagon, particularly if it is sought as evidence of God's favor, is problematic—or at least it would be to many, when considered from particular theological points of view. From the perspective of prosperity theology, worldly success in the form of riches or victories granted to the faithful in keeping with their measure of faith may manifest in fight sports (as in other places) as evidence of God's favor. A fighter's victories are thereby interpreted as reflecting God's approval, here in the form of one's dominance over another. A critical theological response to this might be that such a stance may lead to an overly-focused pursuit of winning, as opposed to virtue.[2] While seeking excellence in one's performance is admirable, if this pursuit becomes cultic and even idolatrous, it is (according to one line of critical theological thought) no longer theologically sound, for while *success* may at times intersect with *excellence*, the two are not necessarily synonymous.[3] Fight sports ministries that encourage excellence and a mutual striving are, in this line of argument, theologically healthier than those that overemphasize success in the form of winning and dominance, particularly as this may intersect with the pursuit of glory. These then would need correction and reformation. Alas, most of the ministries detailed herein do, indeed, explicitly emphasize excellence, a mutual striving, and a commitment to virtue rather than the quest for triumph and glory. They do so just as they practice fight sports ministries without the historic emphasis on how these facilitate gendered ecclesiology and muscular Christianity, and instead offer fight sports ministries as mechanisms of grace, to reach out to those in need of direction or fellowship.

To be sure, these matters are given to debate, historically as in the present age. For example, one Christian who seeks corrections to what he sees as misappropriated priorities involving fight sports and the church is Pastor Brad Williams, who has addressed an open letter to Pastor Mark Driscoll, in an article titled "Dear Driscoll, MMA is Not a Measure of Manhood—Jesus Is."[4] Therein, Williams addresses misplaced priorities against which, he says, Driscoll encourages Christian men to judge themselves. Reviewing Driscoll's earlier quoted assertions (in the previous chapter), and responding to them in their relation to fighting and professional MMA, Williams writes:

> Driscoll claims that men were made for combat, that men will fight to establish dominance, and that getting in touch with your inner feelings and finger painting are sort of unmanly. This bugs me, not only because I think I might enjoy finger painting, but because the behaviors he lists have nothing to do with manhood. Further, he ties this alpha male assertion to Jesus' character, which he also does in his latest UFC apologetic.[5]

Williams' concern is with presenting as essential a single image of Christ against which to judge Christian men's behavior and values, by suggesting there is one way to be "manly" and Christian, and that it involves a willingness to fight and achieve glory. Indeed, this is a point to which we will return later, in considering various models of Christ that may be adapted in Christian or ecclesiastic contexts—those of the warrior or knight, versus that of the shepherd. Williams further quotes Driscoll's observation that when Christ returns He "will come again not in humility but rather in glory," to which Williams responds by noting what he sees as a false dichotomy: that Christ's glory "is not in opposition to his humility"[6] (a point we will explore ahead, shortly). Thus, by focusing on one particular characterization of Christ and upholding it as an ideal to pursue, Williams suggests Driscoll creates an idol, based upon a one-sided or (as Williams sees it) misconstrued image of Christ. Observing Christ's compassion for the weak and his willingness to "endure the cross to save us," Williams chides Driscoll's "view of Jesus as a chest-thumping alpha male," suggesting this does not help modern men understand true Christian values, identity and discipleship—a theological debate worthy of exploration.

What is more, Williams criticizes Driscoll's defense of professional cage fighting in terms that reflect the earlier-shared discussion of Christian ethics and fight sports. Responding to Driscoll's claim that those who reject MMA do so because they either do not understand it or have a misguided notion of who Christ is and what He represents, Williams writes, "I don't reject MMA. I reject the UFC and the beating of a brother in Christ for money and glory or to establish my physical dominance over him."[7] Thus, a debate among modern church leaders emerges, centering on fight sports, gender, glorification, and the understanding of Christ's example, as a model to guide Christian behavior. While the previous discussion of ethics and practice notes that the varied goals of fight sports programs result in differing sets of ethical concerns, and recognizes a range of challenges and possibilities for Christians engaged in competition; and while the previous exploration of gendered ecclesiology and muscular Christianity covers these issues; Williams' discussion reveals additional theological points needing elucidation. These concern the relationship of fight sports to differing ideas of discipleship and theologies of glory.

Fight Sports and the Theology of Glory

Given comments made by some involved in boxing and martial arts about their reasons for pursuing fight sports, saying their fighting is to show God's glory, some reflection on theological matters concerning the seeking of glory, and in particular a glory claiming to reflect God's favor, is in order. To wit, among comments made by some Christians involved in boxing or martial arts, ministries or otherwise, as to why they participation in such sports are to: "bring glory to God"; "bring glory and honor to the Lord"; "glorify God through fighting"; "glorify the Lord with what He's given me"; "glorify Him and make Him known"; "glorify" God's name; and to fight so others will "see God's glory" in their fighting.[8] This manner of speech invites reflection on how it relates to theologies of glory, and how they contrast with other theologies. An important point to make at the outset of this discussion is that nothing herein should suggest a concern with the pursuit of excellence and achieving one's personal best. As the earlier discussion of ethics makes clear, a striving together for excellence, especially, where sports are concerned, in an atmosphere of play, is good. To claim, however, that personal victory over another shows God's favor, or the dominance reflects God's own glory in one's works, is, to those of many theological traditions, irreverent and heterodox. In part, this particular type of "glory talk" is an application of the prosperity gospel that suggests that God offers worldly favor to faithful followers in the form of personal wealth or success, often in measure with one's faithfulness. Those critical of this perspective would suggest that one need only look at the life of Christ and his lack of such "success," measured in worldly standards, to find the prime example of how this manner of assessing favor and the rewards of faithfulness is misappropriated.

To be sure, there are those faith traditions that find merit in the prosperity gospel. Those fighters and ministries that follow this theology may well receive media attention for the very worldly values they exemplify, in a manner that sensationalizes their theological emphases. Others may find the focus on personal victory as a means of reflecting God's favor and glory to be profane and self-centered.[9] As one author writing about Christian involvement in sports suggests, such an approach rests on an understanding of sports in relation to faith that is "triumphalist and self-referential." This writer further notes that a singular focus on achieving successes in sports fails to perceive that opportunities to glorify God may come in moments of failure.[10] In fact, based upon insights by Augustine and others, some theologians reflecting on athletic successes in relation to faith suggest that this priority by some athletes on what amounts to an excessive focus on the self lies at the heart of humanity's fallenness, that "the pattern of athletes invoking the deity every time they win [may be] just another illustration of the doctrine of original sin."[11] Those ministries focused on teaching participants to strive together to do their best, to pursue excellence in a spirit of play, and even to learn humility, pursue a different, some would say more firmly grounded theological approach. Similarly, those competitive fighters that do their best and accept victory without claiming it as evidence of God's favor or a reflection of God's glory would, in this light, avoid the problematic theological entanglements that some suggest result from these misplaced emphases. The glory celebrated, then, is in the opportunity graciously given by God to enjoy an activity involving play, fellowship and a shared striving, whatever the outcome, victory or not.

To understand fully the theology of glory, one may consider how it contrasts with the theology of the cross—an admittedly intricate matter that, nonetheless, merits some elucidation. Indeed, though the theology of the cross concerns mostly the manner by which God offers salvation through Christ and what it teaches about a Christian approach to the world, a discussion of it is useful in considering its contrasting theology, that focused on glory. The theology of the cross sheds light upon God's self-revelation—that people must acknowledge how God chose to be revealed and how God in Christ achieved salvation for all. Christ's very incarnation was an act of humility. The pinnacle of Christ's work on earth, on the cross, turns customary expectations of what God "should" be on their head, for instead of a powerful, dominant, regal figure, we instead find the "foolishness" (a term many theologians of the cross employ) of the cross, where God is actually revealed in an act of submission and humiliation, and a strength is revealed through weakness. The humiliation here is that leading to death on the cross, while the submission is to God's will. Human logic tends to want to ascribe power and glory to that which is godly, but in truth the revealed God is one who achieves salvation in an act of humility, by being brought low. It is this God, then, who on earth identifies with the weak and lowly, and then raises the lowly to victory in an act of divine love. Notably, this is a *divine* act, one based not upon human achievement, but on God's grace. The emphasis herein is on what God's does, apart from any human work or merit; and the focus is on humility, not seeking, or even reveling in, earthly glory. To again raise religious terminology, this theological perspective involves a unique covenant, where God fulfills both sides of the agreement, because human beings are incapable of achieving salvation by their own works, based upon merit. Thus, it is that this cross-focused theology contrasts, in this perspective, with that of the earthly glory-seeking. Its focus is on salvation, sacrifice and grace, in contrast with the latter's focus on self, achievement and grandeur.

From this perspective, it would be a problematic use of theology to justify using victory and dominance over another—in the ring, in the cage, or wherever—as a reflection of God's favor and glory. The theology of the cross teaches that God comes to humanity in the opposite aspect of what we might anticipate—that is, a God whose strength is revealed in weakness and humility. The agenda fulfilled is God's, not human beings'. The saving act is God's, not humans'. Thus, the theology of the cross reflects "God's judgment on human pride" and self-centeredness, for finding splendor in human acts as themselves a means of achieving or reflecting divine favor. The theological paradoxes here, that God reveals power in weakness and glory in lowliness, demonstrate that "the flip side of God's generosity is the painful exposure of human powerlessness and impotence, an experience that human beings want neither to admit nor endure."[12] Once again, showing strength of character, conviction and body are not herein to be considered bad—indeed, in appropriate measure and expression, they are good; but the show of conceit in such strengths as one achieves victory in competition, and the ascription of this to a reflection of God's glory, is another matter. To be sure, there are those theological traditions that find earthly glory to be a sign of divine favor, and there are surely fight sports ministries and professional fighters who ascribe to this view. In contrast, others take another approach—one that emphasizes values more at odds with customary worldly standards—and these, for this very contrast, deserve consideration and articulation.

Thus, fighters or ministry leaders may implicitly model for fans or participants behavior that, according to critics of the theology of glory, demonstrates a flawed understanding of how God works in the world. From this perspective, those that do taut such glory would face scrutiny for how their claims relate to these contrasting understandings (grace versus glory) of what God has revealed, and how God revealed it. The invocation of this sort of "glory talk" begs interrogation in the context of fight sports, in their relation to concepts in Christian theology and understandings of discipleship. The central concern is perhaps best expressed by a theologian of the cross, Gerhard O. Forde, who observes, "We adjust our doctrine of God to fit our glory projects."[13] Otherwise said, "Theologians of glory create a god in their own image and a picture of the human creature after their own longings."[14] Or, as Martin Luther writes, "Because men do not know the cross and hate it, they necessarily love the opposite, namely, wisdom, glory, power, and so on."[15] This leads to a delight in human works, even if one claims God is working "through" them to achieve earthly victory and glory, as it bestows adulation and leads one to "adore oneself as idol."[16] Said otherwise, "One who finds the cause of his joy in himself surely does not have the support of the word of God."[17] The claim that God works to bring others to faith through acts that achieve for God's followers earthly glory, and that this in some way reflects or reveals God's work in the world, belies the example of how God works as revealed in Christ.

This model may in some views contrast with the assumptions underlying the "Jesus didn't tap" approach to theology, espoused by some fighters and ministry leaders, and reflected in some MMA merchandise and online memes depicting Christ-as-fighter, reviewed herein. The "Jesus didn't tap" theology focuses on how Christ refused to "give up" (in martial arts terms, "tap out," or concede) in pursuit of a "victory," holding this up as a model for followers and fighters alike. If by this they mean that Christ went the distance and was willing to suffer to achieve a goal, without compromise, this may be fine. However, if by "Jesus didn't tap" some mean he did not surrender, others might respond that yes, he did. He may not have surrendered to Satan; yet, ultimately, Christ surrendered to God's will, to the cross, even to death.[18] Christ's example shows his followers that they too must surrender, spiritually; they too must face defeat, to die like him so they may be raised like him, unto victory. To hold up as a more suitable model pursuits of earthly glory as more responsive to Christ's example places the focus in the opposite place of where, according to some, Christ's example demonstrates it properly should be placed. Thus, in this theological vein, God glorifies by humbling. This is God's plan, revealed on the cross. God kills to bring to new life. If one's actions, speech, models or slogans suggest otherwise, particularly by conscripting theology to justify the pursuit of earthly glory as somehow evincing God's favor, in fight sports or elsewhere, then one's underlying theology may need reconsideration.

Hence, just as Christ surrendered ("tapped"), so too must Christians "tap," to God. Those suggesting that Jesus did not "tap out" likely mean he did not do so to Satan. Indeed, this is depicted in imagery on t-shirts and online memes, as previously discussed. This understanding may be true enough but might be supplemented with a recognition that the "tapping" that *was* involved was to God's will. "Tapping" is realizing human beings cannot save themselves and need God's mercy. That this surrender involves bringing one low and giving in ("tapping"), in order to be raised high ("glorified"), is a central point of this theology; hence, "it is not man who humbles himself—it is God who humbles him," for "God [instigates] man's humiliation, even if man himself must cooperate with God if this humiliation is to be properly effected."[19] This humility is by necessity a "tapping out" to God. Thus, as Luther says, "humility alone saves."[20] In being humbled—to God's will, by God's law, by the power of God's saving love—believers find a rightful relationship with God—not in acts that seek to achieve earthly glory.

In short, to claim that God draws followers by demonstrating favor through acts of earthly victory and glory, particularly through violent means, runs contrary, many would argue, to God's way as revealed in Christ. This theological perspective and its relation to fight sports may best be expressed in a short reflection on the theology of the cross articulated by Forde, who simply posits its implications in terms of "winners and losers," writing:

> Nobody loves a loser. There is hardly anything worse we can say of a person today than he or she is a loser, a real loser. We want winners. We worship winners. We want to be winners—often at any cost. Yet, by our standards, Jesus was a loser.[21]

This, Forde says, is something we must face to be true to God as revealed in Christ. By refusing to go the traditional route of the winner, that expected of a messiah, Jesus actually "wins" by losing—by refusing to adhere to earthly standards of what it means to achieve victory. Thus, "in a world of destructive, compulsive 'winners,'" Forde asks, "how else could he be victorious except by losing? How else could he get through to us?"[22] It is a statement about what Christ's example offers his followers as a model to follow that God raises this "loser" from the dead, vindicating Christ's approach in the world.

This is not to say that fight sports ministries, or fighters themselves, should encourage losing. The theology of the cross is about more spiritual matters than would easily fit into a reflection on sport or sports ministries. Its corollary, however, in the theology of glory does have something to say in this context. It concerns not an admonition to do one's best, to strive together for excellence, or to feel conflicted about a win, but those who would point to such victories as evidence of God's power and favor and a means by which to bring others into their faith. Thus, the correction it offers is to those who would suggest that a focus on pursuing earthly glory for its own sake is responsive to the model of Christ, as such is set for his followers, making the model of Christ on earth that of a "winner," as opposed to a servant. This is true enough for those who might accept prosperity theology or the theology of glory. The priorities underlying these theological approaches, however, find a counterpoint in the less-often-addressed theological approach outlined here, which provides at least an alternate, if not corrective, approach to the relation of theology to the practice of fight sports and fight sports ministries.

Fight Sports, Ministry and Discipleship

What is at stake in aligning theology with practice is the nature of discipleship understood. How one understands Christ and his message and actions influences how one acts as a Christian and how one represents the Christian message to others by one's example. This is certainly among the matters of concern for many fight sports ministry programs. Correlatively, how one acts presents one's understanding of Christ to the world. The differing approaches to boxing and martial arts ministries, as to the general practice of fight sports themselves, reflect varying understandings of Christ and discipleship. A reflection on the design of fight sports ministries and how leaders represent their conception of Christ is important for understanding the type of discipleship they present.

Christians' understanding of their own role in relation to the church, society and the world is based upon their understanding of the models of Christ presented to them, models that prescribe appropriate behavior. Various models are suggested in the Bible, sometimes in apparent contrast with each other, and scholars and theologians debate which are most appropriate or applicable to people pursuing various callings in the modern age, including in the arena of sports. One such discussion is offered Robert J. Higgs in his book *God in the Stadium: Sports and Religion in America* (1995). There, Higgs discusses the contrasting models of the knight and the shepherd for how they apply to modern sports, and which option, he argues, holds more merit. At one point explicitly discussing these in relation to the theologies of glory and the cross, Higgs' contrasts offer interesting parallels to these theological approaches. If the Christian knight (for all intents and purposes identical with the "warrior" model, discussed herein) is the guiding standard, Higgs contends, followers will be encouraged to seek wealth and status for themselves by means of victory over others. Their defining skills and values relative to this model are often used to dominate and conquer others, more so than to protect, Higgs suggests. Knights fight with knights representing competing interests, resulting in grand pursuits of plunder, spoils, victory and status. In contrast, Higgs presents the model of the shepherd as one whose focus is more "local and limited," befitting those who may protect others (the sheep), but do not otherwise seek status or recognition. The shepherd's intrinsic "meekness and kindness" focuses on the promotion of amity; any use of violence is done solely for the protection of others and the return to peacefulness, with no accumulation of earthly wealth or status sought. As Higgs writes, "Shepherds do not collect trophies."[23] Notably, this characterization comports with the approach suggested in the previous discussion of the ethics of fight sports training.

In fact, in elucidating the contrasts between these two models, Higgs' schematic calls to mind much of the preceding discussions, including the priorities of many of the fight sports ministry leaders interviewed in the previous chapter, and how these may contrast with those of ministries and fighters receiving national attention. How in keeping with these contrasts are those Higgs outlines in a side-by-side chart that juxtaposes the values of the shepherd, symbolized by the staff, with those of the knight or warrior, symbolized by the sword; these contrasts include a focus on "having fun" versus "keeping score," cooperation versus competition, ethics versus rules, wisdom versus winning, humanness versus "manliness," and grace versus glory.[24] Relating these contrasts explicitly to those of the theologies of the cross and glory, Higgs observes that the former (that of the shepherd and its attendant theology of the cross) gives one power to produce change, as opposed to the other (that of the knight or warrior, and the theology of glory) which leads to defining success by the accumulation of earthly riches. Higgs writes that, while pursuit of a life based upon the shepherd model may lead to what many, based upon worldly standards, might consider "wimpy" values, these are in fact more in keeping with true Christian discipleship, as he sees it; he suggests the need to present themselves as powerful in a worldly sense is why many people, particularly in the realms of "athletics, war or business," choose the knightly path and its associated values.[25] Higgs concludes:

> The allegiance of religion and sports in Christendom demonstrates a movement primarily towards the sword [the symbol of the knight, or warrior], so that what is conveyed even by the authority of the Cross is a sense that the shepherd world is inherently inferior, when in fact it is in many ways closer to what is most worthwhile in human life and belief.[26]

Presented in this light, Higgs' discussion suggests that disciples must choose which path they follow, or at least emphasize, in all aspects of their life—including those related to sports and sport ministries. Those virtues believers pursue, be those based upon the model of the shepherd or the knight, influence their style of discipleship, as does their selecting either the way of glory over the gracious implications of the cross. Higgs and others worry that modern culture is drifting ever more towards the ideals of the knight and away from that based upon their understanding of Christ's predominant example, that of the shepherd.

Thus, an integral theological point is at stake by means of the message sent by church-related boxing and marital arts ministries. If one seeks to bring attention to God through an act of human glory, such as in competitive fighting or training to dominate another, then some might say this misses the point of Christ's actions and example, revealed on the cross. (Forde's quote bears repeating here: "We adjust our doctrine of God to fit our glory projects.") Indeed, as one theologian remarks: although "when things and people dazzle and radiate energy, we are instinctively drawn to attention," still "God is a God who works through contraries," and it is for moments of human humility and weakness that God's grace is most perfectly suited.[27] Learning to be servile, to give of oneself, and even be willing to be humbled in the service of others—that is (to many) the message of the cross, and the rightful mission of churches and leaders focused on what the cross teaches of Christian discipleship.

To consider if one's approach appropriately reflects one's ideals, one needs to reflect upon priorities. If one's approach to a sports ministry is guided primarily by Christian ideals more than strictly secular ones, one should be able to articulate how one's approach reflects those ideals, and if one perceives it does not, to then use those ideals as a guide to right one's approach. St. Augustine is helpful in this regard, particularly (and perhaps surprisingly) in his conception of evil, as sports ethicist Mark Hamilton effectively outlines in his "An Augustinian Critique of our Relationship to Sport" (2011).[28] To Augustine, evil is not a thing, but a human choice—a valuing of something out of its proper proportion or as superior to something else which one should hold in higher regard. Often this manifests as a form of "distorted love," where one loves something out of proportion to something that *should* be more highly valued.[29] Thus, this approach involves morality. By carefully considering what we love and pursue more than other things we do not, we may assess whether our values and behavior are proper or evil.

As applied to sports, this approach may reveal if and when someone distorts their values and provide a means to set matters in better balance. Hence, as Hamilton observes, our love for sport becomes distorted through loving the lower things more than the higher. We love winning more than virtue so that there is an overemphasis on winning, thus distorting our affections resulting in evil. Winning matters but it should not matter disproportionately to things that must matter more. [...] Relating to sport in this distorted devoted manner affirms a reductionist view of humans, that we are only our bodies. As physical activities and love for sport overtake love for family, or friends, of God or even personal mental or moral development, sport becomes the primary passion of affection.[30]

Thus, as participants or observers, people may love winning, self, adulation, the thrill of competition, or even compulsive training, above things they should more highly value, such as virtue, fair play, fun, mutual striving, and fellowship. Given what many see as ideals of Christian discipleship and how the giving of oneself is something which should be highly valued, one begins to get a sense of what priorities and principles should guide this "proper balance" to strike in church fight sports ministry programs.

A boxing or martial arts ministry that provides for fellowship, fitness and outreach, while emphasizing opportunities to serve others (to say nothing of God) is a challenge, yet demonstrably possible. Such would be in keeping with many churches' stated mission and theology. To promote an approach to fight sport ministry that is focused on the pursuit of excellence and growth, instead of superiority; to encourage delight in both a participant's own and others' accomplishments; in self-defense focused ministries, to value ending an altercation at the earliest possible opportunity out of concern and love for all involved, even at the expense of pride; to develop the confidence and self-discipline that allows one to choose not to fight; to offer opportunities for involvement for all, regardless of gender, and provide constructive programs for those whose circumstances may find them at-risk and in need of positive reinforcement and community engagement; these may be the soundest approaches for boxing and martial arts ministries based upon such Christian values.

The emphasis and approach of fight sports ministries and their leaders, whatever these are, embody an understanding of discipleship. Many ministries incorporating fight sports are indeed led by those looking to serve others, as shown by those ministry leader interviews contained herein. What is more, the approach many of them take veritably emphasizes service, humility, and even self-sacrifice, whichever of the four program emphases a particular fight sports ministry offers. Those programs reviewed herein that are focused on fitness or recreational sparring do in fact model these values, are presented in the spirit of adiaphora, and are not construed as a means of reclaiming a gendered ecclesiology. Those that teach self-defense help their students learn how to do what is necessary to protect themselves and others, notably while also teaching that it is admirable to set aside pride if necessary to end a confrontation at the earliest possible opportunity. All programs reviewed provide significant opportunities for fellowship, formation, outreach and evangelism. Programs training for competition, as the discussion of ethics suggests, face the most challenges where Christian values and theology are concerned, and the leaders of such programs indicate they are aware of, and respond to these concerns. Programs geared toward competition that reward individual accomplishments, win or lose, limit harm that may come to participants' bodies and minds, and promote mutual striving for excellence are for many preferable, and more in keeping with what they see as reflecting a proper view of Christian discipleship.

That the approach and goals of Christian programs may be different from societal norms and those of secular programs is entirely appropriate. Christianity distinguishes its approach from the norm, and it should be no surprise then that Christian discipleship involves priorities other than those of the secular world. Should boxing and martial arts ministries not adhere to the norms of their non-Christian counterparts, in not emphasizing the pursuit of victory above all else (among other priorities), and even teaching love of all, even one's "opponent," then these may well be necessary ways in which such programs distinguish themselves. This is due to the church's and Christianity's particularity, how it expresses values that may at times differ from and even contrast with those of society at large. As biblical theologian Marcus Borg notes, discussing the concept of discipleship, being a disciple naturally leads one to "become part of the alternative community of Jesus," following a "road less travelled, [wherein] discipleship involves being in a community that remembers and celebrates Jesus," and expressing this "alternative" identity in its actions and values.[31]

Clearly there are secular programs that happen to follow many Christian ideals without being "Christian," as prior discussions of some secular programs attest, even as there are plenty that ascribe to more worldly values. Whatever the case, Christian approaches should strive to be unique not only in their approach and underlying philosophy, but also in their articulation of how that approach explicitly relates to Christian ideals and beliefs. In this way they may explicitly relate to a believer's life of faith and discipleship. Twentieth century theologian Karl Barth, in his classic *The Call to Discipleship*, addresses this matter well, writing:

> the obedience concretely demanded of, and to be achieved by, the disciple, always means that he must move out of conformity with what he hitherto regarded as the self-evident action and abstention of Lord Everyman and into the place allotted to him, so that he is inevitably isolated in relation to those around him, not being able or willing to do in this place that which is generally demanded by the gods who are still fully respected in the world around. At this particular place he is freed from the bonds of that which is generally done or not done, because and as he is bound now to Jesus.[32]

While Barth's subject involves matters of broader consequence than ancillary church ministries, fight sports or otherwise, his point is that a believer's discipleship should nonetheless be expressed to what extent possible in all aspects of life, and perhaps particularly in church programs. The fact that such programs might involve approaches different from the norm, approaches that make them distinct from, and possibly even at odds with many similar secular programs, is entirely fitting. The same is true of their distinction from other church programs more responsive to, as some would see it, the values of this world, such as those modeling the pursuit of glory, instead of the call to a more distinct discipleship. (Notably, Barth rejects the warrior archetype as an appropriate model for Christian discipleship.[33])

To be sure, there are fight sports ministries and fighters whose approach would be more in keeping with the model of the warrior/knight, the unambiguous pursuit of victory, and the theology of glory. Indeed, there are those who explicitly make the case for such approaches to sports, as for their underlying theologies. David Prince, in his aforementioned *In the Arena: The Promise of Sports for Christian Discipleship*, in fact, explicitly writes about the relationship of sports and discipleship in a manner supportive of these approaches. Finding a scriptural basis to perceive Christian discipleship in terms of warfare, even that sports are themselves a form thereof, he advocates not only for supporting the ideal of competition, but also the clear, unequivocal pursuit of victory.[34] Being prepared for spiritual warfare, as Prince emphasizes, means being disciplined, strong, well-trained, ready to persevere and fight evil temptations and sin. In this way, he writes, those attributes athletes use to train themselves to achieve their utmost skill level do bear metaphorical correlation to spiritually training to fight evil.[35] Notably, there may be limits to how to understand this metaphor, as shown in the previous discussion of St. Paul's arguably subversive use of athletic metaphors to contrast those victories sought in earthly competition with those more spiritual victories Christ's disciples should seek. One might do well to take caution, then, when mingling understandings of what it means to fight spiritually with what it means to compete against opponents in sports. To treat victory against evil as the same as one achieved against a competitor risks turning athletic victory into an idol, and further, one that focuses on gaining stature in the world for oneself, in triumphalist fashion. Indeed, Prince notes such concerns, recognizing that a problem arises for some competitors when they "simply attempt to use Jesus for athletic empowerment and success."[36]

It is worth highlighting a paradox previously introduced: that the warrior model is not without biblical witness, even as that of the shepherd appears alongside it, in seeming contrast. Crossan's reflection on this contrast (addressed in Chapter 3) presents a possible resolution, suggesting a difference in the biblical accounts between the historical Jesus and that of the writers who may have imposed prevailing cultural values onto some of their depictions of Christ, thus explaining the apparent dichotomy. Reflecting a similar contrast, St. Paul's use of athletic imagery, as previously discussed, could be perceived as rather subversive, using the "athletic ideal" to reject elitism, and suggest that those who aspire to be disciples should "reject earthly glory," and instead seek a glorious reward as that is found in heaven, while on earth "running the course marked out by the shameful cross."[37] Whatever one's assessment of these issues, what is little in dispute is that one's perceived model of Christ directly influences one's understanding of discipleship and how one approaches all aspects of life.

Fight sports ministries do differ in their underlying models and theologies, and hence advocate, implicitly or explicitly, different styles of discipleship. Perhaps particularly because contemporary culture seems more readily drawn towards the model of the warrior and its attendant theology of glory, that of the shepherd deserves the special attention and consideration afforded above. Indeed, not all ministries pursue the first approach, and for the sake of those fitting the latter an explanation of this model and theology in its relation to fight sports ministries holds merit. The image of a fearless warrior fighting on behalf of the people is laudable, as is that of the shepherd who "lays down his life" for his sheep, in loving sacrifice. Some fight sports ministries and fighters may adopt the warrior model. Others seem more drawn to an approach which contrasts with this more glory-seeking model and emphasizes more that of the shepherding. My own argument finds more authenticity in emphasizing that of the shepherd, along with its attendant emphasis on cooperation over competition, and grace over glory. This emphasis seems to aptly fit many of the fight sports ministry programs featured herein in interviews, and so deserves this detailed consideration. At any rate, leaders and participants should be aware of the differing models and theologies, and their attendant implications.

Perhaps there is something of a paradox to be accepted in considering these models. Martin Luther said of preachers that they "ought to be both warrior and shepherd,"[38] apparently finding value in accepting the paradoxical tension between these models. As we have seen, popular culture's image of church leaders involved in fight sports or fight sports ministries, from those of movies television and literature, regularly portrays such figures as resolving this paradox, presenting these figures as reluctant fighters, whose willingness to fight balances their love of peace. While the historic muscular Christianity movement, as well as popular Christ-as-fighter memes, and national media attention on Christians and fight sports may focus on those that wholeheartedly accept the warrior model, a preponderance of modern practice in fight sports and the church, based upon case studies, seems perhaps open to this balanced understanding. Indeed, some fight sports practitioners may adopt a model of discipleship without a methodical awareness of the range of issues involved, from the ethical to the theological, and hence lack a studied awareness of how theology informs practice and vice versa. Selecting from among models of discipleship may be given to discernment; others matters, such as raising engagement with sports to the level of religious devotion, interpreting victories as signs of God's favor, or treating sport as an essential component of a faithful life (abuses befitting Price's categories of sports supplanting or co-opting religion) are less so. However one responds to the matters outlined above, participants and observers benefit from an explicit awareness of how theology and practice relate.

Harkening comprehensively back to Price's taxonomy of the relation of sports with religion, we see that, yes, when one "co-opts" religion to assert that an athletic victory reflects God's favor and evinces God's glory in that feat, one risks confusing our shared fallen state on earth, and even idolizing triumph and individual achievement. Consideration of the theology of glory, various models of discipleship, and Christian reflections on ethics that emphasize good conduct, mutuality and play are instructive here. Similarly, Price's concern with sports "supplanting" religion, such as by treating it with the devotedness one should reserve for religion itself, is worth considering. Recognizing sports as adiaphora helps participants and observers recall the proper place of such activities in the life of the church and Christians, as a blessing or grace. We have seen the "conscripted" use of sports in some cultural expressions of its relationship with religion, in some fighters' use of religious terminology in the cage or ring names, and even in the use of a religious context to combat what some see as too much feminization of society. That some church responses to or engagements with fight sports might befit sports "conflicting" with religion we see in some church leaders outright opposition to fight sports, both historically or in efforts to control it in the modern day, or in concerns some ethicists' raise when fight sports go too far and either endanger the body or raise the stakes of competition to a level that imposes barriers rather than bridges between combatants, particularly when both are Christian and/or fellow church members. Finally, Price speaks of sports comingling with religion in a manner that aptly describes fight sports ministry programs discussed herein. In "fusing faith and athletics" in a way that creatively remains true to the particularities of the church's mission and Christian faith in order to provide outreach, fellowship, evangelism and opportunities for formation demarks programs that successful comingle religion and sport. That those fight sports ministries reviewed herein mindfully do just this is noteworthy and laudable.

In sum, so long as martial arts and boxing ministries suitably respond to ethical concerns, incorporate proper emphases, and reflect Christian values, they may maintain the balance that makes adiaphora, the "indifferent things," acceptable pursuits in church and Christian life. Clearly there are differing program emphases and approaches, and these lead to differing underlying theologies and understandings of discipleship. Many programs that are more given to more sensational depiction, in practice as in theological foundation, may receive more national media attention, and skew perceptions of what Christian boxing and martial arts programs as a category are about. Part of the effort herein is to demonstrate that this selective attention on these programs, and particular aspects of them no less, may not fully represent the breadth of fight sports ministries programs. By documenting the practice and approach of various unsung fight sports ministries, the aim is to reach a more comprehensive understanding and appreciation of the full range of such programs, to consider them alongside their more prominently covered counterparts, and to see how all such ministries relate to broad cultural, historical, ethical and theological matters. Given the methods and values expressed by many ministries reviewed herein, who bring their programs into prisons or inner cities, or use church-based programs to teach participants (young and old, men and women) an approach to training that encourages all involved to be good stewards of their bodies, supportive of each other's growth, quick to disengage from violence, loving of all (including one's "opponents"), and thankful for pure play as God's gift, these programs may well be not only acceptable as adiaphora, but also genuine and vital expressions of Christian discipleship.

Postscript

I began this analysis of fight sports and the church with a personal reflection. In the preface, I shared how a bullied kid was defended by a bigger youngster in an act (knowingly or not) of mercy and love; how that first kid then reflected on violence and the defense of self and others, and how this relates to Christian discipleship; how his fascination with boxing became a personal journey, both to train in the sport and to reflect theologically upon it; and how this kid, now grown, wished to fully explore something he believed was possible—a proper way to participate in fight sports, including in church ministries, and remain true to Christian values and principles. All of this led to the present work, exploring historical, cultural, ethical, practical and theological aspects of fight sports in relation to the church and its ministries. The aim has been to consider thoughts and guidelines regarding Christian engagement with fight sports for individuals and ministry programs, both for practitioners and observers. Thus, what began with my own experiences and reflections has led to consideration of much larger matters. As Oates writes:

> No other subject is, for the writer, as intensely personal as boxing. To write about boxing is to write about oneself—however elliptically, and unintentionally. And to write about boxing is to be forced to contemplate not only boxing, but the perimeters of civilization—what it is, or should be, to be "human."[1]

Therein lies the outline for this project. Born out of my own past and concerns, and a need to explore how these relate to issues of faith, my objective is to provide insights for those with broad interests in sports, culture and the church to reflect upon and discuss. For those who practice boxing and martial arts, or lead or hope to lead fight sports ministries, my ultimate goal is to help inspire an exploration of the relationship of such activities to matters of faith and Christian discipleship.

Specifically, those with an interest in fight sports and how they intersect with subjects such as history, culture, media studies, gender studies, ethics, sports and society, the American church, and theology will find herein matters worth considering, perhaps considered in a new light. As I explain in the introduction, the juxtaposition of fight sports and the church presents a surprising host of issues for contemplation. My intent is that this book—presented as a scholarly, comprehensive consideration of fight sports and the church, and in particular boxing and martial arts ministries—may stimulate a thoughtful reflection on how the phenomena discussed herein relate to and inform various disciples.

Regarding those who train in fight sports individually, and perhaps apart from a ministry, and wish to reflect upon how faith relates to their own practice, my hope is that this book will prove thought-provoking and useful—the kind of resource I longed for when I was younger and first developing my own interests in boxing and religion. Back then, I would have benefited from a resource that could have helped guide my contemplation on the relation of practice to faith. For those who find themselves in a similar situation, I am confident that they will find discussions and issues raised herein helpful to their own reflections.

For those thinking of beginning a fight sports ministry, or already involved with or running one, the matters examined herein may provide helpful thoughts and guidelines on which to reflect in planning a well-conceived ministry; that is, the ethical, theological and practical issues outlined herein may be of help to a would-be or current leader of such a ministry, to help that leader consider their own responses to the issues and examples raised. Being able to read of the diverse ministerial contexts of existing fight sports programs, and consider how one's own ministry might draw upon, adapt or otherwise respond to program emphases and approaches of others will help not only in drafting of one's own plans, but also to understand how one's approach relates to the field. Seeing how a range of existing ministries developed programs and resources, responded to challenges, and reached their goals may help some refine existing programs, or thoughtfully plan new ministries. Further, knowing the existence of other program and leaders with whom one may dialogue and perhaps even plan joint activities (as was an interest shared by several program leaders during their interviews) is another benefit of this work.

For myself, this book is the end result of that long sought after consideration of how fight sports relate to the church, mentioned in the preface, brought together in one volume. It is an exploration of the issues that have inspired, concerned and interested me since I, as an aspiring fighter and churchgoer, first became interested in boxing. What I find in the end is a genuine path to engage in such activities and remain true to Christian commitments, values and ideals. This is true not only for individual Christians interested in training in fight sports for various purposes (fitness, self-defense, recreation), but also for churches hoping to create fight sports ministries for their own purposes, be that for evangelism, outreach, formation, fellowship, or fun. In short, one may practice or teach fight sports, within a ministry or in a secular setting, in a manner wholly consistent with one's discipleship. This project helps situate that practice historically, culturally, ethically and theologically, so as to understand the phenomenon of fight sports in relation to society and the church. My goal, whether one adheres fully to the particular theological traditions raised herein or not, is at least to provide explicit practical, cultural and theological points to consider, debate and, perhaps, apply.

Chapter Notes

Preface

1. Jacquez Ellul, *Violence: Reflections from a Christian Perspective* (New York: Seabury, 1969), 98.

Introduction

1. Russell Sullivan, *Rocky Marciano: The Rock of His Times* (Chicago: University of Illinois Press, 2002), 148.
2. Christine Thomasos, "Manny Pacquiao Prepares for Fight, Prays for his Opponents," *The Christian Post*, November 10, 2011, accessed April 4, 2017, http://www.christianpost.com/news/manny-pacquiao-prepares-for-fight-prays-for-opponents-61410/print.html.
3. Abby Dorman, "Blood, Sweat, and Jesus: The Power of Sorts Ministries," *Millennial Influx*, March 6, 2015, accessed August 15, 2016, http://www.millennialinflux.com/blood-sweat-and-jesus-the-power-of-sports-ministry/.
4. Nick Watson and Brian Bolt, "Mixed Martial Arts and Christianity: 'Where Feet, Fist and Faith Collide,'" *The Conversation*, January 5, 2015, accessed August 17, 2016, http://theconversation.com/mixed-martial-arts-and-christianity-where-feet-fist-and-faith-collide-34836.
5. "How a Boxing Gym Helps this Baltimore Church Fight for Kids," *PBS*, November 30, 2015, accessed August 17, 2016, http://www.pbs.org/newshour/bb/how-a-boxing-gym-helps-this-baltimore-church-fight-for-kids/.
6. In order: R.M. Schneiderman, "Flock is Now a Fight Team," February 1, 2010; Daniel Junge and Bryan Storkel, "Pastor with a Punch," September 8, 2014; Steve Young and Angus Leader, "Churchgoers Turn the Other Cheek in the Ring," February 2, 2009; Christina Caron, "High School Coach Dies in Church Boxing Match," November 5, 2011"; Chris Erskine, "The Minister can Preach the Virtues of Boxing…," December 17, 2014; Brownie Marie, "Pastor's 'Fight Ministry'…," September 12, 2014; and Nick Watson and Brian Bolt, "Mixed Martial Arts and Christianity," January 5, 2015.
7. A helpful summary comes from the New South Wales "Combat Sports Act 2013," which defines its subject as "any sport, martial art or activity in which the primary objective of each contestant in a contest, display or exhibition of that sport, art or activity is to strike, kick, hit, grapple with, throw or punch one or more other contestants." See: http://www.legislation.nsw.gov.au/#/view/act/2013/96/part1/sec4.
8. Clyde Gentry III, *No Holds Barred: The Complete History of Mixed Martial Arts in America* (Chicago: Triumph Books, 2011), 3.
9. Ibid., 2–3.
10. Thomas A. Green, and Joseph Svinth, "Brazilian Jiu-Jitsu," in *Martial Arts of the World: An Encyclopedia*, ed. Thomas A. Green (Santa Barbara, California: ABC-Clio, 2001), 52–56.
11. Christopher David Thrasher, *Fight Sports and American Masculinity: Salvation in Violence from 1607* (Jefferson, North Carolina: McFarland, 2015), 204, 267 (note 37).
12. Ronald Harris, "Muay Thai," in *Martial Arts of the World: An Encyclopedia*, ed. Thomas A. Green (Santa Barbara, California: ABC-Clio, 2001), 350–354.
13. Gene P. Tansk, "Taekwondo," in

Martial Arts of the World: An Encyclopedia, ed. Thomas A. Green (Santa Barbara, California: ABC-Clio, 2001), 608–617.

14. William J. Long, "Judo," in *Martial Arts of the World: An Encyclopedia*, ed. Thomas A. Green (Santa Barbara, California: ABC-Clio, 2001), 210–217.

15. Kasia Boddy, *Boxing: A Cultural History* (London: Reaktion, 2008), 10–15.

16. *Ibid.*, 15.

17. Arne K. Lang, *Prizefighting: An American History* (Jefferson, North Carolina: McFarland, 2008), 7.

18. *Ibid.*, 8.

19. *Ibid.*, 26.

20. Instrumental in this seems to be the death of a student in Wisconsin: Evan Frank, "Slugging It Out: The Story of Boxing as a High School Sport," *Lake Country Now* (Oconomowoc, Wisconsin), May 6, 2015, accessed August 23, 2016, http://www.lakecountrynow.com/sports/oconomowocfocus/slugging-it-out-the-story-of-boxing-as-a-high-school-sport-b99494819z1-302757381.

21. Rachel Bachman, "College Boxing Clubs Rise from the Canvas," *Wall Street Journal* (New York, New York), Sept. 22, 2015, accessed August 22, 2016, http://www.wsj.com/articles/college-boxing-clubs-rise-from-the-canvas-1442941846.

22. Antoinette Muller, "Why Are We Less Tolerant of Boxing Injuries Than in Other Sports?" *Daily Maverick* (Johannesburg, South Africa), April 1, 2016, accessed August 24, 2016, http://www.dailymaverick.co.za/article/2016-04-01-why-are-we-less-tolerant-of-boxing-injuries-than-in-other-sports/.

23. David Zinczenko, "It Only Looks Dangerous," *The New York Times*, April 1, 2011.

24. Thrasher, 187–188.

25. *Ibid.*, passim.

26. This range is adapted from those suggested by several sources, including: Herman Kauz, *The Martial Spirit: An Introduction to the Origin, Philosophy and Psychology of the Martial Arts* (Woodstock, New York: Overlook Press, 1977); and Bryan Mason, *Beyond the Gold: What Every Church Needs to Know about Sports Ministry* (United Kingdom: Authentic Media, 2011).

27. Jeremy R. Treat, "More Than a Game: A Theology of Sport," *Themelios:* *An International Journal for Students of Theological and Religious Studies* 40, no. 3 (2015): 403.

28. Michael Shafer, *Well Played: A Christian Theology of Sport, and the Ethics of Doping* (Eugene, Oregon: Pickwick, 2015), 1.

29. Nick J. Watson, and Brian Brock, "Christianity, Boxing and Mixed Martial Arts: Reflections on Morality, Vocation, and Well-Being," *Journal of Religion and Society* 17 (2015): 2.

30. David Roark, "A Theology of Sports," *The Village Church* (blog), March 26, 2015, accessed August 27, 2016, http://www.thevillagechurch.net/the-village-blog/a-theology-of-sports/.

31. Joseph L. Price, "From Sabbath Proscriptions to Super Sunday Celebrations: Sports and Religion in America," in *From Season to Season: Sports as American Religion*, ed. Joseph L. Price (Macon, Georgia: Mercer University Press, 2001), 15–38.

32. *Ibid.*, 22.

33. *Ibid.*, 35, 36.

34. As quoted by David H.T. Scott, *The Art and Aesthetics of Boxing* (Lincoln, Nebraska: University of Nebraska Press, 2008), xxiii.

Chapter 1

1. Joyce Carol Oates, *On Boxing* (New York: Harper, 2006), 70.

2. Lang, 5, 26.

3. Boddy, 92–93.

4. Shirl James Hoffmann, *Christianity and the Culture of Sports* (Texas: Baylor University Press, 2010), 119; and William J. Baker, *Playing with God: Religion and Modern Sport* (Massachusetts: Harvard University Press, 2007), 35–36.

5. Clifford Putney, *Muscular Christianity: Manhood and Sports in Protestant America, 1880–1920* (Massachusetts: Harvard university Press, 2001), 11–12.

6. Justin McCarthy, *Modern Leaders: Being a Series of Biographical Sketches* (New York: Sheldon & Company, 1872), 217.

7. Baker, 32; Hoffmann, 119–120, citing another source that quotes Hughes.

8. Walter Besant, *East London* (London: Chatto & Windus, 1912), 330.

9. *Ibid.*

10. *Ibid.*, 172.

Notes—Chapter 1

11. Lang, 12.
12. Michael Abbott, "Bendigo," *Leftlion*, April 1, 2006, accessed September 6, 2016, http://www.leftlion.co.uk/articles.cfm/title/bendigo-part-2/id/1174.
13. Lang, 12–13.
14. Abbott, "Bendigo" (part three), http://www.leftlion.co.uk/articles.cfm/title/bendigo-part-3/id/1175.
15. Tony Ladd and James A Mathisen, *Muscular Christianity: Evangelical Protestants and the Development of American Sport* (Michigan: Baker Books, 1999), 24.
16. It is noteworthy that the practice of fight sports suffered in an earlier era of revivals, during the Second Great Awakening (1800–1840), when rougher forms of sport, such as boxing, were discouraged by evangelicals, leaving the more subdued sport of wrestling as evangelical men's only permissible fight sports outlet (Thrasher, 62).
17. Ladd & Mathisen, 11–13, 34, 231.
18. Baker, 46, 48.
19. *Ibid.*, 48.
20. *Ibid.*, 50–51.
21. Hoffman, 106, 109, 112.
22. Baker, 52–53.
23. *Ibid.*, 53.
24. Jonathan Weier, "The Building of Boys for War: The Militarization of Boys' Work in the Canadian and American YMCAs," in *Children's Literature and the Culture of the First World War*, ed. Lissa Paul, Rosemary Ross Johnston, and Emma Short (New York: Routledge: 2016), 166.
25. John Donald Gustav-Wrathall, *Take the Young Stranger by the Hand: Same-sex Relations and the YMCA* (Chicago: University of Chicago Press, 2000), 15.
26. Pamela Bayless, *The YMCA at 150: A History of the YMCA of Greater New York, 1852–2002* (New York: YMCA of Greater New York, 2002), 34–35.
27. Hoffman, 118.
28. Martin E. Marty, *Pilgrims in their Own Land: 500 Years of Religion in America* (New York: Penguin, 1984), 352–353 (emphasis added).
29. Ladd & Mathisen, 79–83.
30. Stephen Prothero, *American Jesus: How the Son of God Became a National Icon* (New York: Farrar, Straus and Giroux, 2003), 94.
31. *Ibid.*
32. Ladd & Mathisen, 79.
33. Adam Park, "Boxing and the YMCA War Dogs," *Religion in American History* (blog) August 8, 2016, accessed September 16, 2016, http://usreligion.blogspot.com/2016/08/boxing-and-ymca-war-dogs.html; and Thrasher, 143.
34. Ray Pearson, "'Fighting Parson,' Now in Chicago, Lauds Sport at War Camps," *Chicago Daily Tribune* (November 14, 1917), 13; and Ray Pearson, "'Fighting Parson' Puts on the Gloves," *Chicago Daily Tribune* (January 4, 1918), 13.
35. Thrasher, 144.
36. Park.
37. Thrasher, 146–147.
38. Park.
39. Baker, 175.
40. Timothy B. Neary, *Crossing Parish Boundaries: Race, Sports, and Catholic Youth in Chicago, 1914–1954* (Chicago: University of Chicago Press, 2016), 78.
41. Neary, 78; quoting Roger L Treat, from the latter's *Bishop Sheil and the CYO: The Story of the Catholic Youth Organization and the Man Who Influenced a Generation of Americans* (New York: Messner, 1951).
42. *Ibid.*, 76.
43. Baker, 175.
44. Ron Grossman, "Chicago Bishop saw Refuge for Youths in the Boxing Ring," *Chicago Tribune*, September 18, 2015, accessed September 19, 2016, http://www.chicagotribune.com/news/history/ct-bishop-bernard-sheil-pope-francis-flashback-0920-20150918-story.html.
45. Neary, 73.
46. *Ibid.*, 83.
47. Grossman.
48. Baker, 179.
49. Gerald R. Gems, "Sport, Religion and Americanization: Bishop Sheil and the Catholic Youth Organization," in *The International Journal of the History of Sport* 10 (1993): 235.
50. Neary, 8–9.
51. *Ibid.*, 94–95, 101.
52. *Ibid.*, 88.
53. *Ibid.*, 102.
54. *Ibid.*, 126, 128.
55. *Ibid.*, 133.
56. *Ibid.*, 86.
57. "Sheils Resigns, Msgr. Kelly to Head CYO," *Chicago Daily Tribune*, September 3, 1954.
58. Baker, 179–180.
59. Ladd and Mathisen, 127–137; Hoffman, 133–137.

60. Thrasher, 136–138.
61. *Ibid.*, 138.
62. *Ibid.*, 171.
63. It is telling that even scholarly works on the history of fight sports that regularly discuss the church's relation to these whenever possible (such as Thrasher's *Fight Sports and American Masculinity: Salvation in Violence from 1607 to the Present*) discontinue such references in discussions of more modern times, as programs became more local.
64. Bayless, 173.
65. Lang, 13–14.
66. Baker, 27.
67. *Ibid.*, 30–31.
68. Hoffman, 108–109 (including information at footnote 20).
69. Washington Gladden, *Amusements: Their Uses and Abuses* (North Adams, MA: James T. Robinson and Co., 1866), 14–15. Notably, the aforementioned class bias surfaces here again, as Gladden disdainfully refers to Brown's amusements as representing the "peasantry of England."
70. Baker, 91.
71. Ladd & Mathisen, 25.
72. "To Arrest Fitzsimmons," *The Chicago Tribune*, July 21, 1891, 6.
73. "Law and Order Triumph," *The Chicago Tribune*, July 23, 1891, 2.
74. Lang, 38.
75. "Anti Prize Fight Law Valid," *The Chicago Tribune*, July 15, 1895, 4; and "Culberson Prohibits the Big Fight," *The Chicago Tribune*, July 28, 1895, 3.
76. Lang, 38.
77. Dan Streible, *Fight Pictures: A History of Boxing and Early Cinema* (Berkeley, California: University of California Press, 2008), 52.
78. Dan Streible, "Female Spectators and the Corbett-Fitzsimmons Fight Film," in *Out of Bounds: Sports, Media, and the Politics of Identity*, ed. Aaron Baker and Todd Boyd (Bloomington, Indiana: Indiana University Press, 1997), 23.
79. As quoted in Lang, 39.
80. Streible, 64.
81. Ladd & Mathisen, 85.
82. Thrasher, 146.
83. Hoffman, 124.
84. Ladd & Mathisen, 85.
85. Hoffman, 124–125.
86. Robert G. Rodriguez, *The Regulation of Boxing: A History and Comparative Analysis of Policies Among American States* (Jefferson, North Carolina: McFarland, 2009), 32.
87. Lang, 35.
88. Rodriguez, 35.
89. Hoffman, 125.
90. Thrasher, 148.
91. Lang, 53–54.
92. Thrasher, 78, 150–151.
93. Baker, 166–167.
94. Putney, 64.
95. Baker, 166, 169.
96. Lang, 122–123; and Robert K. Christenberry, "My Rugged Education in Boxing," *Life*, May 26, 1952, 114–116ff.
97. Peter Steinfels, obituary for Robert A McCormick, *The New York Times*, February 15, 2000.
98. Richard A. McCormick, "Is Professional Boxing Immoral?" *Sports Illustrated*, November 5, 1962.
99. "Catholic Magazine Calls Boxing 'Merciless, Inhuman,'" National Public Radio, October 27, 2005, accessed September 26, 2016, http://www.npr.org/templates/story/story.php?storyId=4977604.
100. Dino Maragay, "Pope Francis Named 'Champion of Faith' by Boxing Body," *The Philippine Star*, February 4, 2016, accessed September 26, 2016, http://www.philstar.com/sports/2016/02/04/1549633/pope-francis-named-champion-faith-boxing-body.
101. Gentry, 352–353.
102. Bob Woodruff and Ben Newman, "In Jesus' Name, Throw Punches: 'Fight Church' Christian Ministries Believe in Fight Clubs," ABC News, October 3, 2014, accessed September 27, 2016, http://abcnews.go.com/U.S./jesus-throw-punches-fight-church-christian-ministries-fight/story?id=25953786.
103. *Ibid.*

Chapter 2

1. Oates, 72.
2. Ann Douglas, *The Feminization of American Culture* (New York: Alfred A. Knopf, 1977), 77.
3. *Ibid.*, 4–6, 92.
4. *Ibid.*, 126.
5. Kaye Ashe, *The Feminization of the Church?* (Kansas City: Sheed and Ward, 1997), xiv.

Notes—Chapter 2

6. *Ibid.*, 146–147.
7. Leon J. Podles, *The Church Impotent: The Feminization of Christianity* (Dallas: Spence Publishing Company, 1999), x, 8.
8. Patrick M. Arnold, *Wildmen, Warriors, and Kings: Masculine Spirituality and the Bible* (New York: Crossroad, 1991), 64, 68.
9. *Ibid.*, 31–32.
10. *Ibid.*, 70.
11. Robert Moore and Douglas Gillette, *King, Warrior, Magician, Lover: Rediscovering the Archetypes of the Mature Masculine* (San Francisco: Harper Collins, 1991), 75, 93.
12. Joseph Gelfer, *Numen, Old Men: Contemporary Masculinity Spiritualities and the Problem of Patriarchy* (Oatville, Connecticut: Equinox, 2009), 79–80, 89–90.
13. *Ibid.*, 182–196.
14. Nate Pyle, *Man Enough: How Jesus Redefines Manhood* (Grand Rapids, Michigan: Zondervan, 2015), 19.
15. *Ibid.*, 21–22.
16. *Ibid.*, 86, 89, 108.
17. *Ibid.*, 104.
18. *Ibid.*, 37–38, 103.
19. *Ibid.*, 191.
20. David Murrow, *Why Men Hate Going to Church* (Nashville, Tennessee: Nelson Books, 2005), 95–96, 207.
21. Craig Groeschel, *Fight: Winning the Battle that Matter Most* (Grand Rapids, Michigan: Zondervan, 2013), 9, 29, 66, 150.
22. Oates, 11.
23. *Ibid.*, 5.
24. Thomas Hughes, *The Manliness of Christ* (Boston: Houghton, Osgood and Company, 1880), 20.
25. *Ibid.*, 22. As I am quoting Hughes' work and his explication of manliness, the use of exclusive language is intentional and derived, reflecting his approach and style.
26. *Ibid.*, 28–29.
27. Thomas Hughes, *True Manliness* (Boston: D. Lothrop and Company, 1880), 14.
28. *Ibid.*, 13.
29. *Ibid.*, 140, 134.
30. *Ibid.*, 89–90.
31. Thomas Hughes, *Tom Brown's Schooldays* (New York: E.P. Dutton & Co., 1962), 256. (Originally published in 1857; citations refer to the 1962 Dutton edition.)
32. *Ibid.*, 250.
33. *Ibid.*
34. *Ibid.*, 251.
35. *Ibid.*, 269.
36. As quoted and discussed by David Faulkner, "The Confidence Man: Empire and the Destruction of Muscular Christianity in *The Mystery of Edwin Drood*," in *Muscular Christianity: Embodying the Victorian Age*, ed. Donald E. Hall (New York: Cambridge University Press, 1974), 175 and passim.
37. As introduced and quoted by Richard Holt, *Sport and the British: A Modern History* (Oxford: Clarendon Press, 1989), 93
38. *Ibid.*
39. *The Daily Free Press* (Carbondale, Illinois), June 19, 1906, 2.
40. "His Last Fight," *Poverty Bay Herald* (Volume 34, issue 10881), January 26, 1907, 5 (supplement).
41. "Fighting Parson Runs Boxing Club," *The Day* (New London, CT), January 8, 1917, 10.
42. Frederick R. Wedge, *The Fighting Parson of Barbary Coast* (Washington, D.C.: Frederick R. Wedge. 1912), 62.
43. *Ibid.*, 93.
44. *Ibid.*, 115–116.
45. *Ibid.*, 122.
46. *Ibid.*, 125.
47. *Ibid.*, 145.
48. Jack Butler, *Jujitsu for Christ* (Little Rock, Arkansas: August House, 1986), 8–9.
49. *Ibid.*, 20.
50. *Ibid.*, 53.
51. *Ibid.*, 57–58.
52. *Ibid.*, 86.
53. *Ibid.*, 106.
54. *Ibid.*, 166.
55. *Ibid.*, 183.
56. Sally Eckhoff, review of *JuJitsu for Christ*, *Village Voice* literary supplement (April, 1987), 3.
57. *Boys Town*, directed by Norman Tourag (1938; Burbank, CA: Warner Home Video, 2005), DVD.
58. *The Bells of St. Mary's*, directed by Leo McCarey (1945; Chicago, IL: Olive Films, 2013), DVD.
59. *Kid Monk Baroni*, directed by Harold Schuster (1952; Chatsworth, CA: Image Entertainment, 2007), DVD.
60. *Elmer Gantry*, directed by Richard Brooks (1960; Beverly Hills, CA: Metro-Goldwyn-Mayer Home Entertainment, 2001), DVD.
61. "Goodbye, Farewell and Amen,"

M*A*S*H, first broadcast February 28, 1983 (season 11, episode 16) by CBS. Directed by Alan Alda, and written by Alan Alda, Burt Metcalf, et al.; and "As Time Goes By," *M*A*S*H*, first broadcast February 21, 1983 (season 11, episode 15) by CBS. Directed by Burt Metcalfe, and written by Dale Wilcox and Thad Mumford. Both reviewed off commercial DVD, 20th Century Fox, release date February 26, 2013.

62. "Heroes," *M*A*S*H*, first broadcast March 15, 1978 (season 10, episode 18) by CBS. Directed by Neil Cox, and written by Thad Mumford and Dan Wilcox. Reviewed off commercial DVD, 20th Century Fox, release date February 26, 2013.

63. "Dear Sis," *M*A*S*H*, first broadcast December 18, 1978 (season 7, episode 14) by CBS. Directed by Alan Alda, and written by Alan Alda and Larry Gelbart. Reviewed off commercial DVD, 20th Century Fox, release date February 26, 2013.

64. "Fighting Back," *Sons of Thunder*, first broadcast March 13, 1999 (season 1, episode 2) by CBS. Directed by Michael Preece. Reviewed off YouTube.

65. *The Boxer*, directed by Jim Sheridan (1997; Hollywood, CA: Universal Studies, 1998), DVD.

66. *Fight Church*, directed by Daniel Junge and Brian Storkel (2014; Jax Distribution, 2014), DVD.

67. "Jesus Didn't Tap—Christian Apparel and MMA Gear," accessed November 10, 2016, http://jesusdidnttap.com.

68. "Art 4 God," accessed November 16, 2016, http://art4god.com.

69. "Undefeated," on the website "Art 4 God," accessed February 7. 2020, http://www.art4god.com/store/undefeated.

70. David. D. Kirkpatrick, "Wrath and Mercy: Return of the Warrior Jesus," *New York Times*, April 4, 2004, accessed February 7. 2020, https://www.nytimes.com/2004/04/04/weekinreview/wrath-and-mercy-the-return-of-the-warrior-jesus.html.

71. Jack Myers, "Young Men are Facing a Masculinity Crisis," *Time*, May 26, 2016, accessed November 9, 2016, http://time.com/4339209/masculinity-crisis/.

72. Jonathan Gottschall, *The Professor in the Cage: Why Men Fight and Why We Like to Watch* (New York: Penguin, 2015), 82.

73. Walter Ong, *Fighting for Life: Contest, Sexuality, and Consciousness* (Ithaca, New York: Cornell University Press, 1981), 51.

74. Ong, 180.
75. Hughes, *Manliness of Christ*, 109.
76. Ibid., 91.
77. Ibid., 18–19.
78. Ibid., 20.
79. Ibid., 137–139.
80. Ibid., 139–140.
81. For more on this, see Barna William Donovan's *Blood, Guns and Testosterone: Action Films, Audiences, and a Thirst for Violence* (London: Scarecrow Press, 2010). A quick note on style; as Hughes, Myers and others are writing particularly about the experience of men, the use of masculine pronouns in this section is intentional.
82. Boddy, 9.
83. Gottschall, 47–50. Interestingly, Gottschall notes that women likewise face tests of honor, but that these often do not regard their strength and bravery so much as their "sexual propriety" (47).
84. Ibid., 40–45.
85. Geertz is here referencing a concept developed in Jeremy Betham's *Theory of Legislation* (London: Kegan Paul, Trench, Trubner and Company, 1896).
86. Boddy, 9.
87. Leger Grindon, *Knockout: The Boxer and Boxing in American Cinema* (Jackson, Mississippi: University Press of Mississippi, 2011), 3.
88. Frederick V. Romano, *The Boxing Filmography: American Features, 1920–2003* (Jefferson, North Carolina: McFarland, 2004), 1.
89. Ronald Bergan, *Sports in the Movies* (New York: Proteus, 1982), 14.
90. Clay Motley, "Fighting for Manhood: Rocky and Turn-of-the-Century Antimodernism," in *All-Stars & Movie Stars: Sports in Film & History*, ed. Ron Briley, Michael K. Schoenecke, and Deborah A. Carmichael (Lexington, Kentucky: University Press of Kentucky, 2008), 201 and passim.
91. Gottschall, 67.

Chapter 3

1. Oates, 91.
2. For example, see Watson and Brock, Watson and Bolt, and Hoffmann.
3. Watson and Bolt.
4. Mark Galli, "Punches, Smashes, and Bombs: Boxing Gives Us a Window into the Violence Inherent in All Sports,"

Christianity Today, November 11, 2005, accessed October 6, 2016, http://www.christianitytoday.com/ct/2005/november-web-only/52.0a.html.
  5. Shafer, 148.
  6. Hoffmann, 284. Emphasis added.
  7. *Ibid.*, 42–43.
  8. *Ibid.*, 26.
  9. New Revised Standard Version (emphasis added).
  10. Shafer, 90.
  11. Victor C. Pfitzner, "Was St. Paul a Sports Enthusiast? Realism and Rhetoric in Pauline Athletic Metaphors," in *Sports and Christianity: Historical and Contemporary Perspectives*, eds. Nick J. Watson and Andrew Parker (New York: Routledge, 2013), 92.
  12. *Ibid.*, 93.
  13. *Ibid.*
  14. *Ibid.*, 92, 100.
  15. Hoffmann, 42; Shafer, 92.
  16. Victor Pfitzner, *Paul and the Agon Motif: Traditional Athletic Imagery in the Pauline Literature* (Novum Testament Supplement 16) (Leiden, South Holland: E.J. Brill, 1967), 187.
  17. Shafer, 92; Hoffmann, 41.
  18. Shafer, 93.
  19. Pfitzner, "Was St. Paul a Sports Enthusiast?," 101–102.
  20. *Ibid.*, 102–105.
  21. Thrasher, 33.
  22. *Ibid.*
  23. *Ibid.*, 56, 143. Best known of the hymns making liturgical use of Jacob's wrestling with the angel is Charles Wesley's "Come, O Thou Traveler Unknown." Other hymns making such references, although lesser known, include: "Lord, I Cannot Let Thee Go," John Newton; "Shepherd Divine, Our Wants Relieve," Charles Wesley; "I Would Not Be Denied," Charles Price Jones; "With Awe Approach the Mysteries," Jane Marshall; and "Wrestle Like Jacob of Old," H. R. Jeffrey.
  24. Putney, 64.
  25. John Dominic Crossan, *How to Read the Bible & Still Be a Christian: Is God Violent? An Exploration from Genesis to Revelation* (New York: Harper One, 2015), 181.
  26. *Ibid.*, 141.
  27. *Ibid.*, 28.
  28. *Ibid.*, 181.
  29. *Ibid.*, 28 and passim.
  30. *Ibid.*, 66.
  31. R.T. French, *The Gospel of Matthew: The New International Commentary on the New Testament* (Grand Rapids, Michigan: William B. Eerdmans, 2007), 220–221.
  32. Walter Wink, *Engaging the Powers: Discernment and Resistance in a World of Domination* (Minneapolis, Minnesota: Fortress Press, 1992), 175–177.
  33. One prominent example of this advice, as we will soon discuss, is the Gracie family, which operates the Gracie Jiu-Jitsu Academy, a world-renowned franchise of martial arts schools.
  34. Walter Wink, *Jesus and Nonviolence: A Third Way* (Minneapolis, Minnesota: Fortress, 2003), 3.
  35. *Ibid.*, 5–6.
  36. *Ibid.*, 83.
  37. Crossan, 245.
  38. Both concepts are often intermingled in ethicists' writings, albeit explicitly recognized as individual (though related) concepts, as in Shafer 147ff and before.
  39. Hoffmann, 116, 169, 184.
  40. Shafer, 147; Hoffmann, 184.
  41. Muller.
  42. Schafer, 148–149.
  43. Watson and Brock, 8.
  44. Mark Galli, "Should We Ban Boxing?," *Christianity Today* 49, no. 10, October 28, 2005, http://www.christianitytoday.com/ct/2005/octoberweb-only/52.0c.html; "Punches, Smashes, and Bombs" (cited above); and "Transformed by a Left Hook," *Christianity Today* 49, no.12, December 2, 2005, http://www.christianitytoday.com/ct/2005/novemberweb-only/53.0d.html; all accessed October 17, 2016.
  45. Putney, 56–57.
  46. Hoffmann, 173.
  47. Shafer, 146.
  48. *Ibid.*, 152.
  49. Bayless, 15 and passim.
  50. Charles Kingsley, "Nausicca in London," in *Good Words*, ed. Rev. Donald Macleod (London: Daldy, Isbister & Co., 1874), 23.
  51. Rodger Oswald, "Biblical Foundations of Sports Ministry: Defining the Phenomenon," in *Recreation and Sports Ministry: Impacting Postmodern Culture*, ed. John Garner (Nashville, Tennessee: Broadman & Holman, 2003), 35.
  52. *Ibid.*
  53. Hoffmann, 199–200.
  54. *Ibid.*, 198.

55. *Ibid.*, 199–201.
56. *Ibid.*, 213.
57. *Ibid.*, 198–99.
58. Shafer, 156.
59. *Ibid.*, 151.
60. *Ibid.*, 158.
61. *Ibid.*, 157.
62. Nick J. Watson and John White, "'Winning at all Costs' in Modern Sport: Reflections on Pride and Humility in the Writings of C.S. Lewis," in *Sport and Spirituality: An Introduction* (New York: Routledge, 2007), 64.
63. Drew Hyland, "Competition and Friendship," *Journal of the Philosophy of Sport* 5 (1979): 35.
64. Hoffman., 147.
65. *Ibid.*, 145, 156.
66. *Ibid.*, 164.
67. Greg Linville, "Ethics Competition in Church Setting," in *Recreation and Sports Ministry: Impacting Postmodern Culture*, ed. John Garner (Nashville, Tennessee: Broadman & Holman, 2003), 175.
68. Shafer, 121.
69. Linville, 173.
70. *Ibid.*, 178–179. Once again, the use of non-inclusive word choices reflects those of the author quoted, somewhat necessary given Linville's construction of "Christmanship."
71. Shafer, 140.
72. Hoffman, 161.
73. Somewhat similar to this is Gottschall's (136) citation of a child psychologist, who notes that for boys "rough play" may occur "more in the spirit of fun than of anger" (a point which will come up once again, later).
74. Hyland, 29.
75. *Ibid.*, 33–34.
76. *Ibid.*, 35.
77. Shafer, 141.
78. *Ibid.*, 137.
79. Johan Huizinga, *Homo Ludens* (Boston: Beacon Press, 1950), 13.
80. *Ibid.*, 12.
81. *Ibid.*
82. As evidence of this, note the systematic discussions of Huizinga's elements of play in: Shafer, pp. 201–209; Hoffman, pp. 273–278; Robert K. Johnston, *The Christian at Play* (Grand Rapids, Michigan: William B. Eerdmans, 1983), 33–49; Ruth Caspar, "Play Springs Eternal" *The New Scholasticism* 52, no. 2 (1978): 188–190; and others.
83. Shafer, 184, 180–181.
84. *Ibid.*, 238, 240.
85. Hoffman, 282.
86. Treat: 395.
87. Hoffman, 267–268.
88. Treat: 397.
89. Caspar, 193–194.
90. Treat: 399.
91. *Ibid.*: 403.
92. Shafer, 232, 234–235.
93. Susan Saint Sing, "The Energy of Play," in *Theology, Ethics and Transcendence in Sports*, eds. Jim Parry, Mark Nesti and Nick Watson (New York: Routledge, 2011), 205.
94. Arthur F. Holmes, "Towards a Christian Play Ethic," *Christian Scholar's Review* 11, no. 1 (1981): 45.
95. Caspar, 197.
96. Shafer, 143–144.
97. *Ibid.*, 144.
98. Hoffmann, 173. To review Shafer's response to Hoffman, see his remarks in Shafer, 145–146. Hoffman's observation that well-to-do churches' "elaborate" and "lavish" fitness facilities evince misplaced priorities when poverty abounds, and should therefore be reexamined for the message they send about church values, is fair enough (Hoffman, 173). Granted, there are likely excessive fitness-focused ministries needing reform. However, it is worth noting, particularly in light of the rather humble facilities in use by many of the programs reviewed in the upcoming case studies chapter, that Hoffman's caution should not be applied too broadly. In this light, it is important to remember the more modest programs of local congregations and inner cities, that provide important opportunities for Christian fellowship and formation, and safe-havens for at-risk youth in urban areas to gather in a supportive environment.
99. "Training Programs," at the Gracie Jiu-Jitsu Academy, accessed October 20, 2016, http://www.gracieacademy.com/training_programs.asp.
100. "KeepItPlayful," a blog of Ryron Gracie, "The KeepItPlayful Movement," posted January 2, 2013, https://keepitplayful.wordpress.com/2013/01/02/the-keepitplayful-movement/.
101. Shafer, 233–237.
102. *Ibid.*, 232, 234–235.
103. Gottschall, 136, using a quotation by a child psychologist.

104. Hyland, 34–35.
105. Hoffman, 263.
106. *Ibid.*, 263, 288 (in the latter citation, referencing philosopher Randolph Freezell).
107. Here, using terms from Samuel Wells' discussion of the theology of Stanley Hauerwas, as quoted by Shafer, 130.
108. Hoffman., 286.
109. *Ibid.*, 284.
110. As quoted and discussed by Nick J. Watson, "Muscular Christianity in the Modern Age: 'Wining for Christ' or 'Playing for Glory'?," in *Sport and Spirituality: An Introduction* (New York: Routledge, 2007), 90.
111. Shafer, 145.

Chapter 4

1. Oates, 49.
2. Gottschall, 230.
3. To identify ministries to include in this study, the author searched for news stories about church related fight sports programs, and also searched the internet for websites and social media accounts that directed the author to various ministries. The author then contacted leaders of fight sports ministry programs and requested a phone interview, and interviewed all who responded and were willing to participate in this project. Although the author contacted the leaders of some ministries documented in *Fight Church*, none replied.
4. Rev. Jarrod Lanning (pastor of Trinity Lutheran Church, North Carolina), phone interview with the author, September 26, 2016.
5. "Taekwondo, Like Agriculture, Can be Beneficial at Any Age," *North Carolina Field and Family*, January 31, 2013, accessed December 6, 2016, http://www.ncfieldfamily.org/nc-living/taekwondo-like-agriculture-can-be-beneficial-at-any-age/.
6. *Ibid.*
7. Christian Karate Association, accessed December 5, 2016, http://christiankarate.wixsite.com/welcome. Now at https://www.christiankarate.org/.
8. Steve Wilson (founder and chief instructor, Christian Karate), phone interview with the author, September 22, 2016.
9. See Psalms 144:1, 18:34.
10. Rev. Thomas Richards (pastor of St. Paul's Lutheran Church, Tannersville, Pennsylvania), phone interview with the author, September 25, 2016.
11. Andrew Truong (instructor, Rock Church's Trinity MMA, Vista, California), phone interview with the author, October 1, 2016.
12. Charles Clark (boxing program instructor, Cross for Christ boxing gym, True Foundation Outreach Center, Columbus, Mississippi), phone interview with the author, September 23, 2016. Clark's new program focuses on everything from fitness (he specifically mentions the body as a temple of God) to training and preparation for competition, noting that his program involves prayer, Bible readings, and a focus on character development. Offered as part of a broader ministry facility, he encourages participants to attend church, which some do, but, as he admits, most do not.
13. Mike Mosley (boxing program instructor, Fist of God boxing, Created for So Much More Worship Center, Baltimore, Maryland), phone interview with the author, September 29, 2016.
14. Rev. Servando Perales (founder and coach at Victory Boxing Club of Omaha, Nebraska), phone interview with the author, August 7, 2017.
15. Cristino Felix (president of Christian Boxing Academy in Jersey City, New Jersey), phone interview with the author, March 8, 2018.
16. *Ibid.*
17. "How a Boxing Gym Helps this Baltimore Church Fight for Kids."
18. *Ibid.*
19. Kimberly Bays, "Ministry Reaching At-Risk Teens Through Boxing, " *Philadelphia Neighborhoods*, February 10, 2010, accessed December 17, 2016, https://philadelphianeighborhoods.com/2010/02/10/kensington-ministry-reaching-at-risk-teens-through-boxing/.
20. Melissa Kormar, "Bibles and Boxing Gloves," *Star*, December 9, 2014, accessed December 17, 2016, http://www.starnewsphilly.com/2014/dec/9/bibles-and-boxing-gloves/#.WFCcUXeZPMU.
21. Bays.
22. Rev. Craig Cerrito (assistant pastor, Rock Ministries, Calvary Chapel of Kensington, Pennsylvania), phone interview with the author, September 19, 2016.
23. Bays.

24. *Ibid.*
25. Cerrito interview.
26. *Ibid.*
27. Kormar.
28. Catholic Charities of Boston, "About the Program," accessed December 9, 2016, http://www.ccab.org/?q=TeenCenter.
29. Paul Doyle (boxing program instructor, formerly of the Teen Center at St. Peter's Church in Dorchester, Massachusetts [part of Catholic Charities of Boston], and now of the Colonel Marr Boys & Girls Club of Dorchester), phone interview with the author, September 27, 2016.
30. *Ibid.*
31. Jan Brogan, "Boxing, Not Fighting, Is the Focus at Dorchester Teen Center," *Globe Correspondent*, May 14, 2013, accessed December 20, 2016, https://www.bostonglobe.com/lifestyle/2013/05/13/boxing-not-fighting-focus-dorchester-teen-center/09LgsNKuSbE5P8VyQGq-5hP/story.html.
32. *Ibid.*
33. Doyle interview.
34. Eoin Cannon, "Boxing Takes Hold at St. Peter's: Former Pros, Cops Teach Kids the Ropes," *Dorchester Reporter*, April 4, 2013, accessed December 21, 2016, http://www.dotnews.com/2013/boxing-takes-hold-st-peter-s-former-pros-cops-teach-kids-ropes.
35. Doyle interview.
36. Cannon.
37. Brogan.
38. *Ibid.*
39. Mike Joyce (vice president of programming, Boys and Girls Club of Dorchester, Massachusetts), phone interview with the author, September 22, 2016.
40. Brogan.
41. Cannon.
42. Brogan.
43. Felix interview.
44. Christian Boxing Academy, accessed May 16, 2018, https://www.cbainvictory.com.
45. *Ibid.*
46. Felix interview.
47. *Ibid.*
48. Cristino Felix, personal correspondence with the author, January 30, 31, and February 2, 2020. And Valerie Velazquez-Stetz, "Blue Suicide Hits Home for JCPD Lt. Felix," *The Blue Magazine* online (no date), accessed February 2, 2020, https://www.thebluemagazine.com/blue-suicide-hits-home-for-jcpd-lt-felix.
49. Perales interview.
50. Paula Determan, *The Cry of a Warrior* (Spring Hill, Tennessee: Holy Fire Publishing, 2013), 18.
51. Perales interview.
52. Determan, passim.
53. *Ibid.*, 44.
54. Perales interview.
55. *Ibid.*
56. Determan, 71.
57. Perales interview.
58. Determan, 62.
59. Perales interview.
60. Escape Ministries, accessed May 18, 2018, http://escape-out.org.
61. Ruben Silvas (boxing coach with West Side Boxing and Fitness, a part of Escape Ministries, in Holland, Michigan), phone interview with the author, March 14, 2018.
62. *Ibid.*
63. *Ibid.*
64. *Ibid.*
65. Sonia Ramos (founder, president and CEO of Boxing for Christ in San Jacinto, California), phone interview with the author, December 12, 2018.
66. Boxing for Christ, accessed December 18, 2018, http://boxingforchrist.com.
67. Ramos interview.
68. *Ibid.*
69. *Ibid.*
70. *Ibid.*
71. *Ibid.*
72. Pastor Mark Morrow (pastor and head of SonRise Church and Church Street Boxing, in Salem, Oregon), phone interview with the author March 14, 2018.
73. *Ibid.*
74. Anna Reed, "Church Mixes Worship and Boxing," *The (Salem) Statesman Journal*, April 15, 2017, accessed March 15, 2018.
75. Morrow interview.
76. Victory Ministry and Sports Complex, accessed December 19, 2016, http://victoryjoplin.com/wp/.
77. Teejay Britton (director, Victory Gym and Fitness Center, Joplin, Missouri), phone interview with the author, December 15, 2016.
78. *Ibid.*
79. Jason Peake, "The Pugilist Preacher: Britton Inspires In and Out of the Cage,"

Joplin Globe, May 17, 2016, accessed December 23, 2016, http://www.joplinglobe.com/sports/local_sports/the-pugilist-preacher-britton-inspires-in-and-out-of-the/ article_f1f5c2ff-5bc4-5625-9b6b-f1b5d542fb22.html.

80. Britton interview.

81. Truong interview.

82. Michael Birch (instructor, Rock Church's Karate Ministry, San Diego, California), phone interview with the author, September 27, 2016.

83. Christian Karate, "Character Qualities," accessed December 20, 2016, http://www.christiankarate.org/character-qualities.

84. Wilson interview.

85. Rev. J. Brown (director of church relations, Concordia University, Texas, and former pastor of Praise Lutheran Church, and associate pastor at Concordia Lutheran Church, both in Fort Wayne, Indiana), phone interview with the author, September 24, 2016. Brown has since moved to Texas to serve as Director of Church relations at Concordia University Texas, leaving the ministries he started in the hands of others. He is considering beginning another karate ministry in Texas, either in a church or in a storefront facility.

86. *Ibid.*

87. Richards interview.

88. *Ibid.*

89. Lanning interview.

90. "Taekwondo, Like Agriculture, Can be Beneficial at Any Age."

91. Lanning interview.

92. Anchor's introduction to the video news package, accompanying Woodruff and Newman.

93. Video news package, accompanying Woodruff and Newman.

94. Schneiderman.

95. *Ibid.*

96. Molly Worthen, "Who Would Jesus Smack Down?," *New York Times Magazine*, January 6, 2009. Driscoll later resigned as pastor of Mars Hill and began serving a church in Scottsdale, Arizona.

97. *Ibid.*

98. As quoted in Nate Wilcox, "Redeeming MMA for Christians: A Controversial Mega-Church Pastor if Pro-MMA," *Bloody Elbow*, February 12, 2012, accessed December 21, 2016, http://www.bloodyelbow.com/2012/2/12/2793395/redeeming-mma-for-christians-a-controversial-mega-church-pastor-is.

99. *Fighting Politics*, directed by Emily Vahey (Media Fly Films, 2009). To see the video clip, visit the Fighting Politics page on YouTube, accessed December 20, 2016, https://www.youtube.com/watch?v=ddFbELpXTcg.

100. Worthen. To review a video clip wherein Driscoll apparently remarks on the incident Worthen recounts, or a strikingly similar one, see the Fighting Politics page on Facebook, accessed December 26, 2016, https://www.facebook.com/fightingpolitics/videos/vb.50629466340/10150139034965573/?type=2&theater.

101. Jessica Johnson, "Christians and Cage Fighting, from Fight Church to Mark Driscoll," *Religion Dispatches*, September 29, 2014, accessed December 23, 2016, http://religiondispatches.org/christians-and-cage-fighting-from-fight-church-to-mark-driscoll/.

102. The aforementioned PBS piece about the boxing ministry in Baltimore is the exception.

103. See "Gang Fight Nebraska," NET Nebraska website, http://netnebraska.org/basic-page/television/gang-fight-nebraska; and "Return to Victory," by Mike Tobias, July 5, 2017, http://netnebraska.org/article/news/1084416/return-victory-boxing.

104. Examples of these news stories appear in the footnotes of sections covering the various ministries included herein.

Conclusion

1. Hoffman, 75.

2. Robert J. Higgs, *God in the Stadium: Sports and Religion in America* (Lexington, Kentucky: University of Kentucky Press, 1995), 297.

3. *Ibid.*, 298–9.

4. Brad Williams, "Dear Driscoll, MMA is Not a Measure of Manhood—Jesus Is," *Christ and Popular Culture*, November 17, 2011, accessed December 30, 2016, http://christandpopculture.com/mark-driscoll-mma-is-not-the-measure-of-manhood-jesus-is/.

5. *Ibid.*

6. *Ibid.*

7. *Ibid.*

8. This collection of comments is assembled from news articles, online videos, the documentary *Fight Church*, and other sources used for this study.

9. Shirl Hoffman, "Prayers Out of Bounds," in *Theology, Ethics and Transcendence in Sports*, ed. Jim Parry, Mark Nesti, and Nick Watson (New York: Routledge, 2011), 56.

10. Prince, David E., *In the Arena: The Promise of Sports for Christian Discipleship* (Nashville, Tennessee: B&H Books, 2016), 54–56.

11. Christopher H. Evans and William R. Herzog II, "The Faith of Fifty Million: A Kingdom on Earth?" in *The Faith of Fifty Million: Baseball, Religion and American Culture* (Westminster John Knox Press: Louisville, Kentucky, 2002), 218–219.

12. Mark C. Mattes, "Theology of the Cross," in *Dictionary of Luther and Lutheran Traditions*, ed. Timothy J. Wengert, Mark A. Granquist, Mary Jane Haemig, Robert Kolb, Mark C. Mattes and Jonathan Strom (Grand Rapids, Michigan: Baker Academic, 2017), 737, 735.

13. Gerhard O. Forde, *On Being a Theologian of the Cross: Reflections on Luther's Heidelberg Disputation, 1518* (Grand Rapids, Michigan: William B. Eerdmans Publishing, 1997), 89.

14. Robert Kolb, "Luther on the Theology of the Cross." In *The Pastoral Luther: Essays on Martin Luther's Practical Theology*, ed. Timothy J. Wengert (Grand Rapids, Michigan: William B. Eerdmans, 2009), 39.

15. As quoted in Forde, 93.

16. *Ibid.*, 39–40.

17. Walther von Loewenich, *Luther's Theology of the Cross*, trans. Herbert J.A. Bouman (Minneapolis, Minnesota: Augsburg Publishing House. 1976), 125.

18. See Luke 22:42b and Philippians 2:8.

19. Alister E. McGrath, *Luther's Theology of the Cross: Martin Luther's Theological Breakthrough* (New York: Basil Blackwell, 1985), 154.

20. von Loewenich, 129.

21. Gerhard O. Forde, "Loser Takes All: The Victory of Christ." In *A More Radical Gospel: Essays on Eschatology, Authority, Atonement, and Ecumenism*, ed. Mark C. Mattes and Steven D. Paulson (Grand Rapids, Michigan: Wm. B. Eerdmans, 2004), 98.

22. *Ibid.*, 100.

23. Higgs, 4.

24. *Ibid.*, 313–314.

25. *Ibid.*, 300–302.

26. *Ibid.*, 312.

27. Peter L. Steinke, *Preaching the Theology of the Cross* (Minneapolis, Minnesota: Augsburg Publishing, 1983), 32.

28. Mark Hamilton, "An Augustinian Critique of our Relationship to Sport," in *Theology, Ethics and Transcendence in Sports*, eds. Jim Parry, Mark Nesti and Nick Watson (New York: Routledge, 2011).

29. *Ibid.*, 28–33.

30. *Ibid.*, 29, 31.

31. Marcus J. Borg, *Meeting Jesus Again for the First Time: The Historical Jesus & the Heart of Contemporary Faith* (New York: Harper Collins, 1994), 135–136.

32. Karl Barth, *The Call to Discipleship*, trans. G. W. Bromiley, ed. K.C. Hanson (Minneapolis, Minnesota: Fortress Press, 2003), 45.

33. *Ibid.*, 43.

34. Prince, 50.

35. Prince, 47–50.

36. Prince, 53.

37. Pfitzner, "Was St. Paul a Sports Enthusiast?," 105.

38. Timothy J. Wengert, "Introducing the Pastoral Luther," in *The Pastoral Luther: Essays on Martin Luther's Practical Theology*, ed. Timothy J. Wengert (Grand Rapids, Michigan: Wm. B. Eerdmans, 2009), 15. An important note to add is that the use of "shepherd" here is related to that of "pastor."

Postscript

1. Oates, preface.

Bibliography

Abbott, Michael. "Bendigo." Leftlion. April 1, 2006. Accessed September 6, 2016. http://www.leftlion.co.uk/articles.cfm/title/bendigo-part-2/id/1174.
"Anti Prize Fight Law Valid." *The Chicago Tribune,* July 15, 1895.
Arnold, Patrick M. Wildmen, *Warriors, and Kings: Masculine Spirituality and the Bible.* New York: Crossroad, 1991.
"Art 4 God." Accessed November 16, 2016. http://art4god.com.
"As Time Goes By." *M*A*S*H.* First broadcast February 21, 1983 (season 11, episode 15) by CBS. Directed by Burt Metcalfe, and written by Dale Wilcox and Thad Mumford. Reviewed off commercial DVD, 20th Century Fox, release date February 26, 2013.
Ashe, Kaye. *The Feminization of the Church?* Kansas City: Sheed and Ward, 1997.
Bachman, Rachel. "College Boxing Clubs Rise from the Canvas." *Wall Street Journal* (New York, New York), Sept. 22, 2015. Accessed August 22, 2016. http://www.wsj.com/articles/college-boxing-clubs-rise-from-the-canvas-1442941846.
Baker, William J. *Playing with God: Religion and Modern Sport.* Cambridge, Massachusetts: Harvard University Press, 2007.
Barth, Karl. *The Call to Discipleship.* Translated by G. W. Bromiley. Edited by K.C. Hanson. Minneapolis, Minnesota: Fortress Press, 2003.
Bayless, Pamela. *The YMCA at 150: A History of the YMCA of Greater New York 1852–2002.* New York: YMCA of Greater New York, 2002.
Bays, Kimberly. "Ministry Reaching At-Risk Teens Through Boxing," *Philadelphia Neighborhoods,* February 10, 2010. Accessed December 17, 2016. https://philadelphianeighborhoods.com/2010/02/10/kensington-ministry-reaching-at-risk-teens-through-boxing/.
The Bells of St. Mary's. Directed by Leo McCarey. 1945. Chicago: Olive Films, 2013. DVD.
Bergan, Ronald. *Sports in the Movies.* New York: Proteus, 1982.
Besant, Walter. *East London.* London: Chatto & Windus, 1912.
Birch, Michael. Instructor, Rock Church's Karate Ministry, San Diego, California. Phone interview with the author. September 27, 2016.
Boddy, Kasia. *Boxing: A Cultural History.* London: Reaktion Books, 2008.
Borg, Marcus J. *Meeting Jesus Again for the First Time: The Historical Jesus & the Heart of Contemporary Faith.* New York: HarperCollins, 1994.
The Boxer. Directed by Jim Sheridan. 1977. Hollywood, CA: Universal Studies, 1998. DVD.
Boys Town. Directed by Norman Tourag. 1938. Burbank, CA: Warner Home Video, 2005. DVD.
Britton, Teejay. Director, Victory Gym and Fitness Center, Joplin, Missouri. Phone interview with the author. December 15, 2016.
Brogan, Jan. "Boxing, Not Fighting, Is the Focus at Dorchester Teen Center." *Globe*

Correspondent, May 14, 2013. Accessed December 20, 2016. https://www.bostonglobe.com/lifestyle/2013/05/13/boxing-not-fighting-focus-dorchester-teen-center/09LgsNKuSbE5P8VyQGq5hP/story.html.

Brown, Rev. J. Director of church relations, Concordia University, Texas, and former pastor of Praise Lutheran Church, and associate pastor at Concordia Lutheran Church, both in Fort Wayne, Indiana. Phone interview with the author. September 24, 2016.

Butler, Jack. *Jujitsu for Christ*. Little Rock, Arkansas: August House, 1986.

Cannon, Eoin. "Boxing Takes Hold at St. Peter's: Former Pros, Cops Teach Kids the Ropes." *Dorchester Reporter*, April 4, 2013. Accessed December 21, 2016. http://www.dotnews.com/2013/boxing-takes-hold-st-peter-s-former-pros-cops-teach-kids-ropes.

Caron, Christina. "High School Coach Dies in Church Boxing Match." *USA Today*, November 5, 2011.

Caspar, Ruth. "Play Springs Eternal." *The New Scholasticism* 52, no. 2 (1978): 187–201.

Catholic Charities of Boston. "About the Program." Accessed December 9, 2016. http://www.ccab.org/?q=TeenCenter.

"Catholic Magazine Calls Boxing 'Merciless, Inhuman.'" National Public Radio. October 27, 2005. Accessed September 26, 2016. http://www.npr.org/templates/story/story.php?storyId=4977604.

Cerrito, Rev. Craig. Assistant pastor, Rock Ministries, Calvary Chapel of Kensington, Pennsylvania. Phone interview with the author. September 19, 2016.

Christenberry, Robert K. "My Rugged Education in Boxing." Life, May 26, 1952.

Christian Karate Association. "Character Qualities." Accessed December 20, 2016. http://www.christiankarate.org/character-qualities.

Christian Karate Association. Accessed December 5, 2016. http://christiankarate.wixsite.com/welcome.

Clark, Charles. Boxing program instructor, Cross for Christ boxing gym, True Foundation Outreach Center, Columbus, Mississippi. Phone interview with the author. September 23, 2016.

Crossan, John Dominic. *How to Read the Bible and Still Be a Christian: Struggling with Divine Violence from Genesis through Revelation*. New York: Harper One, 2015.

"Culberson Prohibits the Big Fight." *The Chicago Tribune*, July 28, 1895.

The Daily Free Press (Carbondale, Illinois). June 19, 1906: 2.

"Dear Sis." *M*A*S*H*. First broadcast December 18, 1978 (season 7, episode 15) by CBS. Directed by Alan Alda, and written by Alan Alda and Larry Gelbart. Reviewed off commercial DVD, 20th Century Fox, release date February 26, 2013.

Determan, Paula. *The Cry of a Warrior*. Spring Hill, Tennessee: Holy Fire Publishing, 2013.

Donovan, Barna William. *Blood, Guns and Testosterone: Action Films, Audiences, and a Thirst for Violence*. London: Scarecrow Press, 2010.

Dorman, Abby. "Blood, Sweat, and Jesus: The Power of Sports Ministries." *Millennial Influx*. March 6, 2015. Accessed August 15, 2016. http://www.millennialinflux.com/blood-sweat-and-jesus-the-power-of-sports-ministry/.

Douglas, Ann. *The Feminization of American Culture*. New York: Alfred A. Knopf, 1977.

Doyle, Paul. Boxing program instructor, formerly of the Teen Center at St. Peter's Church in Dorchester, Massachusetts (part of Catholic Charities of Boston), and now of the Colonel Marr Boys & Girls Club of Dorchester. Phone interview with the author. September 27, 2016.

Eckhoff, Sally. Review of *JuJitsu for Christ*. *Village Voice* literary supplement, April, 1987: 3.

Ellul, Jacquez. *Violence: Reflections from a Christian Perspective*. New York: Seabury, 1969.

Elmer Gantry. Directed by Richard Brooks. 1960. Beverly Hills, CA: Metro-Goldwyn-Mayer Home Entertainment, 2001. DVD.
Erskine, Chris. "The Minister can Preach the Virtues of Boxing…" *Los Angeles Times*, December 17, 2014.
Evans, Christopher H. and William R. Herzog II. "The Faith of Fifty Million: A Kingdom on Earth?" In *The Faith of Fifty Million: Baseball, Religion and American Culture*. Westminster John Knox Press: Louisville, Kentucky, 2002.
Faulkner, David. "The Confidence Man: Empire and the Destruction of Muscular Christianity in The Mystery of Edwin Drood." In *Muscular Christianity: Embodying the Victorian Age*, edited by Donald E. Hall (New York: Cambridge University Press, 1974).
Felix, Cristino. Former President of Christian Boxing Academy in Jersey City, New Jersey. Phone interview with the author. March 8, 2018. And personal correspondence with the author. January 30, 31, and February 2, 2020.
Fight Church. Directed by Daniel Junge and Brian Storkel. 2014. Jax Distribution, 2014. DVD.
"Fighting Back." *Sons of Thunder*. First broadcast March 13, 1999 (season 1, episode 2) by CBS. Directed by Michael Preece. Reviewed off YouTube.
"Fighting Parson Runs Boxing Club." *The Day* (New London, CT), January 8, 1917.
Fighting Politics. Directed by Emily Vahey. 2009. Media Fly Films.
Forde, Gerhard O. "Loser Takes All: The Victory of Christ." In *A More Radical Gospel: Essays on Eschatology, Authority, Atonement, and Ecumenism*, edited by Mark C. Mattes and Steven D. Paulson. Grand Rapids, Michigan: Wm. B. Eerdmans, 2004.
Forde, Gerhard O. *On Being a Theologian of the Cross: Reflections on Luther's Heidelberg Disputation, 1518*. Grand Rapids, Michigan: William B. Eerdmans Publishing, 1997.
Foreman, George. *God in My Corner*. Nashville, Tennessee: Thomas Nelson, 2007.
Frank, Evan. "Slugging it Out: The Story of Boxing as a High School Sport." *Lake Country Now* (Oconomowoc, Wisconsin), May 6, 2015. Accessed August 23, 2016. http://www.lakecountrynow.com/sports/oconomowocfocus/slugging-it-out-the-story-of-boxing-as-a-high-school-sport-b99494819z1-302757381.
French, R.T. *The Gospel of Matthew: The New International Commentary on the New Testament*. Grand Rapids, Michigan: William B. Eerdmans, 2007.
Galli, Mark. "Punches, Smashes, and Bombs: Boxing Gives Us a Window into the Violence Inherent in All Sports." *Christianity Today* (online), November 11, 2005. Accessed October 17, 2016. http://www.christianitytoday.com/ct/2005/november-web-only/52.0a.html.
Galli, Mark. "Should We Ban Boxing?" *Christianity Today* (online). October 28, 2005. Accessed October 17, 2016. http://www.christianitytoday.com/ct/2005/october-web-only/52.0c.html.
Galli, Mark. "Transformed by a Left Hook." *Christianity Today* (online). December 2, 2005. Accessed October 17, 2016. http://www.christianitytoday.com/ct/2005/novemberweb-only/53.0d.html.
Gelfer, Joseph. *Numen, Old Men: Contemporary Masculinity Spiritualities and the Problem of Patriarchy*. Oatville, Connecticut: Equinox, 2009.
Gems, Gerald R. "Sport, Religion and Americanization: Bishop Sheil and the Catholic Youth Organization." In *The International Journal of the History of Sport* 10 (1993): 233–241.
Gentry III, Clyde. *No Holds Barred: The Complete History of Mixed Martial Arts in America*. Chicago, Illinois: Triumph Books, 2011.
Gladden, Washington. *Amusements: Their Uses and Abuses*. North Adams, MA: James T. Robinson and Co., 1866.
"Goodbye, Farewell and Amen." *M*A*S*H*. First broadcast February 28, 1983 (season 11, episode 16) by CBS. Directed by Alan Alda, and written by Alan Alda, Burt Metcalf, et al. Reviewed off commercial DVD, 20th Century Fox, release date February 26, 2013.

Gottschall, Jonathan. *The Professor in the Cage: Why Men Fight and Why We Like to Watch.* New York: Penguin, 2016.
Green, Thomas A., and Joseph Svinth. "Brazilian Jiu-Jitsu." In *Martial Arts of the World: An Encyclopedia,* edited by Thomas A. Green. Santa Barbara, California: ABC-Clio, 2001.
Grindon, Leger. *Knockout: The Boxer and Boxing in American Cinema.* Jackson, Mississippi: University Press of Mississippi, 2011.
Groeschel, Craig. *Fight: Winning the Battles that Matter Most.* Grand Rapids, Michigan: Zondervan, 2013.
Grossman, Ron. "Chicago Bishop saw Refuge for Youths in the Boxing Ring." *Chicago Tribune,* September 18, 2015. Accessed September 19, 2016. http://www.chicagotribune.com/news/history/ct-bishop-bernard-sheil-pope-francis-flashback-0920-20150918-story.html.
Gustav-Wrathall, John Donald. *Take the Young Stranger by the Hand: Same-sex Relations and the YMCA.* Chicago: University of Chicago Press, 2000.
Hamilton, Mark. "An Augustinian Critique of our Relationship to Sport." In *Theology, Ethics and Transcendence in Sports,* edited by Jim Parry, Mark Nesti and Nick Watson. New York: Routledge, 2011.
Harris, Ronald. "Muay Thai." In *Martial Arts of the World: An Encyclopedia,* edited by Thomas A. Green. Santa Barbara, California: ABC-Clio, 2001.
"Heroes." *M*A*S*H.* First broadcast March 15, 1978 (season 10, episode 18) by CBS. Directed by Neil Cox, and written by Thad Mumford and Dan Wilcox. Reviewed off commercial DVD, 20th Century Fox, release date February 26, 2013.
Higgs, Robert J. *God in the Stadium: Sports and Religion in America.* Lexington, Kentucky: University Press of Kentucky, 1995.
"His Last Fight." *Poverty Bay Herald* (Volume 34, issue 10881). January 26, 1907.
Hoffman, Shirl. "Prayers Out of Bounds." In *Theology, Ethics and Transcendence in Sports,* edited by Jim Parry, Mark Nesti, and Nick Watson. New York: Routledge, 2011.
Hoffman, Shirl James. *Christianity and the Culture of Sports.* Waco, Texas: Baylor University Press, 2010.
Holmes, Arthur F. "Toward a Christian Play Ethic." *Christian Scholar's Review* 11, no. 1 (1981): 41–48.
Holt, Richard. *Sport and the British: A Modern History.* (Oxford: Clarendon Press, 1989.
"How a Boxing Gym Helps this Baltimore Church Fight for Kids." PBS. November 30, 2015. Accessed August 17, 2016. http://www.pbs.org/newshour/bb/how-a-boxing-gym-helps-this-baltimore-church-fight-for-kids/.
Hughes, Thomas. *The Manliness of Christ.* Boston: Houghton, Osgood and Company, 1880.
Hughes, Thomas. *Tom Brown's Schooldays.* New York: E.P. Dutton & Co., 1962.
Hughes, Thomas. *True Manliness.* Boston: D. Lothrop and Company, 1880.
Huizinga, Johan. *Homo Ludens: A Study of the Play Element in Culture.* Kettering, Ohio: Angelico Press, 2016.
Hyland, Drew. "Competition and Friendship." *Journal of the Philosophy of Sport* 5 (1979): 27–37.
Jesus Didn't Tap—Christian Apparel and MMA Gear. Accessed November 10, 2016. http://jesusdidnttap.com.
Johnson, Jessica. "Christians and Cage Fighting, from Fight Church to Mark Driscoll." *Religion Dispatches.* September 29, 2014. Accessed December 23, 2016. http://religiondispatches.org/christians-and-cage-fighting-from-fight-church-to-mark-driscoll/.
Johnston, Robert. *The Christian at Play.* Grand Rapids, Michigan: William B. Eerdmans, 1983.

Bibliography 187

Joyce, Mike. Vice president of programming, Boys and Girls Club of Dorchester, Massachusetts. Phone interview with the author. September 22, 2016.

Junge, Daniel, and Bryan Storkel. "Pastor with a Punch." *New York Times*, September 8, 2014.

Kauz, Herman. *The Martial Spirit: An Introduction to the Origin, Philosophy, and Psychology of the Martial Arts*. Woodstock, New York: Overlook Press, 1977.

"KeepItPlayful," a blog of Ryron Gracie. "The KeepItPlayful Movement." Posted January 2, 2013. https://keepitplayful.wordpress.com/2013/01/02/the-keepitplayful-movement/.

Kid Monk Baroni. Directed by Harold D. Schuster. 1952. Hollywood, California: Image Entertainment, 2007. DVD.

Kingsley, Charles. "Nausicca in London." In *Good Words*, edited by Rev. Donald Macleod. London: Daldy, Isbister & Co., 1874.

Kirkpatrick, David. D. "Wrath and Mercy: Return of the Warrior Jesus." *New York Times*, April 4, 2004. Accessed February 7. 2020. https://www.nytimes.com/2004/04/04/weekinreview/wrath-and-mercy-the-return-of-the-warrior-jesus.html.

Kolb, Robert. "Luther on the Theology of the Cross." In *The Pastoral Luther: Essays on Martin Luther's Practical Theology*. Edited by Timothy J. Wengert. Grand Rapids, Michigan: William B. Eerdmans, 2009.

Kormar, Melissa. "Bibles and Boxing Gloves." Star, December 9, 2014. Accessed December 17, 2016. http://www.starnewsphilly.com/2014/dec/9/bibles-and-boxing-gloves/#.WFCcUXeZPMU.

Ladd, Tony, and James A. Mathisen. *Muscular Christianity: Evangelical Protestants and the Development of American Sport*. Grand Rapids, Michigan: Baker Books, 1999.

Lang, Arne K. *Prizefighting: An American History*. Jefferson, North Carolina: McFarland, 2008.

Lanning, Rev. Jarrod. Pastor of Trinity Lutheran Church, North Carolina. Phone interview with the author. September 26, 2016.

Linville, Greg. "Ethics Competition in Church Setting." In *Recreation and Sports Ministry: Impacting Postmodern Culture*. Edited by John Garner. Nashville, Tennessee: Broadman & Holman, 2003.

Long, William J. "Judo." In *Martial Arts of the World: An Encyclopedia*. Edited by Thomas A. Green. Santa Barbara, California: ABC-Clio, 2001.

Maragay, Dino. "Pope Francis Named 'Champion of Faith' by Boxing Body." *The Philippine Star*, February 4, 2016. Accessed September 26, 2016. http://www.philstar.com/sports/2016/02/04/1549633/pope-francis-named-champion-faith-boxing-body.

Marie, Brownie. "Pastor's 'Fight Ministry'…" *Christianity Today*, September 12, 2014.

Marty, Martin. *Pilgrims in Their Own Land: 500 Years of Religion in America*. New York: Penguin, 1984.

Mason, Bryan. *Beyond the Gold: What Every Church Needs to Know about Sports Ministry*. United Kingdom: Authentic, 2011.

Mattes, Mark C. "Theology of the Cross." In *Dictionary of Luther and Lutheran Traditions*, edited by Timothy J. Wengert, Mark A. Granquist, Mary Jane Haemig, Robert Kolb, Mark C. Mattes and Jonathan Strom. Grand Rapids, Michigan: Baker Academic, 2017.

McCarthy, Justin. *Modern Leaders: Being a Series of Biographical Sketches*. New York: Sheldon & Company, 1872.

McCormick, Richard A. "Is Professional Boxing Immoral?" *Sports Illustrated*. November 5, 1962.

McGrath, Alister E. *Luther's Theology of the Cross: Martin Luther's Theological Breakthrough*. New York: Basil Blackwell, 1985.

Moore, Robert, and Douglas Gillette. *King, Warrior, Magician, Lover: Rediscovering the Archetypes of the Mature Masculine*. San Francisco: HarperCollins, 1991.

Morrow, Mark. Pastor and head of SonRise Church and Church Street Boxing, in Salem, Oregon. Phone interview with the author. March 14, 2018.

Mosley, Mike. Boxing program instructor, Fist of God boxing, Created for So Much More Worship Center, Baltimore, Maryland. Phone interview with the author. September 29, 2016.

Motley, Clay. "Fighting for Manhood: Rocky and Turn-of-the-Century Antimodernism." In *All-Stars & Movie Stars: Sports in Film & History*, edited by Ron Briley, Michael K. Schoenecke, and Deborah A. Carmichael. Lexington, Kentucky: University Press of Kentucky, 2008.

Muller, Antoinette. "Why Are We Less Tolerant of Boxing Injuries Than in Other Sports?" *Daily Maverick*, April 1, 2016. Accessed August 24, 2016. http://www.dailymaverick.co.za/article/2016-04-01-why-are-we-less-tolerant-of-boxing-injuries-than-in-other-sports/.

Murrow, David. *Why Men Hate Going to Church*. Nashville, Tennessee: Nelson Books, 2005.

Myers, Jack. *The Future of Men: Masculinity in the Twenty-First Century*. San Francisco: Inkshares, 2016.

Myers, Jack. "Young Men Are Facing a Masculinity Crisis." *Time*, May 26, 2016. Accessed November 9, 2016. http://time.com/4339209/masculinity-crisis/.

Neary, Timothy B. *Crossing Parish Boundaries: Race, Sports, and Catholic Youth in Chicago, 1914–1954*. Chicago: University of Chicago Press, 2016.

Oates, Joyce Carol. *On Boxing* (Updated and Expanded Edition). New York: Harper Perennial, 2006.

Oswald, Rodger. "Biblical Foundations of Sports Ministry: Defining the Phenomenon." In *Recreation and Sports Ministry: Impacting Postmodern Culture*, edited by John Garner. Nashville, Tennessee: Broadman & Holman, 2003.

Park, Adam. "Boxing and the YMCA War Dogs." *Religion in American History* (blog). Posted August 8, 2016. http://usreligion.blogspot.com/2016/08/boxing-and-ymca-war-dogs.html.

Peake, Jason. "The Pugilist Preacher: Britton Inspires In and Out of the Cage." *Joplin Globe*, May 17, 2016. Accessed December 23, 2016. http://www.joplinglobe.com/sports/local_sports/the-pugilist-preacher-britton-inspires-in-and-out-of-the/article_f1f5c2ff-5bc4-5625-9b6b-f1b5d542fb22.html.

Pearson, Ray. "'Fighting Parson' Puts on the Gloves." *Chicago Daily Tribune*, January 4, 1918.

Pearson, Ray. "'Fighting Parson,' Now in Chicago, Lauds Sport at War Camps." *Chicago Daily Tribune*, November 14, 1917.

Perales, Rev. Servando. Founder and coach at Victory Boxing Club of Omaha, Nebraska. Phone interview with the author. August 7, 2017.

Pfitzner, Victor. *Paul and the Agon Motif: Traditional Athletic Imagery in the Pauline Literature* (Novum Testament Supplement 16). Leiden, South Holland: E.J. Brill, 1967.

Pfitzner, Victor C. "Was St. Paul a Sports Enthusiast? Realism and Rhetoric in Pauline Athletic Metaphors." In *Sports and Christianity: Historical and Contemporary Perspectives*, edited by Nick J. Watson and Andrew Parker. New York: Routledge, 2013.

Podles, Leon J. *The Church Impotent: The Feminization of Christianity*. Dallas: Spence Publishing Company, 1999.

Price, Joseph L. "From Sabbath Proscriptions to Super Sunday Celebrations: Sports and Religion in America." In *From Season to Season: Sports as American Religion*, edited by Joseph L. Price. Macon, Georgia: Mercer University Press, 2001.

Prince, David E. *In the Arena: The Promise of Sports for Christian Discipleship*. Nashville, Tennessee: B&H Books, 2016.

Prothero, Stephen. *American Jesus: How the Son of God Became a National Icon.* New York: Farrar, Straus and Giroux, 2003.
Putney, Clifford. *Muscular Christianity: Manhood and Sports in Protestant America, 1880–1920.* Cambridge, Massachusetts: Harvard University Press, 2001.
Pyle, Nate. *Man Enough: How Jesus Redefines Manhood.* Grand Rapids, Michigan: Zondervan, 2015.
Ramos, Sonia. Founder, president and CEO of Boxing for Christ in San Jacinto, California. Phone interview with the author. December 12, 2018.
Reed, Anna. "Church Mixes Worship and Boxing." *The (Salem) Statesman Journal,* April 15, 2017. Accessed March 15, 2018. https://www.statesmanjournal.com/story/life/faith/2017/04/12/sonrise-church-boxing-salem-oregon/100300090/
Richards, Rev. Thomas. Pastor of St. Paul's Lutheran Church, Tannersville, Pennsylvania. Phone interview with the author. September 25, 2016.
Roark, David. "A Theology of Sports." *The Village Church* (blog), March 26, 2015. Accessed August 27, 2016. http://www.thevillagechurch.net/the-village-blog/a-theology-of-sports/.
Rodriguez, Robert G. *The Regulation of Boxing: A History and Comparative Analysis of Policies Among American States.* Jefferson, North Carolina: McFarland, 2009.
Romano, Frederick V. *The Boxing Filmography: American Features, 1920–2003.* Jefferson, North Carolina: McFarland, 2004.
Sammons, Jeffrey T. *Beyond the Ring: The Role of Boxing in American Society.* Chicago, Illinois: University of Illinois Press, 1990.
Schneiderman, R.M. "Flock Is Now a Fight Team." *New York Times.* February 2, 2010.
Scott, David H.T. *The Art and Aesthetics of Boxing.* Lincoln, Nebraska: University of Nebraska Press, 2008.
Shafer, Michael. *Well Played: A Christian Theology of Sport and the Ethics of Doping.* Eugene, Oregon: Pickwick Publications, 2015.
Shirley, Phil. *The Soul of Boxing: What Motivates the World's Greatest Fighters?* United Kingdom: HarperCollins, 2000.
Silvas, Ruben. Boxing coach with West Side Boxing and Fitness, a part of Escape Ministries, in Holland, Michigan. Phone interview with the author. March 14, 2018.
Sing, Susan Saint. "The Energy of Play." In *Theology, Ethics and Transcendence in Sports,* edited by Jim Parry, Mark Nesti and Nick Watson. New York: Routledge, 2011.
Steinfels, Peter. Obituary for Robert A McCormick. *The New York Times.* February 15, 2000.
Steinke, Peter L. *Preaching the Theology of the Cross.* Minneapolis, Minnesota: Augsburg Publishing, 1983.
Streible, Dan. "Female Spectators and the Corbett-Fitzsimmons Fight Film." In *Out of Bounds: Sports, Media, and the Politics of Identity,* edited by Aaron Baker and Todd Boyd. Bloomington, Indiana: Indiana University Press, 1997.
Streible, Dan. *Fight Pictures: A History of Boxing and Early Cinema.* Berkeley, California: University of California Press, 2008.
Sugden, John. *Boxing and Society: An International Analysis.* New York: Manchester University Press, 1996.
Sullivan, Russell. *Rocky Marciano: The Rock of His Times.* Chicago: University of Illinois Press, 2002.
"Taekwondo, Like Agriculture, Can Be Beneficial at Any Age." *North Carolina Field and Family.* January 31, 2013. Accessed December 6, 2016. http://www.ncfieldfamily.org/nc-living/taekwondo-like-agriculture-can-be-beneficial-at-any-age/.
Tansk, Gene P. "Taekwondo." In *Martial Arts of the World: An Encyclopedia.* Edited by Thomas A. Green. Santa Barbara, California: ABC-Clio, 2001.
Thomasos, Christine. "Manny Pacquiao Prepares for Fight, Prays for his Opponents." *The Christian Post,* November 10, 2011. Accessed April 4, 2017. http://www.

christianpost.com/news/manny-pacquiao-prepares-for-fight-prays-for-opponents-61410/print.html.

Thrasher, Christopher David. *Fight Sports and American Masculinity: Salvation in Violence from 1607 to the Present.* Jefferson, North Carolina: McFarland, 2015.

"To Arrest Fitzsimmons." *The Chicago Tribune,* July 21, 1891.

"Training Programs." At the Gracie Jiu-Jitsu Academy. Accessed October 20, 2016. http://www.gracieacademy.com/training_programs.asp.

Treat, Jeremy R. "More Than a Game: A Theology of Sport." *Themelios: An International Journal for Students of Theological and Religious Studies* 40, no. 3 (2015): 392–403.

Truong, Andrew. Instructor, Rock Church's Trinity MMA, Vista, California. Phone interview with the author. October 1, 2016.

Velazquez-Stetz, Valerie. "Blue Suicide Hits Home for JCPD Lt. Felix." In *The Blue Magazine* online. (No date.) Accessed February 2, 2020. https://www.thebluemagazine.com/blue-suicide-hits-home-for-jcpd-lt-felix.

Victory Ministry and Sports Complex. Accessed December 19, 2016. http://victoryjoplin.com/wp/.

von Loewenich, Walther. *Luther's Theology of the Cross.* Translated by Herbert J.A. Bouman. Minneapolis, Minnesota: Augsburg Publishing House. 1976.

Watson, Nick, and Brian Bolt. "Mixed Martial Arts and Christianity: 'Where Feet, Fist and Faith Collide.'" *The Conversation.* January 5, 2015. http://theconversation.com/mixed-martial-arts-and-christianity-where-feet-fist-and-faith-collide-34836.

Watson, Nick J. "Muscular Christianity in the Modern Age: 'Wining for Christ' or 'Playing for Glory'?" In *Sport and Spirituality: An Introduction.* New York: Routledge, 2007.

Watson, Nick J., and Brian Brock. "Christianity, Boxing and Mixed Martial Arts: Reflections on Morality, Vocation and Well-Being." *Journal of Religion and Society* 17 (2015): 1–22.

Watson, Nick J., and John White. "'Winning at all Costs' in Modern Sport: Reflections on Pride and Humility in the Writings of C.S. Lewis." In *Sport and Spirituality: An Introduction.* New York: Routledge, 2007.

Wedge, Frederick R. *The Fighting Parson of Barbary Coast.* Washington, D.C.: Frederick R. Wedge, 1912.

Weier, Jonathan. "The Building of Boys for War: The Militarization of Boys' Work in the Canadian and American YMCAs." In *Children's Literature and the Culture of the First World War,* edited by Lissa Paul, Rosemary Ross Johnston, and Emma Short. New York: Routledge: 2016.

Wengert, Timothy J. "Introducing the Pastoral Luther." In *The Pastoral Luther: Essays on Martin Luther's Practical Theology,* edited by Timothy J. Wengert. Grand Rapids, Michigan: Wm. B. Eerdmans, 2009.

Wilcox, Nate. "Redeeming MMA for Christians: A Controversial Mega-Church Pastor if Pro-MMA." *Bloody Elbow.* February 12, 2012. Accessed December 21, 2016. http://www.bloodyelbow.com/2012/2/12/2793395/redeeming-mma-for-christians-a-controversial-mega-church-pastor-is.

Williams, Brad. "Dear Driscoll, MMA is Not a Measure of Manhood—Jesus Is." *Christ and Popular Culture.* November 17, 2011. Accessed December 30, 2016. http://christandpopculture.com/mark-driscoll-mma-is-not-the-measure-of-manhood-jesus-is/.

Wilson, Steve. Founder and chief instructor, Christian Karate. Phone interview with the author. September 22, 2016.

Wink, Walter. *Engaging the Powers: Discernment and Resistance in a World of Domination.* Minneapolis, Minnesota: Fortress Press, 1992.

Wink, Walter. *Jesus and Nonviolence: A Third Way.* Minneapolis, Minnesota: Fortress, 2003.

Woodruff, Bob, and Ben Newman. "In Jesus' Name, Throw Punches: 'Fight Church' Christian Ministries Believe in Fight Clubs." *ABC News* (abcnews.go.com), October 3, 2014. Accessed September 27, 2016. http://abcnews.go.com/US/jesus-throw-punches-fight-church-christian-ministries-fight/story?id=25953786.

Woodward, Kath. *Boxing, Masculinity and Identity: The "I" of the Tiger*. New York: Routledge, 2007.

Worthen, Molly. "Who Would Jesus Smack Down?" *New York Times Magazine*, January 6, 2009.

Yi, Joseph E. *God and Karate on the Southside: Bridging Differences, Building American Communities*. Lanham, Maryland: Rowman & Littlefield Publishers, 2009.

Young, Steve, and Angus Leader. "Churchgoers Turn the Other Cheek in the Ring." *USA Today*, February 2, 2009.

Zinczenko, David. "It Only Looks Dangerous." *The New York Times*, April 1, 2011.

Index

Numbers in **_bold italics_** indicate pages with illustrations

adiaphora 25, 148–150, 160, 164–165
Adkins, Scott 38
American Medical Association 83
Aquinas, Thomas 2
Arnold, Patrick M. 49
Ashe, Kay 48–49

Baker, William J. 21
Baptist church 41, 58, 143
Barth, Karl 161–162
Beals, Brandon 143
Beecher, Henry Ward 39
The Bells of St. Mary's 8, 64–66, **_67_**
Bendigo _see_ Thompson of Nottingham, William
Bentham, Jeremy 80
Bergman, Ingrid 64, **_66_**, **_67_**
Besant, Walter 28–29
Biddle, Anthony J. Drexel 42
Birch, Michael 115, 137
Blackman, John 22
Boddy, Kasia 79–80
body as temple 85, 91–95, 101, 105–106, 112–115, 179n12
Bonhoeffer, Dietrich 18
Borg, Marcus 161
The Boxer 24, 73–74
Boxing for Christ (San Jacinto, CA) 10, 130–133, **_131_**, **_133_**
Boy's Town 8, 63, **_64_**, **_65_**
Brazilian jiu-jitsu (BJJ) 4, 12, 13, 15, 85, 107, 135, 136
British Medical Association 83
Britton, Teejay 135–137
Brock, Brian 18
Broughton, Jack 14
Brown, Pr. J. 139, **_140_**
Buress, Paul 74–75
Butler, Jack 24, 60–63

Campus Crusade for Christ 36
Carpentier, George 41
Catholic Charities of Boston 120

Catholic church 7, 10, 33–36, 4, 44, 45, 74, 75, 111, 120–121
Catholic Youth Organization (CYO) 7, 8, 23, 24, 33–37, 38, 44, 53, 71, **_71_**, 147
Cerrito, Rev. Craig 119
Chan, Jackie 37
character development 31, 33, 36, 38, 43, 85, 95–98, 100, 108, 112, 138, 142, 179n12
Chase, Rev. William 42
Christenberry, Robert H. 43
Christian Boxing Academy (Jersey City, NJ) 116–117, 122–124, **_123_**
Christian Karate Association 10, 38, 113–114, **_114_**
Christology 9, 17, 48
Christopher, William 69, **_71_**
Church Street Boxing (Salem, OR) 134–135
Cityline Church (New Jersey) 124
Clark, Charles 115–116
Colonel Marr Boys & Girls Club (Dorchester, MA) 120, **_121_**
Concord Karate Club (Fort Wayne, IN) 10, 139
Congregational church 39
Conway, Fr. Richard 120–121, **_121_**
Corbett, James 40
Crosby, Bing 63–64, **_66_**
Cross for Christ Boxing Gym 11, 115
cross, theology of the 25, 153–159, 163
Crossan, John Dominic 89, 91, 93, 162–163
Culberson, Charles 40

David (biblical figure) 43, 49, 88, 114
Day-Lewis, Daniel 73
Dempsey, Jack 41
Dickens, Charles 24, 57, 63
Dio Chrysostom 87
discipleship 4, 6, 9–10, 16, 17–18, 20, 22, 23, 25, 27, 29, 31, 34, 38, 45–46, 50, 78, 88, 96, 97, 113, 139, 146, 148, 152, 155, 157–165, 167, 169
Dobson, James C. 143
Dobson, Ryan 143

Index

Douglas, Ann 48, 81
Doyle, Paul 120-122, **121**
Driscoll, Mark 143-144, 151-152
Duffel, Fr. John 45

ecclesiology 17, 23, 47-52, 147, 151, 152, 160
Ellroy, James 25
Ellul, Jacques 2, 5, 89, 115
Elmer Gantry 69, **69**
Episcopal Church 42, 43
Esau (biblical figure) 50
Escape Ministries (Holland, MI) 10, 128-130
evangelical religion 10, 11, 30-31, 68, 111, 143, 149
evangelism 6, 9, 17, 29, 36, 45, 47, 49, 51, 84, 104, 111, 139, 145, 161, 164, 169

Felix, Cristino 116-117, 122-124
Fellowship of Christian Athletes 36
feminization 11, 17, 23, 47-49, 52, 54, 64, 66, 74-75, 81, 142, 143, 144, 145, 147, 164
Figg, James 13-14
Fight Church 11, 45, 74-75, 81, 88, 142-143, 144
The Fighting Parson of Barbary Coast 58-60, 63
Fist of God boxing ministry (Cherry Hill, MD) 11, 115-116, 117
Fitzsimmons, Bob 40-41
Flanagan, Fr. Edward J. 63, **64**, **65**
Focus on the Family 143
Forde, Gerhard O. 155, 156, 159
Foreman, George 7, 19
Francis, Pope 44
Frank, Jason David 76

Galli, Mark 93-94, 109
Gardner, Hezekiah Orville 30
Geertz, Clifford 80
Gelfer, Joseph 49-50
Gentry, Clyde III 21
Girard, Rene 79
Gladden, Washington 39
glory, theology of 17, 20, 25, 96, 108, 109, 144, 148, 151-159, 162, 163, 164
Going My Way 63-64
Goliath (biblical figure) 43, 88
Gottschall, Jonathan 77, 78, 79, 80, 112
Gracie Jiu-Jitsu 13, 37, 106-108
Green Hornet 37
Grindon, Leger 81
Groeshel, Craig 51

Hall, Jim 40
Hamilton, Mark 159-160
Higgs, Robert J. 157-159
Hocker, Pr. Preston 45, 75, 142-143
Hoffman, Shirl James 21, 96-101, 103-104, 109
Holyfield, Evander 125
hopkido 112
Hughes, Thomas 23, 28-29, 39, 48, 53-57, 63, 69, 74, 76, 78-80, 147, 150

Huizinga, Johan 102-103
Hyers, Tom 39
Hyland, Drew 101, 109

imago dei 24, 85, 91-95, 101, 104, 106
Ireland, Archbishop John 40

Jacob (biblical figure) 43, 50, 88, 177n23
Jeffries, James 41
Johnson, Jack 41
Joyce, Mike 122
judo 12, 13, 37, 38
Jujitsu for Christ 60-63
Junge, Daniel 11

karate 10, 12, 13, 15, 37, 60, 63, 73, 111, 114, 115, 137, 139, 140
The Karate Kid 13, 72
Kickboxer 37
kickboxing 10, 12, 14-15, 111, 119, 135
Kid Monk Baroni 66-68
Kingsley, Charles 28, 57, 95
knight model 25, 151, 157-159, 162

Ladd, Tony 21
Lancaster, Burt **69**
Lang, Arne K. 21
Lanning, Pr. Jarrod 112-113, 141
The Leather Saint 68
Lee, Bruce 37
Lewis, Lenox 125
Lewis Law 42
Linville, Greg 99-100
Lombardi, Vince 98
Luther, Martin 155, 156, 163
Lutheran church 10, 112, 114, 139, 140, 141

Malone, Henry 51
manliness 27, 48, 53-54,
The Manliness of Christ 28, 48, 53-54, 63, 78-80, 81, 158
Marciano, Rocky 7, 19
Martinez, Luis Alberto 51
*M*A*S*H* 69-72, **71**
Mason, Bryan 22
Mathisen, James A. 21, 110
McCormick, Fr. Richard A. 43-44
Melancomas 87
Merriam, William 40
Merton, Thomas 2
Methodist church 37, 39, 41
millennial theology 32
Moody, Dwight 31
Morin, Trinidad 128
Morrow, Pr. Mark 134-135
Mosley, Mike 115-117
muay thai 12, 13, 135
Mulcahy, Father John Francis Patrick 24, 69-72, **71**
Muldoon, William 42-43
Murrow, David 51

muscular Christianity 8, 9, 19, 21, 23, 27–34, 39, 42, 46, 47–48, 52–53, 54, 56, 57, 63, 68, 73, 77, 78, 82, 95, 101, 105, 147, 152
Myers, Jack 77, 78, 79
The Mystery of Edwin Drood 57

New Jersey State Athletic Commission 45
New York State Athletic Commission 42
The New York Times 11, 43, 76, 143–144
Nimoy, Leonard 6
Norris, Chuck 13, 37, 72
Novak, Paul 51

Oates, Joyce Carol 3, 27, 47–48, 52, 83, 111–112, 122, 167
Ong, Walter 77–78, 80
Orr, Paul 119
Osborne, Buddy 118

Pacquiao, Manny 7, 19
Perales, Rev. Servando 116, 125–128, **126**
play 17, 24, 30, 80, 84, 85, 94, 99–109, 112, 119, 137, 142, 149, 152–153, 164–165
Podles, Leon J. 48–50
Presbyterian church 41, 43
Price, Joseph L. 19–21, 38, 86, 149, 150, 164
Prince, David E. 22, 162
Protestant 10, 21, 49, 74, 111, 148
Public Broadcasting System (PBS) 11, 145
Putney, Clifford 21
Pyle, Nate 50–51, 150

The Quiet Man 68

Ramos, Danny **133**
Ramos, David 130, **131**
Ramos, Sonia 130–134, **131**, **133**
Reformed church 128
Renken, John 75, 143
retributive violence 88–90, 93
Richards, Pr. Thomas 114–115, 140–141
Rock Church (San Diego, CA) 10, 115, 137, **138**
Rock Ministry of Calvary Chapel (Kensington, PA) 10, 118–120
Rocky 7–8, **8**
Rooney, Mickey **64**, **65**

St. Augustine 7, 153, 159
St. John the Divine Cathedral 20, 43, 88
St. Paul 6, 7, 20, 24, 85–87, 89, 162, 163
Sammons, Jeffrey T. 21
Saunders, Bishop Willard 118
Sawyer, Stephen 76
Shafer, Michael 16, 21, 92–93, 97, 100, 101, 108
Sheil, Bishop Bernard J. 33–36
shepherd model 17, 25, 82, 151, 157–159, 162–163, 182n38
Silvas, Ruben 128–130
social gospel 30, 39
SonRise Church (Salem, OR) 10, 134–135

Sons of Thunder 24, 72–73
Sports Ambassadors 36
Stallone, Sylvester **8**
Statham, Jason 37
Storkel, Bryan 11
Sullivan, James 39
Sullivan, Scott 75
Sunday, Billy 31–32, 48, 53, 69, 74, 76, 124, 147, 150

taekwondo 12, 13, 37, 111
Taylor, Dr. B.W.R. 42
Teen Center at St. Peter's Church (Dorchester, MA) 10, 120–122
Tennessee Champ 68
Terry, John 22, 51
Thomas, Frank **64**
Thompson of Nottingham, William (Bendigo) 29, 74
Thrasher, Christopher David 21
Tiger Schulmann's Karate and Martial Arts 37
Tom Brown's School Days 23, 28, 53, 55
Tracy, Spencer 63, **64**, **65**
Trinity Martial Arts Club (Fort Wayne, IN) 139
Trinity MMA 115, 137, 138
True Manliness 53
Truong, Andrew 115, 137, **138**
Tunney, Gene 41
Tyler, Richard "Dickie" **67**

The Ultimate Fighter 37, 44–45
Ultimate Fighting Championship (UFC) 12, 51, 81, 143, 144, 151, 152
USA Boxing 119, 124, 127, 128, 130, **133**

Van Damme, Jean-Claude 37
Venture for Victory 36
Victory Boxing Club (Omaha, NE) 10, 116, 125–128, **126**, 145
Victory Ministry and Sports Complex (Joplin, MO) 11, 135–136

Wahlberg, Mark 120
Walker Law 42
Walker, Texas Ranger 72–73
Ward, Micky 120
Warrior 37
warrior model 23, 25, 27, 49–52, 54, 69, 74–75, 76, 82, 96, 116, 137, 145, 147, 151, 158, 162–164
Waterman, Ron 51
Watson, Nick 18
The Way of the Dragon 37
Wayne, John 68
Weber, Stu 51
Wedge, Rev. Frederick 32, 58–60
West Side Boxing and Fitness (Holland, MI) 10, 128–130
Willard, Jess 41
Williams, Pr. Brad 151–152

Williamson, Wendy 22, 51
Wilson, the Rev. Steve 113–114, *114*, 138–139
Wilson, Woodrow 32
Wink, Walter 90
Wise, Rev. John 88
World Boxing Council (WBC) 44
World War I 32, 37

World War II 33, 35, 37, 43
wrestling 12, 15, 32, 43, 54, 85, 88

Young Men's Christian Organization (YMCA) 7, 8, 23, 30–33, 35, 36, 37, 38, 53, 58, 88, 95, 147

www.ingramcontent.com/pod-product-compliance
Lightning Source LLC
Chambersburg PA
CBHW021355300426
44114CB00012B/1233